CW00542149

The word lonesome expresses a sadness, a blue note, a sour note. Even though the music bares the trace of struggle and of pain, it is also the means of uplift, transcendence to joy and celebration. Meeting and experiencing sadness of tragedy in art, literature or music is very often the transformation of that experience to its corresponding opposite, the release of joy and freedom.

One is forced to put the requirements of the music before all personal considerations, to play honesty from the heart with no motive other than the selfless expression of joy and beauty for their own sake. It is this quality that has driven and inspired me all of my musical life. I have found that you can never possess it, you can only yield to it. It demands honesty and humility.

Martin Hayes,
from the sleeve notes of The Lonesome Touch 1997

THE
UNTHANKS

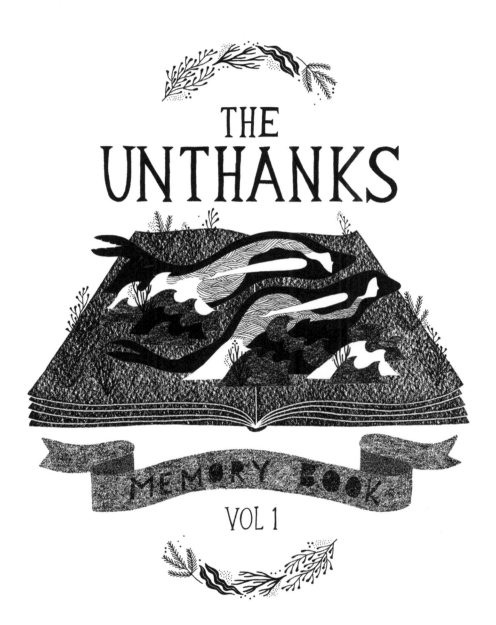

MEMORY BOOK

VOL 1

Front cover illustration by Natalie Rae Reid
Compiled, edited and designed by Cally and The Unthanks,
with able technical assistance from Nik Rose.
Proof reading by Andrew Cupples.
Printed and bound by Hollinger Print, Norwich.
Huge thanks to all the fans and fellow artists who have contributed
to this book, and to the family, friends, past band members, photographers,
writers and editors who have helped us with the materials in this book.

First published in 2016 by RabbleRouser Music

mail@the-unthanks.com
www.the-unthanks.com

All photo are taken by and sourced from the personal archives and albums of
The Unthanks family and band members (past and present) and have been used
by kind permission.
The following photos deserve separate credit and thanks: In all cases
we have tried to credit as accurately as ten year old archives allow, however,
if you spot any errors to this please get in touch via the website.

Photo Credits

7, 74, 78, 79, 106, 108 Alex Telfer
9, 87, 90, 91 Judith Burrows
14, 15 (except Otley shots) Stephen Redfern
18 (bottom left), 19 (top and middle left), 21, 131 Allan Wilkinson
24, 159 Andy Gallacher
37 Lewis Arnold
36 (except Journal Award photos), 38, 39 Karen Melvin
47, 156 Jamie Drew
75, 81, 109 (centre left), 135, 136, 143 (bottom), 163, 168, 169, 176 Ken Drew
86 Fung Wah Man, courtesy of The People Speak
107, 110 Pip
130 Mark Winpenny
138, 139 (album / book shots) Ken Pattison
142, 145, 146, 152 (bottom), 153, 154, 155, 167 (except centre left), 177 Sarah Mason
145, 146, 148, 157, 158 Drew Meakin
148 Alice Bentley (illustrations)
149 Gary Calton
162 Reed Ingram Weir
174 Dan Graham
175 Samuel Ashdown
186 Alexander Guzman

With grateful thanks to all the magazines and newspapers
who have kindly granted reproduction rights.

© 2016 RabbleRouser Music
ISBN 978-0-9571717-6-3
All rights reserved. No part of this publication may be reproduced, stored in a retrieval system or
transmitted in any form or by any means electrical, mechanical or otherwise without first seeking
permission of the copyright owners and publishers. The Unthanks have asserted their rights under
the Copyright, Designs and Patents act, 1988 to be identified as Authors of this work.
A Cataloguing-in-Publication Data record for this book is available from the British Library.

MENU

The real Winterset – just a couple of miles from where Adrian and Chris grew up in South Yorkshire, taken by Adrian's dad, Max, sometime in the 70s.

FOREWORD
HEARING VOICES
Paul Morley

Suddenly, I heard the voice and voices of the Unthanks coming from a space outside. It was one, or two, of those sounds you wait for all your life, or that's waiting for you, and there is perhaps an inevitability you will find it, but you don't really know how you do. Where did they come from? One second they were nowhere to be seen or heard, and then, there they were.

There it is. A new voice, a new sound, something else, full of sense and reason, something that refreshes you and all of the other sounds you love, which it now becomes part of; a personal history of sound, and song, which will live with you for the rest of your life.

I found them to some extent a few years ago in an unpromising pile of compact discs I was working through, looking for new music, as you do, in the final stages of a world before music streaming etc, where everything became available at once and the new is not like it was. I'd lost heart, to be honest, in going through the regular pile of CDs that I got sent, still working, to some extent, as a rock critic, or someone who had a regular column about music, writing about what it was, where it had been, where it might be going. Like that might still be happening.

The CD pile of newcomers I was sent was mostly, to my ears, becoming a pile of clichés, of reruns and replays, of the same old and/or the same new, and represented

a loss of energy, a lack of inspiration and drama, that was beginning to infect me or at least disappoint me. Music from the 70s – the 1770s and 1870s as much as the 1970s – was sounding fresher and stranger than the magic spoiling over-supply of newcomers, who were too locked inside the 1970s and perhaps needed some sense of the 1770s and 1870s to make them seem more 21st century, more part of a labyrinthine world spinning out of control, a conceptual projection of itself, where everything past, present and future was beginning to happen at once.

Then I played, without much initial hope, music by a group I did not know, with a name that hinted at some sort of wintery, nocturnal glamour, from an album with a title that suggested interesting minds with a fascination for the odd even perverse, and song titles that implied an awareness of forces beyond the world of everyday realities. As soon as I played it, for once, I did not want to stop within a few seconds. I wanted to see and hear where I was going next; where this performance, and the group were clearly made up as a performance, the performance of a lifetime, was going to take me.

The music looked backwards and forwards at the same time. It clearly came with knowledge of the 1970s – whether music produced by Joe Boyd, Bob Johnston or Manfred Eicher – but there was also for goodness' sake the 1770s, ghostly even eerie but larger than life, and also a sense that this group, if that's what they were, knew more than a little about the Ralph Vaughan Williams linking via near extinct folk song of Tudor polyphony and continental modernism, about how minimalist composers could conjure a sound that was outwardly static but inwardly in constant motion (or vice versa), a sonic product of action. And then there was the voice, the voices, the day brightening harmonies, the heart and soul, in real and unreal time, shy and lonely, epic and modest, putting into words what cannot be put into words, poised between despair and bliss, feeling ideas rather than thinking them, pain linked to pain, singing in such a way that as a listener I seemed to be dreaming the song they were singing.

I heard the Unthanks, and there was something familiar about them, something at the back of my mind, or at the distant edges of a dream I once had. There were echoes of stories I'd heard, of other compelling singers and players going against the grain that lived inside my memory, but I had never come across anything quite like them before. This was a few years into the 21st century, when I felt perhaps there was little waiting for me that combined voice, sound, song, magical thinking, location and atmosphere in ways that were different enough to be something of a shock, a revelation. I recognised them to some extent, but I knew nothing about them, and they came as all great sounds and songs do from an out there that was outside where I'd been before or even thought of going.

They were being presented and talked about as traditional, as folk, active members of a half-forgotten or half-remembered community, a series of communities, where songs are an integral part of the process of living, not created merely to be dressed up and sold and mapped out as part of a commercial career. They were industrious regional musicians committed to preserving the energies and identities, and collecting the songs, of an intimate, underestimated music that seemed constantly in danger, a music scarred by the past, used to being exiled and replaced by glossy new trends and shiny new styles, apparently doomed to exist only as a historic, insular testament to a dead genre.

Folk by its very nature had survived centuries, through war and peace, across cultural fads and technological and industrial distortion, as a unifying, affirmative force, a counter-cultural form of protest, propaganda, locally connected, handmade, full of gradually accumulating tensions, mourning and spurning, rogues and brides, farewells and turtles doves, bawdy, bittersweet, bloodied, rustic, sordid, thrilling, whimsical, radiant,

fairy tales painted black and blue, an erotic insatiability, a festive renewal, a teaching tool, a winding path, a theatrical masquerade, a natural phenomenon like flora and fauna, carrying human bodies, people hit by fate, out of history into the present, leaving beautiful traces and celebrating throbbing life. But with so much going on at the beginning of the 21st century, most of that to do with pleasure, escape and self-gratification, it was easy to overlook it, and for most forget about it altogether, as though it was nothing but a decaying, sentimental yearning for an uncharming bygone past. There are those, though, who refuse to forget about it, who understand and use the strength and adaptability that has carried it through time; as much as it is from and of the past, when blended with modern elements and allowed to evolve, it also achieves the ultimate, mysterious prize of all great music — timelessness.

Rachel and Becky Unthank had the grace and bearing, and bravado and fearlessness, and accents and desperate, plain, open hearted, introspective melancholy of folk singers, and were enthusiastic folk dancers, and they seemed at their happiest, however wounded, gloomy and disturbing the message, when telling a tale through many discursive verses, and the music that unfolded around and through them was obviously best labelled as folk even as it skewed categories and mixed ingredients.

They were of a line that had come from where folk rock and a certain portion of the topsy-turvy psychedelic end of rock and pop had emerged out of pre-Dylan traditional folk and blues, illuminated by Dylan and Joni's reach for the supernatural through the natural as they outwitted a changing world. It was a line that just recently had got mixed up with something that was being called psych folk, new folk, freak folk, avant-folk, harking back to the likes of Shirley Collins, Tyrannosaurus Rex and Pearls Before Swine and what they harked back to. An acoustic, or mostly acoustic, highly singable music that had an idiosyncratic awareness of punk aesthetics and the indie dynamic that followed, of the free spirited shape shifting jazz of Miles and the impressionistic ambient, chill and trip hop that followed. Where a form of folk could be in vogue, or at least mentioned in polite company, and still raise spirits, or at least not seem lost in the past, of no use in a racing, crashing and increasingly argumentative and punishing modern world.

Folk though wasn't the first thing that struck me when I first heard the Unthanks, following my instinct and making my mind up in a matter of seconds that this was the sort of music I loved, whatever it was called, whatever the apparent genre, wherever they came from, however suspicious the rigid folkloric purists living down memory lane.

The Unthanks introduced themselves — to me as I listened for the first time — with these subtly ornamented sunshine and rain snow and mist sea and breeze tender and pensive sister and stranger voices that wonderfully needed the world and flowed so deliciously through vowels and nimbly stepped over the sticks and bones of consonants, voices representing a different world of tastes and wishes, of hurt and hope, fear and romance, love and spirit, lust and innocence, sly and serpentine, from the black soiled green loaded countryside but somehow cosmic, that seemed simultaneously surrealist and natural, raw and soothing, solemn and sensual, soft and powerful voices imbued with a sense of mortality that so gloriously controlled mood and occupied space, that were using songs to explore the flexibility of boundaries, as treasures to possess, and I didn't think folk.

I thought North, a far North, a far out North, a pure North, a north beyond the north, of winter and resistance, bleak beauty and dark thoughts, brightly bursting brass bands, frosty breath, grief and defiance, ancient and modern, lost villages and rough, tangled towns, clouds piled endlessly beyond the hills. I thought of an abstract, splendidly remote country with its own woods, valleys, myths and rivers where the fantastic wondering solo turns Martin Carthy, Nick Drake, Robert Wyatt, David Sylvian and Tim Buckley move in and out of the shadows, dwellings are named after Fotheringay, Pentangle and Planxty, and the family names are Carpenter, Wilson and Waterson, and here come the discreet family Unthanks, following certain well-trodden paths, but discovering their own, and opening up new views, crossing borders, breaking thresholds, exploring coastlines, heading out, home-sick and worldly, fight and flight in their voices.

I thought wistful, metaphysical, an undefined sadness, transformation, grave, glowing, gothic, down to earth but with alien markings, shivers down the spine, dreamlike waterfalls, secret notions, songs like individual flowerings on a common stem, a beautiful representation of the virtues of independence. I thought this was music that was going to make me, as a writer, go over the top; music that I loved, as a writer, because it reminded me that music's meanings are always slippery, and require some chasing down, and always stay tantalisingly out of reach, however over the top you go. You go over the top often into battle because you want to find a way to explain and explore how much you love this music, to get to the heart of the matter, as much as you can, where life for a moment, and maybe longer, as the years fly by, in some close corner of the brain, is made incandescent, without simply saying before moving on to the next thing; I like this music, and I give it five stars.

More Unthank albums and collections of songs imagined, borrowed, found, adapted, appreciated and converted have followed their very first; there have been perfectly judged cameo contributions to the works and compilations of others, even a name change of sorts, a minor but provocative change of identity. There's been acclaim, guest appearances, collaborations, nominations and awards, and all of the biographical detail that comes with this sort of performance and presence, which of course if you fancy you can track down elsewhere. A chronology, a discography, a biography, general guides, playlists, videos and recommendations, examples and explanations of honest, guileless intentions; places you can begin on your own journey to the heart of the matter and beyond.

They have always remained to me a mystery, with added elements of the slightly mystical, showing little signs of slowing down even when they disappear into their own private space. A mystery, somewhere else, however much I talk to them, or find out about them and their earthly concerns, practical struggles and undimmed ambitions, as a family, household, business, workers, scenario, ensemble, travellers, label, self-promoters, as he and she, as a work in progress. I receive emails from them, and even in some form or another actually work with them, but the mystery grows. I have no idea how they do what they do, how it all comes together in their heads, in the studio, in performance, in life, in the space outside. I prefer the mystery, not knowing and not wanting to know where they come from or who they really are. I prefer the mystery of how they find the time and what the voice does and turns into and how the two things become connected.

I prefer the mystery I hear in the voice, and voices, sweet with decision, the sound of togetherness, determination, love, a sad sublime sound that is folk and unfolk, discreet and unyielding, words that are poetic and documentary, telling us in the most enchanting detail like news bulletins from deep inside the endless imagination where we've been and how we got here and how alive we've been, and helping us to understand in the knotty middle of the latest human and now near post-human machine-guided versions of turmoil, sensation, fear and danger … what on earth's to become of us.

AN INTRODUCTION

Adrian McNally

Summer 2005. I was up super early and already at my desk. I don't recall why. 6.30am or so. 6 Music was piping through my newly acquired digital radio, the station still in its infancy. Phill Jupitus was playing something a bit 'worldy', or should it be 'worldly', hell-bent as he seemed to be on doubling the station's music diversity in the space of his breakfast show each day.

He either didn't back-announce the track, or I didn't hear him, so I sent a text in, asking if he would say what the last song was. Next minute — in fact probably less than a minute — my phone was ringing.

He'd only gone and rung me up.

"Adrian? Hello, it's Phill. It was the Celtic Skatalites mate. Fantastic, isn't it?"

Phill Jupitus, in my phone. No producer's voice on the line first.

"Oh! Er, erm, yes, really great. Thanks so…"
"Anything else you want to know? You'll find them on the net…"
"Thanks… er, well, you might…"

"Sorry, got to go man. Thanks so much for listening."
"Oh, yeah, sure. It's so nice of you to…"
"Bye mate."

Gone.

Wow. What a guy.

Two or three years later, we would find ourselves collaborating with him in a Somerset barn, for Charles Hazlewood's reimagining of *The Beggar's Opera*.

Not even 7am and my day would not get any better. But then it occurred to me, I could have seized the opportunity, told him about Rachel and Becky, asked him if he'd mind me sending him a CD. In truth, even though it was over in a flash, it did cross my mind in the space of the phone call. My instinct was not to. Jupitus the famous DJ comedian had trusted me as a member of the public, to behave normally, so that he could behave normally too, and not like a celebrity, by just going ahead and ringing me up. To have taken advantage would have been a betrayal. We have to play our part if we want our celebrities to be real.

That didn't stop me writing to him though! I let a few days go and then sent him a letter, reminding him of and thanking him for his call, before explaining the copy of *Cruel Sister* enclosed, a debut album I had produced and released, by a young band called Rachel Unthank & The Winterset. It wasn't him I was taking advantage of. Just our circumstantial, unexpected contact.

Within a week, he had played the opening track, 'On A Monday Morning', and then in time our version of 'River Man', and amazingly, 'Rap Her To Bank' — an unaccompanied mining song, on BBC 6 Music.

It was our first piece of exposure beyond the folk scene. That was the start. We were off.

A month or two later. Rachel and I sat in the car outside the Co-op in Corbridge, mouths open, eyes wide, fingers pointing. Absolute shock that *Cruel Sister* was Folk Album of the Year in *Mojo* Magazine. Until then, we hadn't thought it was going anywhere.

Since then, we've been very lucky to lead a life in music, mixing family and friendship with creative journeys that have largely been into the unknown, at least for untrained enquirers like us. We hope you will enjoy this book as an insight into those adventures. It is not a historically comprehensive biography. Allow us to save you from that. A high percentage of the reality of being in a band is monumentally dull to experience firsthand, let alone to read about.

There is a danger however, in presenting just the highlights and the fun bits, of painting a glorified picture that appears so rosy, it may engender either envy or the desire to puke. I'd like to acknowledge briefly, before the show begins, that for every successful venture, there has been blood, sweat and tears, and sacrifice. But we all know that, I think. Because there is always another side to any form of success, that people don't see. For us, being in an independent, self-managed, self-releasing band, fighting the tide of a music industry disappearing out to sea, and remaining artistically ambitious in the face of it, has taken us to the edge of sanity, and maybe not all the way back!

So with that acknowledged here in the intro, before the book starts, we needn't concern ourselves any further with the trials and tribulations.

We are of course incredibly lucky to have such excellent fans, and in that sense, we have had it much easier that many artists, more talented and committed than us, that have fallen by the wayside of the drastic changes our industry has experienced in the last twenty years.

We wanted to give you a say in fact, though this was not without its dangers too. While we've kept the pages relatively free of fancy five star reviews (using largely only non-critique based press features that hopefully serve to tell parts of the journey) there is nevertheless praise from fellow artists and fans who were encouraged to have a part in our story. We were careful to ask contributors to write about their own relationship with music, so that their stories would say at least as much about them, as about us; about the power of music to impact our lives, its social and political functions, its capacity to heal or inspire. Inevitably however, for a book about The Unthanks, contributors pay compliments that it may appear we have gone looking for.

Of course, I'm protesting too much. We enjoy what people have to say and it can be immensely touching or gratifying. But mainly I would prefer to believe that if we receive plaudits, it is also the music that is receiving the love. Personally, my motivation to engage with folk music is the hope that we might contribute to the furtherance of it being heard, of it being regarded as having relevance, wisdom, truth and beauty. We push ourselves and summon the bravery to be musically creative with traditional song in the hope of communicating it to a wider audience, in the hope of being an open door for folk music, for people who might otherwise not have considered it a genre that could speak to them. The music merely passes through us. It might sound cloyingly self-effacing, but it's the truth. Performers who genuinely love music are just the conduit. To respond to praise in any other way is dangerous, because every performer will hear a lot more silence in their lifetime than applause.

So let's hear it for music. The transcendental, transporting music we all love, overwhelming our souls with truth and beauty, giving us the means to experience and make sense of feelings together — feelings we might not otherwise have the bravery or imagination to share or articulate. Where would we be without it?

Thank you for affording us the means to make some, for over ten years now. While we're working out where that takes us next, we hope you enjoy this, our Memory Book.

Adrian

I
GROWING UP IN CLOGS

Rachel Unthank

Our first experience of performing was of clog dancing. From the age of five we were part of Addison Rapper and Clog Dance team. The men, including our dad, did rapper dancing, spurned from the pit villages of Northumberland and County Durham. Five men, armed with swords (long palette-like pieces of metal with a wooden handle on each end – a tool from the pits), would join together in a circle. It is a compact, fast and flashy dance with stepping and interweaving of the swords, an occasional somersault over the swords, ending with an interwoven star which is held up high. I found it thrilling as a child. So much more dangerous and risky than Morris dancing. The

women in the team clog danced, so from the age of five we donned wooden soled leather shoes and were taught to dance.

We practised every Friday night in a church hall in Ryton, Gateshead, where we grew up. I remember the diagonal patterns of the sprung wooden floor, ineffectual orange glowing electrical heaters hanging from the ceiling, and using the china teacups for water during the break. We used to perform at folk festivals, village shows, ceilidhs, events at the local brewery, shop precincts… all sorts of places, but one of my favourite excursions would be a dance tour.

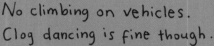

No climbing on vehicles.
Clog dancing is fine though.

A dance tour would involve dance teams from across the country getting together for a day, or weekend, of organised dance spots. I remember going to the Lake District on many occasions, boarding a bus with a kaleidoscope of dance teams. There would be us, Morris dancers with their bells and hankies, the scarier border Morris men with their ragged outfits and big sticks, with feathers in their top hats. There were North West Clog teams, very different to our own – a processional kind of dance in clogs, sometimes with tasselled sticks or huge arcs of garlands of flowers, and always accompanied by a host of musicians and a big bass drum, that went right through you, shaking your bones and making your heart jump. I remember being captivated with some stripy legged, red cheeked clog dancers called Lizzy Dripping. At each stop, usually near a pub, everyone would file off the bus and take their turn to perform. We would take our turn, sometimes a routine worked out for the whole team, or sometimes a solo spot. Even before we could dance, my brother, sister and I would be kitted out in a tiny version of the team kit. We were proud to wear it. It identified us with our team. We were part of the gang. I remember confidently waltzing into a roughish pub somewhere locally, my dad in his burgundy corduroy short trousers and yellow sash, top hat and tails, with a rubber chicken in his top pocket. Then teenaged-me, dressed in a quilted skirt, embroidered pinny, fussy blouse and shawl, with total confidence and completely unabashed. For the first time, I clocked that there was no way that I would ever have been brave enough to go into that pub had I not been in my kit. It dawned on me that this costume was a disguise, an armour. That being a part of whatever this was, gave me confidence and put me at ease.

Becky and I have recently started dancing in a clog team again, in a room above a pub in Newcastle. And, when we come downstairs, my dad and brother are playing tunes, in the music session below. All three of us kids have drifted back.

2

A NORTHUMBRIAN WAY

Rachel Unthank

Packed pubs, full of joyful noisy singers, that bristle with exciting harmonies. Respectfully hushed ballad sessions, unravelling dark tales. Energetic, late night ceilidhs, whirling, swinging, ranting, and polka-ing the night away. Giddy family parties of shared songs and wine and silliness. Storytelling festivals, with tall tales, and thought-provoking wonder, ghost stories huddled around fires. Music sessions full of fiddles and concertinas and whistles where tunes almost fly. A myriad of bizarrely dressed clog, Morris and rapper teams, parading through and taking over the streets. It's hard to know where to start.

When I think back to our childhood, I can see that being exposed to all these different aspects of tradition, and experiencing song, music, dance and stories, both taking part and observing, helped mould our own attitudes and philosophy towards performing. Of all these experiences, perhaps the biggest influence has been the Northumbrian Ceilidh. A Northumbrian Ceilidh is a very unique, special kind of ceilidh and for me, brings together so much of what I enjoy. There is

social dancing as you would expect, but also there will be singers, musicians, storytellers, clog dancers... all sorts of things.

Our parents used to take our family to the Northumbrian Ceilidhs at Whitby Folk Week. I remember them warmly, and also remember the tickle of anticipation, as their popularity meant you had to arrive early to make sure you got in. And, being early is not something Unthanks have ever been very good at.

The ceilidhs used to take place in the Whitby Friendship Rowing Club, in a hot, packed room overlooking the harbour. The ceilidh was led by concertina player Alistair Anderson and the band was a remarkable trio of musicians called The Shepherds — actual Northumbrian shepherds, who seemed ancient and kind of noble, to me. They consisted of the high sweet Northumbrian pipe playing of Joe Hutton, Will Atkinson's rasping and rhythmic harmonica, and the lilting fiddle playing of Willie Taylor, who had one finger missing. We used to love ceilidh dancing and

Brother Matt with Rachel and Dad in Addison Kit.

Alistair made sure of telling the grown ups not to avoid our dance set, or mistakenly presume that we wouldn't know the dances, because he said, we knew what we were doing.

After a couple of dances everyone would go back to their seats, clustered around tables, packed in around the dance floor, and it would be time for a turn. Alistair would often play, swinging his concertina around in his eccentric, virtuosic and joyful fashion, and we would hear a host of different performers. Always a song, maybe a ballad from Hannah Hutton, wife of the piping shepherd, or a Geordie music hall song from madcap genius Johnny Handle. And, then it would be time to dance again. And so the evening would go on, dancing the night away, punctuated with different performers taking the floor for a song or a story or a tune, mixing up humour, mournful ballads, plaintive airs and lively dance tunes.

Now, when I look back, I appreciate the bringing together of different generations, where kids and older generations were all valued. We were entrusted to take part, to be quiet when appropriate, to watch, to learn, and be capable of joining in too. My brother was fascinated, inspired and in awe of the aforementioned three fingered playing shepherd, and there was a sense that they took delight in seeing little kids dancing to their tunes.

I think we learned a lot at those Northumbrian Ceilidhs. I see these different threads of the tradition, that were laid out for us there to experience — music, song, storytelling and dance — finding their paths and weaving their way into our current performances. Maybe it seems at odds to explore dark, brooding songs, and then, throw in a bit of clog dancing to cheer everyone up, but to us these things have always sat comfortably beside each other, and are part of the tapestry of

Becky dancing at Whitby Folk Week.

When the age gap was
a little more apparent!

emotion that is there to be explored as performers. I suppose as children we were exposed to songs and tales of hardship and heartache, disasters and death, tunes aching with yearning and beauty, but this would always be coupled and handled with the indomitable spirit that our region is renowned for – humour, lightheartedness and a spiritedjoyfulness, expressed through its music hall songs that make fun of catastrophe, through the high energy of rapper and clog dance, and the sprightly tunes that accompany them.

I now also celebrate that immersive quality of a Northumbrian Ceilidh that brings together a community of people, performers and non performers, and lets them take part in an event that they are all a part of. This holistic approach runs deeply through our own singing weekends, where people come and join us to sing, to take part in something, an event, where everybody contributes a small part of themselves that as a whole is much bigger, which as a result is nourishing and makes people feel connected.

We went to a ceilidh at the wedding reception of some close family friends recently, Northumbrian style, naturally. I observed my own kids and their cousins sat wide eyed watching their grandad rapper dance, and their delight at being whisked around the floor by an auntie, or granny during a ceilidh dance. During the final dance, I looked around the circle, the coming together of families and generations, moving together united by the music. If you stepped into a village hall in some remote place in a different country, you might be more inclined to wonder at and prize this special culture. It is special.

Our first photo shoot by Stephen Redfern in Adrian's flat, Slaithwaite, 2003

RR002

A SHORT INTRODUCTION TO... rachel unthank

1 THE SANDGATE DANGLING SONG

2 TWENTY LONG WEEKS

3 RAVEN GIRL

4 THE SNOW IT MELTS THE

SOONEST

5 BALKANS

6 MY BONNY LAD

engineered and produced by adrian mcnally
published by RabbleRouser Music 2004 RR002
tracks 3,5,6 © rachel and becky unthank 2004
tracks 1,2,4 © rachel unthank 2004
www.rabblerousermusic.com

A SHORT INTRODUCTION TO... rachel unthank

RR002

1 THE SANDGATE DANGLING SONG (trad)
2 TWENTY LONG WEEKS (Alex Glasgow)
3 RAVEN GIRL (unknown/esther Watson/r&b unthank)
4 THE SNOW IT MELTS THE SOONEST (trad)
5 BALKANS (trad/arr sandra kerr/r&b unthank)
6 MY BONNY LAD (trad/arr r&b unthank)

Rachel Unthank is a young singer steeped in the Traditions of the North-East of England. Born and brought up on Tyneside in a family very much involved in the North East folk scene, Rachel's upbringing is reflected in her sense of responsibility to carry and spread the tradition that has been passed on to her.

A one-time BBC Radio 2 Young Tradition Semi Finalist, her act is both accomplished and charming, combining a beguiling mix of youthful energy and assured experience. Rachel's main asset is a illusive and emotive voice; illusive in that it surprises at every turn; emotive in that it is capable of soul, sweetness and fire in equal measures. There are probably stronger singers in a purely technical sense, but Rachel seems to sing from somewhere true. Her voice is enhanced by an understanding and appreciation of traditional music that is rare in one so young. A successful 2003 culminated in a main stage performance at Sidmouth International Festival with her sister Becky Unthank. Becky appears on two tracks of this recording.

This CD was made to coincide with the Nu Routes tour, a series of profile-raising concerts promoting the evolution of new acoustic and traditional music throughout the UK. On the tour, Rachel supports Michael McGoldrick, Ed Boyd and John Joe Kelly, with the concerts climaxing in a collaboration between Rachel and Michael's band. In 2004, Rachel will release a debut album proper. We hope you enjoy this taster.

all enquiries: Adrian McNally, RabbleRouser Music. www.rabblerousermusic.com
01484 840369 adrianmcnally@aol.com

All rights of the producer and of the owner of the recorded work are reserved. Unauthorised copying, public performance, broadcasting, hiring or rental of this recording prohibited.

rachel and becky unthank

"ASSURED AND POISED..SINGERS TO KEEP YOUR **EYE** OPEN FOR"
LIVING TRADITION
TRADITIONAL **UNACCOMPANIED SONG** FROM
THE NORTH EAST OF ENGLAND AND AROUND THE **WORLD.**
"a beguiling mix of youthful energy
and **assured experience"**

Rachel and Becky Unthank are sisters steeped in the traditions of the North-East of England. Although they've been singing all their lives, 2004 is seeing a fast rise to notoriety, with performances with Michael McGoldrick and an impressive festival calendar that includes Cambridge and Towersey. The progress will continue in late 2004 with the long-anticipated release of their debut album. Born and brought up in Tyneside by a family very much involved in the local North East folk scene, Rachel and Becky have been going to and performing at folk clubs and festivals for as long as they can remember. Their upbringing is very much reflected in their sense of responsibility to carry and spread the tradition that has been passed on to them, while their performances also feature traditional song from around the world. As singers, musicians and clog dancers of 26 and 19 respectively, their act is both accomplished and charming, combining a beguiling mix of youthful energy and assured experience.

A successful 2003 included Bromyard Festival, Whitby and Darlington Spring Thing, and culminated in a main stage performance at Sidmouth International Festival. In 2004, Rachel was chosen to support **Michael McGoldrick** and Friends on the Nu Routes tour - a serious of profile raising concerts promoting the evolution of new traditional music. Singing unaccompanied in front of packed houses, Rachel was a real hit, and ended the show each night by joining Michael, Ed Boyd and John Joe Kelly on stage for a final finale. Rachel and Becky will release a debut album proper later in the year. They are booked for **2004 festivals Cambridge, Towersey, Gosport, Holmfirth, Saddleworth, Wallingford Bunfest and Otley.**

all enquiries:
Adrian McNally, RabbleRouser Music. Also representing Last Night's Fun, Flook, Malinky.
01484 840369 adrian@rabblerousermusic.com

Above: A hastily made sampler, released to sell on a short tour supporting Michael McGoldrick. Below: An early duo performance at Otley Folk Festival, 2004. With Adrian on guitar.

ALBUM LAUNCH

SUNDAY Civic Hall 4.30-6pm

HOLMFIRTH FOLK FESTIVAL - THE LAUNCH OF DEBUT ALBUM
"CRUEL SISTER" - A ONE-OFF CONCERT WITH SPECIAL GUESTS
FROM THE ALBUM, FREE BUBBLY & CD SIGNING
www.rachelunthank.com

Rachel Unthank & The Winterset
Cruel Sister

3
CRUEL SISTER

The launch of the long awaited debut album:
Cruel Sister

- one-off concert with 15+
special guests from the album,
including:
Chris Sherburn
Rosie Morton
Damien O'Kane
Will Hampson
Bryony Griffith
And lots of Unthanks!

- the first chance to buy and have
signed Cruel Sister

- free bubbly and other surprises!

- www.rachelunthank.com

SUNDAY

Civic Hall 4.30-6pm
Holmfirth Folk Festival

Rachel Unthank & The Winterset
Jackie Oates, Belinda O'Hooley, Becky Unthank, Rachel Unthank

Cruel Sister
RabbleRouser Music (RR005)

Rachel Unthank & The Winterset

FOLK ALBUM OF THE YEAR
MOJO MAGAZINE

The
Cruel Sister
Tour

"Rachel Unthank is brilliant" KATE RUSBY
"I simply can't recommend them enough" BOB HARRIS, BBC RADIO 2
"simply gripping...their ambition knows no bounds" FROOTS

+ support

BUSH HALL, LONDON
Saturday 25th Feb 2006

310 Uxbridge Road London W12 7LJ Tickets £10, Doors 7.30pm www.ticketweb.co.uk 08700 600 100

www.rachelunthank.com "gold dust for the folk world" folking.com "this is music lived, not learned" Folk On Tap

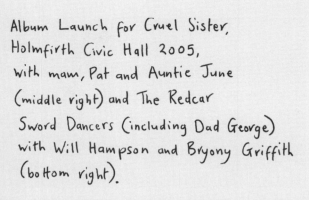

Album Launch for Cruel Sister,
Holmfirth Civic Hall 2005,
with mam, Pat and Auntie June
(middle right) and The Redcar
Sword Dancers (including Dad George)
with Will Hampson and Bryony Griffith
(bottom right).

AN ARTIST WRITES...

No 1. Nick Hornby, Author

What a strange, difficult year 2016 has been. If you're reading this in two or five or ten years' time, perhaps that sentence will seem incomprehensible, but I suspect not; the events of the year will be felt, in hundreds of different ways, for a long time to come. At the beginning of the year we lost two of the greatest, most vital and most influential musicians of the last fifty years, people who in their own different ways made music that seemed more modern than everything that had gone before; and in the cataclysmic referendum in June, we discovered that we were not the country that we thought we were, and that we didn't know each other –or even like each other –as much as we thought we did. The referendum, as it turned out, was a foreshadowing of the terrifying result in the US Presidential Election. Trump's victory announced the return of the sort of demagoguery we thought had died out in the first half of the 20th century. Everything went backwards; a large number of people seemed to want it that way.

On the face of it, English folk music is the last place to turn if we want to heal our wounds. Haven't we had enough, on both sides of the Atlantic, of white people droning on about the past, pretending that we are living in simpler (if, frankly, more miserable) times? Unless you want to argue that Drake or Lady Gaga or Deerhunter are, at their heart, folk musicians, it's hard to make the case that the genre speaks to everyone: it doesn't. That's why we have folk clubs, rather than folk stadia. I am one of the people to whom folk doesn't speak, until one night a few years ago when I heard The Unthanks on a well-known music television show. (I don't know why I'm being coy. I'm not the BBC. And even the BBC let you mention

TV shows. It was *Later... With Jools Holland*.) They played 'Here's The Tender Coming', and it felt like the world stopped turning for a few minutes –but not in a let's-go-back–to-the-nineteenth-century way. Rather, they managed to find a time and a place outside the brightly-lit studio full of wires and bands, a place for anyone who loves melody, arrangements, voices, the sound of the human spirit.

The Unthanks are authentic, but only to themselves, rather than to a received notion of what authenticity is; Rachel and Becky sing in accented English, but it is the accented English they speak in. They are not Jane and Joanna Barleycorn. And the music would have confused those Dylan fans who booed during the 1966 tour because he'd gone noisy. The Unthanks'music is rarely noisy, although it swells and dips and stirs, but it isn't folk, really. It's something altogether fresher, stranger, and yes, more contemporary: the voices come from the north-east, the music underneath from elsewhere, from modern orchestral jazz, from the more ambitious end of pop music. The Unthanks have covered Robert Wyatt, the Beatles, Antony and the Johnsons, King Crimson and Tom Waits; they've worked with orchestras and brass bands. In recent years, the band have provided some of my most memorable live experiences, sat among warm, devoted, frequently transported audiences, in venues that are sometimes transformed into churches, if they weren't churches already. The Unthanks make secular spiritual music for everyone, and, at the end of the year when some of us have been troubled by some of the uglier definitions and manifestations of Englishness, it is an enormous consolation to realise that this – I want to say this above all –is the sound of my country.

Opposite
The Winterset
at
Cambridge
Folk Festival
2007

Outtakes from Cruel Sister shoot
by Adrian, River Tyne, Warden.

AN ARTIST WRITES...

No 2. Ade Edmondson, actor and writer

I first saw The Unthanks at The Borderline in London –
a cramped, sweaty rock venue, which was full of sweaty urban
folkies for the evening. I was at the back of the crowd, so when
Rachel and Becky put their clogs on and started clogging, all I
could see was their two shiny faces, smiling, but looking rather
serious at the same time, bobbing up and down to the sound of
wood on wood. It held the room. That's when I fell in love with
them…

RACHEL UNTHANK & THE WINTERSET

Cruel Sister Rabble Rouser RR005

So conditioned have we been in recent times
to hearing folk songs delivered in winsome,
prettified female voices, this comes as quite a
shock. A very welcome shock. More Eliza
Carthy than Cara Dillon, Rachel Unthank
sings with rare boldness in a Geordie accent
that's so in your face it almost seems harsh,
but it carries the finest virtues of any singer
of traditional material and that is to convey
the story in an honest and direct fashion. It is
tempered to a degree by the softer vocal
accompaniment of her sister Becky, while
likeminded free spirits Jackie Oates on viola
and Belinda O'Hooley on piano complete a
band clearly passionate about the songs.
Becky Unthank even achieves something I
thought well-nigh impossible with her
charged performance of *Riverman* – that Nick
Drake actually wrote a good song.

It's an opportune time to be listening to
their choked performance of *On A Monday
Morning*, following so closely the death of its
author, Cyril Tawney. Peter Bellamy's remains
the definitive version, but you feel the pain
of the Unthanks, hungover in the bus queue.
They also bring a fresh feel to Dave Goulder's
January Man, a song that's been round the
blocks quite a few times over the years, but
they really come into their own with their
highly individual interpretations of traditional material. Rachel's unaccompanied reading
of *The Fair Flower Of Northumberland* is simply gripping, there's a proud Geordie anthem
with Becky's *Rap Her To Bank*, and the mum-
mers play theme *The Greatham Calling On
Song* is joyous.

Their ambition knows no bounds, and if
they do labour slightly during the mammoth
telling of *Cruel Sister*, their willingness to
embrace difficult material like Alex Glasgow's *Twenty Long Weeks* without any
attempt at sweetening the pill, is part of
what makes it such a gratifying album. For
this reason the one track I have a real problem with is *Raven Girl*, the poppy harmonies
– apparently inspired by hearing some
French singers – seem gimmicky and go
against the grain of the rest of the album.
That apart, it's terrific stuff.

www.rachelunthank.com

Colin Irwin

THE SPITZ FESTIVAL of FOLK

SEPTEMBER 2007

ALASDAIR ROBERTS - CIRCULUS
LISA KNAPP - LONE PIGEON
JOHN POWER - THE SEE SEE - RALFE BAND
OYSTERBAND - MARY HAMPTON
THE YOUNG REPUBLIC - DAWN LANDES
CHARLIE PARR - FRANK TURNER
RACHEL UNTHANK & THE WINTERSET
DEVON SPROULE - MOON MUSIC ORCHESTRA
FOLK ORCHESTRA - INDIGO MOSS
PARIS MOTEL - MR DAVID VINER

www.spitz.co.uk

GIG REVIEW With Shelley Marsden

Rachel Unthank and the Winterset @ The Spitz, London, 24 November

RACHEL UNTHANK begins a
song but coughs and splutters
after the second note. She apolo-
gises, has a giggle with sister
Becky, and calmly starts again.
With their between-song banter
(pianist Belinda O'Hooley, the
comedian of the group whose
hilarious allusions to her sexual
orientation have them cracking
up), their self-conscious clog-
dancing and the 'hands-on-hips'
stance on stage, Rachel Unthank
are the antithesis of practised and
sickly-sweet traditional music.

There is none of the preten-
sion of 'folkdom' in this packed-
out room, and Rachel Unthank
astonish the small but expectant
crowd with the raw power of their
vocals and musical talent. Jackie
Oates' fiddle-playing is mesmeriz-
ing, as are the melancholy notes of
Rachel's cello.

They have the courage to
experiment with unusual arrangements and at the same time are
obviously in love with traditional
music. One of the highlights is
Becky Unthank's haunting version of Antony and the Johnson's
'For Today I Am A Boy'. I didn't
expect to be so exhilarated and
refreshed by the talent and inge-
nuity of four down-to-earth northern lasses.

Rachel Unthank & The Winterset

Cruel Sister
(RabbleRouser Music RR005)

FOLK ALBUM OF THE YEAR
MOJO MAGAZINE 2005

"Simply gripping..their ambition knows no bounds" *FROOTS*
"when they strike gold, the results are electrifying" *NET RHYTHMS*
"joyous..freshingly forthright and in-yer-face" *MOJO*
"one day all music will sound like this" *PHIL JUPITUS, BBC 6 MUSIC*

www.rachelunthank.com   www.myspace.com/rachelunthank

Autumn/Winter 2006

Rachel Unthank & The Winterset

07.09 **DURHAM** GALA THEATRE 0191 3324041 www.galadurham.co.uk
09.09 **BROMYARD** FOLK FESTIVAL 01885 490323 www.bromyard-folk-festival.org.uk
14.10 **HALIFAX** SQUARE CHAPEL ARTS CENTRE 01422 349422 www.sq-chapel-arts.demon.co.uk
15.10 **LOUGHBOROUGH** FOLK FESTIVAL 01509 231914 www.loughboroughtownhall.co.uk
10.11 **NEW FOREST** FOREST ARTS CENTRE 01425 612393 www.forest-arts.co.uk
11.11 **BRISTOL** FOLKHOUSE 0117 9262987 www.bristolfolkhouse.co.uk
18.11 **CAMBRIDGE** THE JUNCTION 01223 511 511 www.junction.co.uk
19.11 **BASINGSTOKE** THE ANVIL 01256 844244 www.theanvil.org.uk
24.11 **LONDON** THE SPITZ 020 7392 9032 www.spitz.co.uk
25.11 **DUBLIN** THE COBBLESTONE 01-8721799 www.musicee.ie
27.11 **YORK** NATIONAL CENTRE FOR EARLY MUSIC 01904 658338 www.ncem.co.uk
28.11 **EDINBURGH** LEITH FOLK CLUB 0131 478 7810 www.leithfolkclub.com
29.11 **GLASGOW** ÒRAN MÓR 0141 357 6200 www.oran-mor.co.uk
30.11 **STIRING** THE TOLLBOOTH 01786 2740000 www.stirling.gov.uk/tolbooth
01.12 **ALNWICK** PLAYHOUSE 01665 510785 www.alnwickplayhouse.co.uk
02.12 **NOTTINGHAM** THE MAZE 0115 947 5650 www.cosmicamerican.com
03.12 **NEWCASTLE** CUMBERLAND ARMS 01912656151 www.thecumberlandarms.co.uk

www.rachelunthank.com
www.myspace.com/rachelunthank

Belinda O'Hooley
voice and piano
Becky Unthank
voice and dancing
Rachel Unthank
voice, cello and dancing
Jackie Oates
voice and 5 string viola

"one day all music will sound like this..just beautiful, beautiful music" *PHIL JUPITUS, BBC6 MUSIC*
"I just love it. I simply can't recommend them enough" *BOB HARRIS, BBC RADIO 2* "This is music lived, not learned" *FOLK ON TAP* "gold dust for the folk world" *FOLKING.COM* "Rachel Unthank is brilliant" *KATE RUSBY*
"Simultaneously graceful and unflinching" *METRO NEWS*

Pick of the Week in The Guardian Guide
RACHEL UNTHANK & THE WINTERSET, BUSH HALL, LONDON, FEBRUARY 2006 CRUEL SISTER TOUR

AN ARTIST WRITES...

No 3. Cally, Rag & Bone Man

SONGS OF AGES

"We have a different Nick Drake cover here," said Naomi at Rykodisc as she handed me a handwritten silver CD by an artist I hadn't heard of. I hurriedly slipped it into my case and pressed her on the purpose of my visit – to get hold of a copy of Norma Waterson's re-pressed album *The Very Thought Of You*. It was 2005, I had long been manager of Nick Drake's estate and I was on the hunt for cover versions. John Wood; Nick's producer/friend/ engineer highly recommended Norma's version. As publishers of Nick's songs, Ryko had a copy waiting for me. I adored The Watersons, still do to this day, so this was an exciting prospect, a personal landmark.

My days of late-night under-the-blanket John Peel broadcasts were heightened by the many sessions performed by The Watersons, and The High Level Ranters. These were the arid desert days of the mid 1970s, and I was an impoverished Art School student in Watford. Weekly trips to 'The Old Man's Shop' on the Clarendon Road threw up many a vinyl gem; records were piled to the ceiling, the shop smelled of wee, and my hands were filthy after lengthy crate-digging sessions. Old singles were 30p and one day in 1975 I left with one that would move my world on. It was knackered, had a stained plain sleeve, was on the Topic label, and it looked great (which was why I bought it). After one play of 'The Collier's Rant' by Louis Killen everything else sounded different.

If we were to avoid being shipwrecked on Soft Rock we had to venture bravely in 75; the most exotic music was imported, a great deal from Jamaica and Germany, very little homegrown in the UK apart from those distant shores of Canvey Island and 'the North-East'. Killen was from the north-east, his voice was strong and true, the single hit me like a sledgehammer; as brave and as bold as Big Youth or Popol Vuh, exotic, beguiling, fortifying.

Later, back in my office: Norma's album was no disappointment, then on fishing out that silver handwritten CD I spied *Cruel Sister* scrawled in felt pen on it. I put it on, got to 'River Man' and the room went ghostly still.

There are few versions of Nick's songs I enjoy. So many are sportive attempts of conquer without submission. His songs are often difficult to pull off, many have-a-go-heroes try, yet few seem to have closely listened to the song before starting out. Cruel sisters The Unthanks resisted the tricky time signature and the ornate embellishments; their version was open, sparse and very much their own. Becky sang a lonely version from the top of a moor, perhaps right next door to Louis Killen.

Their Bairns was born, I dived in full of anticipation. Nothing had prepared me for Lull 1; gratifyingly I was never quite the same after that either. Here, in one tiny song, was the economy and sparseness of Lee Perry, the confidence of Popol Vuh, and, in its simplicity, the epic grandeur of Peter Hammill, my entire listening diet in one tiny song, and people ask why they mean so much?

That year, our first-ever dog; a chocolate brown standard poodle, a hound that nursed my family back from the brink, a dog that asked for nothing and gave so much, was gently pulled off the vet's table as she entered the long sleep. I tried to drive home through the rain and tears, hearing "Sleep bonnie bairnie behind the castle, bye, bye, bye, bye, thou shalt have a golden apple, bye bye, bye, bye".

That's why.

Geordie folkster Rachel Unthank tells Shelley Marsden about some of her favourite things..

UNTHANK you for the MUSIC

FOLK SPECIAL

If you like your sounds traditional then you should fall in love with Rachel Unthank and the Winterset. Brought up in families where music means everything, they are four unassuming lasses who have taken the folk world by storm. They sing in their own accent (Geordie) and their powerful, unpolished songs breath new life into an often self-important and unadventurous traditional scene.

Their debut album Cruel Sister, was released last year. It not only gave them instant recognition (Mojo magazine awarded them Best Folk Group of 2005) but dragged folk music into the 21st century. The Guide chats to the group's alarmingly young and talented singer (and sometime sword dancer) Rachel Unthank, about folk festivals, cheese and why she still finds it 'weird' to be interviewed.

What's the first piece of music that sent shivers down your spine?

One of my favourite spine tingling pieces of music is a track by Solas called Feathered Hen. I shared a room at university and it used to be our going-to-sleep tune.

What has been your most memorable gig so far?

Probably the album launch for Cruel Sister. It was at Holmforth folk festival, which we've being going to since kids. We weren't sure if any one would come but it was packed. We had the musicians off the album including most of my family, so there was a cast of thousands. There were balloons, cake, bubbly, sweets and mass audience participation of popping party poppers, which sounded like fire works. I even did long sword dancing onstage, a first for me, with Redcar sword dancers.

There was a very special atmosphere. That would be closely followed by our last gig in London at Bush Hall, which was very exciting. The shabby chic of the place and the vibe from the audience made for a really memorable evening for us.

You've caused a huge splash in the folk pond. Why, is your sound so different?

There are lots of people making splashes all the time for loads of different reasons. We just try to represent the songs we sing as honestly as possible. For me personally, it's all about communicating the story of the song to the audience. The mixture of traditional material and the different influences we all bring to the band hopefully create a fresh perspective.

Working with the Winterset, Becky Unthank, Jackie Oates and Belinda O'Hooley, we all pull in different directions and I think that creates a healthy and creative environment in which to play music.

Really, we just try to do something that we would enjoy listening to ourselves, which has its roots in tradition but sounds like it's just hatched.

You've had a hectic time since Cruel Sister – are you enjoying it?

Of course! Playing so many different gigs and at all my favourite festivals is a dream come true. Any accolades and media attention from people we've listened to for years and respect is wonderful and bonkers all at the same time. I find this bit weird too. Who gives a monkeys about what I think?! I talk nonsense most of the time so to think that people will actually read this makes me nervous.

The best bit is being given the opportunity to what you love to do best and the weirdest and loveliest is that people come along and share that with you.

Apart from music, can you tell me about some of your favourite things?

Cheese (mmmmmmmm), shoes, winter beaches, cake, hats, mojitos, sparkles (yes I'm a predictable girl), my cello, swimming and my new ukulele all make me very happy, but my most favourite thing in the world is a family party where we all have a sing and a right good giggle.

If you'd never become a singer, what would you be doing now?

I studied History and theatre studies at University but I'm not really cut out to be a historian or an academic, I'm not studious enough.

All I ever wanted to be was a folk singer really, so I feel quite lucky to be doing what I am. I also do a lot of teaching in schools, I'm passionate about passing our traditions on and there's nothing quite like returning from a tour to a bunch of primary children.

They certainly keep your feet firmly on the ground. Failing all that I'd be happy swinging on a star and bringing moonbeams home in my jar, but as the song says, I'd probably be better off as I am!

What four musicians (alive or resurrected) would you invite to your fantasy dinner party?

Bjork. Jack Elliot (deceased), father of a well known folk singing family from Birtley in the North East who I never met; I would ask him to teach me his songs and tell me tales about life working in the mines. Robert Wyatt. Billie Holiday.

I don't know much about these characters. They have all had and have interesting lives in completely different ways. As you may have gathered by now, I love a good story and I think they would all have a good yarn to tell. I would love to hear about their inspiration, why they do what they do (or did) and hear them describing their music to each other.

I toyed with the idea of some teenage grunge/rock heartthrobs but decided that in retrospect they'd probably make for dull conversationalists compared to this lot. Now I'm starting to think about the food...there would definitely be a cheese course.

✳ *Rachel Unthank and the Winterset's debut album, Cruel Sister, is out now.*

23

4
FIRSTS
Adrian McNally

Adrian McNally didn't make an onstage appearance as an Unthank until 2009, but it was in 2002 that he met Rachel and Becky, and first started encouraging and enabling them to become full time singers, before dreaming up and developing The Winterset. Here, Adrian looks at how he fell into folk music and met Rachel and Becky.

The First Time I Heard A Folk Song

As a kid growing up in a house full of music, I'd heard plenty of folk song from America, from Dylan and Guthrie, and in the vernacular from Joni and co. I was getting into Nick Drake and John Martyn too by mid-teens. I'd also heard plenty from Ireland and had already fallen for the Irish tune-based tradition in the form of early Planxty and Bothy Band records, realising that diddly tunes actually weren't all the same and finding the complexity and forward momentum in them transfixing. But the first time I heard an English folk song came late and was a different matter altogether.

It was very late in fact, and I was worse for wear, but in a quiet and amiable way, at the house of a close friend's older brother. My friend Chris (a different one) and I were at uni, and we were on a weekend trip to see his two nephews and brother Paddy, up in the wild west of County Durham. It's the only area of the country that has ever reminded me of where I grew up – its more or less rural and pretty, but the villages that grew up to serve the mines which are gone now, have left the communities in them devoid of purpose and identity. Paddy and his family had plenty of purpose however, as community arts and theatre people. Ten years later I discovered a link with Rachel and Becky, who knew them because Becky went to their workshops as a child. It had been a nice evening. Dinner, drink, doobies, probably all courtesy of Paddy, as we were skint students. He had been playing us a tape of the indigenous music of somewhere in South America that he had returned from, after the latest of his funded trips on which he would go and learn to make some traditional exotic instrument and then return home to make and furnish County Durham's more curious teenagers with. Something like that. It was gone 2am and we were way past the point of usefulness when he switched tapes and despite my state, the next words stayed with me for years to come without actually hearing them again. "Farewell Durham, Yorkshire too, Nottingham the same to you. Scotland, South Wales, say adieu. Farewell Johnny Miner."

Bang. That was it. Music was never the same again. I was changed. This music was about where I was from. It was about my grandad, and half the adults of the village I grew up in. I discovered years later that it was a song by Ed Pickford on a tape of Bob Fox and Benny Graham's How Are You Off For Coals?.

Memories of lads, same age as me (11 or 12), walking up the street with their wheelbarrows containing a pitiful half bucket of coal scraps that took them all day to pick, came flooding back.

Until then, I thought the only people who could write about where they were from had to be from Detroit Rock City, or Panama, or Paradise City (these mid-eighties soft rock song references doing anything for you?). And that if you came from somewhere rainy, provincial and anglo, you had to either write introspective, existential songs of yearning or write about pendragons and topographical oceans.

Never had it occurred to me that you could write about the dole, and the pits of Northern England, in your own accent, let alone that it could sound electric, let alone that anyone would want to listen. It was OK to sing in your own accent if you were from New Jersey, but not Newcastle, Middlesbrough or Sheffield, otherwise why would Sting have adopted quasi-Jamaican vowels and why did David Coverdale and Joe Elliott sing like the mid-Atlantic offspring of Steve Tyler and Janis Joplin, all of whom I loved?

The idea that the communities I belonged to could have a voice, a vernacular and a say was super exciting. I thought about Farewell Johnny Miner, privately, a lot, but without doing anything about it for a while, until this happened...

The First Time I Experienced A Folk Club

I went to Holmfirth Folk Festival a fair bit in my teens, as it was local. This didn't involve any actual festival attendance however. It only involved sitting in The Nook pub, drinking and lapping up the sessions, which to my ears, and before the dawn of the Nineties Irish theme pub doom (ha! I actually meant to write 'boom', but my autocorrect changed it to 'doom'... I think I'll leave it!) was exotic and wild music. One afternoon, the Nook was just too packed, and I was forced to try the Elephant and Castle instead. It too was chocka, and for a bit of breathing space, I slipped into the back room, only to discover what I came to learn was a singing session. Here the real damage was done. If Farewell Johnny Miner had lit the fuse, this was the bomb. By the time I came out a couple of hours later, more or less everyone in the room had sung, alone, without instruments. A really old woman, a fella with the complexion and physicality of an outdoor manual worker, a black teenage lass with a Barnsley accent... OK, there was a few middle aged blokes with beards, but every time I thought I'd seen the least likely candidate get up and bring the room to a standstill with a performance of extraordinary emotional resonance, a rough looking skinhead lad in a tracksuit would stand up and top it.

My heart raced, and my blood was hot. You know that terrible burning you get if you suddenly realise something terrible and unavoidable, or the lightning adrenalin your body pushes through you to respond to a dangerous situation? Well, I felt like that the whole time I was in there. Now of course, its commonplace, not just to me, but in general the folk way is far less of a closed shop than it was then. At that moment, it was utterly extraordinary — the most profound experience of my life to that point in fact — that these ordinary looking people had a voice, had art, had heritage, had shoulders to stand on, had the facility to express emotion and attitude in a way they might not have had the facility to do in verbal discourse. Had each other. It was more powerful and evocative than any play I'd ever seen, any film, any speech, any form of public address whatsoever.

Some of them were fantastic performers. A fat chap in a baseball cap — voice of an angel. A frail old woman — voice like the devil itself. But then, the paradox of the ones who didn't have a very good voice at all, technically. Could barely hold a tune even. Some of them made the best performances of all. The only yardstick by which to measure was the effective conveyance of the sentiment in the song — devastating, funny, angry... whatever. The beauty was truth. The truth was beautiful.
I haven't been the same since.

The First Time I Heard Rachel Sing

By this point, I was already immersed in the scene, working with Irish singer and guitarist Denny Bartley and Yorkshire Anglo Concertina player Chris Sherburn. I was so impressed by their musicality and conviction that I dropped everything and became their manager, agent, sound man, record producer and record label. My feckless approach in my early twenties had come good. Being pragmatic enough to realise that only a tiny handful of the people who try have any meaningful success in the music industry, I hedged my bets and had a go at everything, such that by 1996 I was running a music magazine in Manchester, working for a booking agency, and doing bits of live and studio sound here and there. None of it made me any money, my parents despaired, I was miserable, and in hindsight, if ever I was going to get anywhere, I should really have ploughed all my energies into just one area, otherwise how do you beat the rest to the top?! Little did I know that the music industry (as we knew it) was about to lose its 'top'and die a slow, lingering death. With the resulting shift to DIY, I was ideally multi-skilled to flourish in the emerging culture of doing things the small, independent, cottage industry way. By the time I met Rachel and Becky, my cottage industry template was already in place.

That's the background then to explain why in 2002 I was with Chris and Denny, by now known as Last Night's Fun, at Warwick Folk Festival, where I met Rachel dressed as a green witch (her, not me), properly for the first time.

We had sort of met very briefly a couple of times before, and had confusing and quietly profound but unspoken effects on each other. Our romantic interest declared and slightly hungover the next day, in a not-particularly-nice pub beer garden, Rachel was called on to sing. She remained seated on a concrete step, where I sat beside her, so her voice was very close to me and she sang softly and quietly. But not sweetly. I don't remember what she sang. Only the effect.

It didn't tell me what to think. Her voice, that is. Or feel. Not that it was passive either (this is also what Martin Freeman had to say about Rachel when we first met him — that her believability as a storyteller is down the fact that she doesn't tell the listener what to think – she's never believed me but funnily enough was happy to take it from a brilliant and famous actor!) There was a maternal warmth, but a resigned dispassion, as cool and certain as the North Sea. She was only 25, but she sounded like a woman, not a girl. It was basically the calmest and most authoritative noise I'd ever heard and in an instant I was sure she could and should be a star. Or rather, that people must hear her.

I'm describing this now, like I have rationalised and tinted the memory with hindsight, but its genuinely how I felt from the moment she drew breath. Of course I had to temper my response, otherwise I'd have scared her to death with my intensity, I'm sure. It was such a surprise to me. To spend time with, she was like a jack-in-a-box, bouncing around the place in boisterous and breezy fashion. I guess maybe it's easy to live in the moment when you can call up and purge the depths of despair and vent the joy of living within the medium of song.

As it turned out, Rachel wasn't just a calm singer. She could also be a right loudy-head, influenced by the shanty singing men she grew up watching, as well as by the monumental conviction of women singers like Sheila Stewart and June Tabor. I had seen all too many aspiring young vocalists who clearly wanted to emulate the same unquestionable fire and sheer volume as say, Peter Bellamy, but without having either the emotional maturity or control of their voice to be any more than a cartoon caricature. It seemed to me that Rachel had learned not just her vernacular from her elders, but had understood the value of the songs, the value of what she had been taught, giving her a sense of duty and love for the songs. It is easy, or easier, I think, to whip up the storm inside you, when you believe in the gravity of the song, because you are simply there to show it, to give it. You're lucky as hell, basically, to momentarily be at one with it. Knowing Rachel as I do now, I know that she feels this luck. This culture she was offered, and which worked its magic on her at a formative age, giving her something to offer the world that in theory, anyone can give, but only if you see its value.

The First Time I Saw Rachel and Becky Perform

I don't remember actually! That is, it happened too gradually. I probably first heard them sing together at a family party, or even just to themselves. Becky was just seventeen, and would hide, vocally, behind her sister, elder by seven years. Rachel would back off to allow her to come through, and Becky would just back off too. But she could be a loudy-head too. I hear now in our early albums, that she too was influenced by those bawdy men and women. Or was she influenced by Rachel being influenced. I don't know, but it's funny to listen back, now that the voice of her own that she has found is so sensual, so lazy and liquid.

Times have changed. At the very moment I am writing this, Becky is probably just coming off stage in Shetland, on the last night of a collaboration with members of Portishead, Lau and Mogwai. She definitely doesn't hide behind Rachel anymore, or need to!

I do remember their first proper folk club booking as a duo, at South Shields Folk Club, probably 2003. They'd bumbled through a few festival spots which they gladly snapped up for free tickets, but perhaps were not taken as seriously as I would have liked! But no pep talk was required for that first proper show on home soil. They had to work hard to get a set of proper length together, and with adrenalin pumping from the sense that this was it – no longer were they kids – they were quite brilliant, or at least I thought so at the time. It was a big deal for them, but in psychological terms more than in vocational ones. In a folk club or singing session, you get up if you're asked, you sing a song from where you are in the room, and then you sit back down again, having shared with the room… something, hopefully. If you have grown up in this egalitarian democracy of singing, then taking the journey from the folk club floor, up and on to the stage, setting yourself apart by suggesting that people pay to hear you sing, is a very big step indeed.

And that is where I will stop, or try to. This piece is only an attempt at pre-band history.

The only other pre-band thing I would like to reflect on is to remind myself of the adult I was before Rachel and Becky swerved into view. I could say that I was a typical example of a failed musician with washed up dreams, but even that would be an exaggeration, because I hadn't even tried, let alone failed. After playing in a daft pub band as a teenager with Chris Price, I went to uni and didn't play the piano again for 14 years. I didn't even play it well before I stopped. I didn't have chops of any sort that might come back with a bit of practice. Nevertheless I still had the regret of a failed musician, that I hadn't tried, that the music industry back then had seemed so impenetrable that it wasn't even worth trying to unlock the imagination I was sure I had, having listened to so much good music as a kid. I knew I had potential, I was very sad that I had never tried to explore it, and I thought I was well past the point at which I ever would.

It wasn't that long ago at all that I was that person, and in the majority camp of would-be musicians who never get beyond their bedroom and wonder why. The reason most don't is because they never have the right idea, at the right time. I don't mean that in a marketing sense. To be successful, you don't just have to make good music, it has to be something that enough people at that time are going to get and want to invest in. I just got lucky, that in Rachel and Becky, I happened on two people I believed in so much that it unlocked the creative seam in me. Their authority, their believability, their uniqueness, was a sound basis for an understandable idea – one that has seen me go from cooking up a band but appointing a pianist because I wasn't confident or capable enough to take the stool myself, to writing my first score despite being unable to read music, being forced by necessity and the encouragement of Rachel and Becky to eventually become an onstage member, to this year scoring ninety minutes of music for a symphony orchestra to play with us. My 30-year-old self, let alone my 18-year-old self, would find this utterly ridiculous. However modest or however memorable our contribution turns out to be, my own personal leap is beyond measure, and my gratitude for it is beyond measure, to Rachel and Becky. Thank you.

Tuesday 27 OCTOBER

LIVERPOOL Folk & Roots FESTIVAL 2009
21ST – 28TH NOVEMBER

THE UNTHANKS

ROY BAILEY

MARTIN SIMPSON

STORMALONG JOHN

HUGHIE JONES

THE RANDOM FAMILY

THE SIXTEEN TONNES

DENIS JONES & LIZ GREEN

LIZZIE NUNNERY

PLUS EXHIBITIONS, WORKSHOPS & MUCH MORE

WWW.LIVERPOOLFOLKANDROOTS.COM

THE COMPANY STORE

NAME Becky Unthank

VISITING Jools Holland

TIME IN 7.00

EXTENSION NO.

VALID ON DAY OF ISSUE ONLY. PLEASE RETURN THIS PASS TO RECEPTION

(handwritten) TV debut.

10.00 BBC
Regional News

10.35 Make ...
The market for ... lighten dark skin is now worth millions of pounds – and Anita Rani wants to find out why. The presenter explores the pressures that impel those with darker skins to "lighten up", and also the risks taken by those using illegal products.
Director Kevin Jarvis; Exec producer William Lyons (S) (AD) 923824

11.15 Film 2009 with Jonathan Ross
Writer Nick Hornby discusses *An Education*. Plus a location report from Michael Caine's upcoming drama *Harry Brown*, and reviews of *9* and *Dead Man Running*.
Director Howard Brenner; Series producer Tom Webber (S) 911718
Get your RT Guide to Films 2010: page 39

11.45 The Graham Norton Show
4/11. Anarchic talk show with celebrity guests.
Shown yesterday at 10.35pm (S)   693466
Followed by **Weatherview** (S)

12.35–3.20am Sign Zone Signed. Repeats not indicated.
See Hear Results of a health survey. With voiceover. (S) 9830190

1.05 Last Chance to See 4/6. Stephen Fry and Mark Carwardine search for Komodo dragons. (S) (AD) 9382995

2.05 Saving Britain's Past 2/7. Tom Dyckhoff visits the Park Hill flats in Sheffield. (S) 2933003

2.35 MasterChef: the Professionals The two winners from the fourth quarter-final go head to head. (S) 1855577

3.20–6.00am BBC News (S)

Watch again or catch up on BBC iPlayer at bbc.co.uk/iplayer

◄ For regional variations see overleaf

...ts to find o... ...ared within their lifetim...
...ec producer Andrew Cohen (S) (A...

HORIZON: radiotimes.com/horizon
BBC FOCUS MAGAZINE: out monthly, £3.60

10.00 Later Live...with Jools Holla...
7/10. Maxwell performs in the *Later...* studio...
first time since his 1996 debut, showcasing tra...
his *Black Summers' Night* album; Stereopho...
return for a ninth time on the eve of the rele...
their *Keep Calm and Carry On* album. Plus s...
Canada's Diana Krall, the Lake District's Wild...
and Northumberland folk band the Unthank...
extended version is on Friday at 11.35pm.
Director Janet Fraser Crook; Series producer Alison Howe
Simulcast in HD on the BBC HD channel (see page 83)
BEHIND-THE-SCENES PICS: radiotimes.com/later

10.30 Newsnight With Kirsty Wark. (S)
Followed by **Weather** (S)

11.20 The World's Greatest Money...
Maker: Evan Davis Meets Warren ...
Ukulele-playing investor Warren Buffett can...
on the Forbes 2009 world billionaires list w...
estimated fortune of $37 billion. Despite hi...
wealth, the "Sage of Omaha" lives modest...
native Nebraska, and runs his $150 billion...
with just 20 staff. **See choice, page 68.**
Shown yesterday at 9pm (S)

12.20–3.20am BBC News (S)

HD BBC HD Freesat 108 Sky 143 Virgin108 (see p...

Watch again or catch up on BBC iPlayer at bbc.co.uk/i...

Films ▣ Premiere Star Ratings

SUNDAY ...GHT LIVE!

Chic folk... Rachel Unthank

RACHEL UNTHANK & THE WINTERSET
at Camden Jazz Cafe, London

THEY'RE rank outsiders for this year's Mercury Music Prize... but judging by the reaction of the audience in Camden, Rachel and The Winterset ought to be planning how to spend the winner's £20,000 already.

Anyone who thinks folk music means knitting wholemeal porridge with your finger in your ear should stop reading immediately. This lot sing of booze, sex and longing as convincingly as any rock 'n' roll outfit... ...ine-fighting on the Tyne. John Sergeant

Featuring Rachel on lead singing duties along with kid sister Becky, accompanied by Niopha on vocals and violin and Steph on piano and vocals, RU&TWS sing spine-tingling songs that might just make folk truly fashionable again in the 21st Century.

And having been truly blown away by the outfit at this gig, I find it baffling that all the talk about the Mercury Award has so far gone to underground dubstep outfit Burial, hot new talent Adele and fantastic but veteran indie outfits Radiohead and Elbow.

Playing mostly from their second album *The Bairns*, this quartet were utterly beguiling from start to finish and proved that folk is genetically hard-wired into the British soul. Bringing nu-feminist attitude to centuries-old songs like *I Wish*, their sparkling North Eastern wit also tempered the naturally doom-laden lyrics of their tales of woe from the underclasses of yesteryear. And time and again the girls voiced pitch-perfect, exquisite, bittersweet harmonies – and when they went totally acapella on *Ma Bonny* and their cover of Robert Wyatt's *Sea Song*, the four voices together fair made the hairs leap to attention on the back of your neck with it's otherworldliness.

Rachel has the clearer, more traditional voice while Becky's is more smoky, but they all sing in their natural Northumbrian accent, which makes it all the more charming. Oh and they even manage to make clog dancing sexy onstage. Yes, you read correctly. "You must recognise us," quips Rachel at one point. "We were in Lord of the Rings. As hobbits."

We can only hope they'll be as famous and legendary one day. But without the hairy feet, of course.

SET LIST
On A Monday Morning
Blue Bleezing Blind Drunk
Lousy Cutter (Blues Gan Oot O' The Fashion)
I Wish
Lull (Newcastle Lullaby)
Blackbird
Ma Bonnie Lad
Sea Song
Feltin Lonnin
My Donald
Sandgate Dangling Song
Farewell Regality

JODY THOMPSON

V1
...ky103 Virgin 103

...ening News
...and Mary Nightinga...
...cky Mantin. (S)

...and Laurel that ...
...rl makes plans
...ining Cain's m...
...a Harding
...Rokhsaneh G...
...etcalfe Mat...
...Wylde Ly...
...gle
...gle Ede...

5
NIOPHA KEEGAN

My mother and father were Irish immigrants in England, hailing from Leitrim and Wexford. They met in England whilst doing their nurse training in Maidstone, Kent and later moved to St Albans in Hertfordshire where I was born. They decided to settle there to raise their family. My father was always homesick and missed Irish culture and the "Irish way of life" so my parents consciously submerged the family into the small Irish community in St Albans and the larger Irish Diaspora in London. I remember as a child spending a lot of time travelling into the "big smoke", always to areas such as Kilburn and Cricklewood- the hub of the London/Irish community.

My brother Niall is 7 years older than me and started Irish music lessons when he was 5 so it was inevitable that I too started tin whistle lessons at the same age. My godfather, Peter Fahy was one of the biggest musical influences on my brother and I. Peter lived in St Albans with his American wife Katie and they were our closest family friends. Peter had a real passion for

Irish music. He wrote and collected tunes and spent many years travelling around Ireland going to festivals and sessions playing his music, so we were very lucky that he dedicated some of his time to share his music with us. I still have handwritten tunes that Peter gave me, my favourite being 'The Blackbird' slow air. I have vivid memories of Peter visiting our family home. He would ask me what tunes I had been learning and he'd often lilt a tune to me and I would try to learn it on the whistle from his singing.

My mum and dad had gruelling jobs and three children which meant they had to work opposite shifts — Dad on day shifts, Mum on nights, to cut down on childcare costs. However my father had a real passion for Irish music and my mother was a human dynamo. Working nights, picking us all up from different schools and taking us to various different music lessons and dance lessons every night of the week. On a weekly basis I had — private classical violin lessons, private Irish music lessons, orchestra rehearsals, ceilidh band lessons,

Peter and I at my first holy communion

response, "Yeah I suppose so." He responded with "Well your talents lie elsewhere, I believe. How about if you come and play the fiddle for my Feis instead (a Feis is an Irish dancing competition)? To be honest when you dance you resemble a baby elephant!"

I was of course devastated with this statement and didn't go near dance class for a good few weeks but I then learned that I would be paid a lot of money to play for the dancing at the Feis and all was forgiven. I think the period of time that I played, not only for Mr. Bracken's class Feis but some other regional competitions as well, saw the most improvement and development in my fiddle playing. I would play for twelve hours a day, practically non-stop, both Friday and Saturday. The best practice I ever did. Although I was a terrible dancer it helped me with my sense of rhythm and feel for music. I'm the person you'll find tapping their foot and nodding in time to music in the corner at a party rather than busting a groove on the dancefloor.

piano lessons and Irish dance lessons. That was just me! My brother had the same amount of classes but with different tutors and likewise my sister. I really don't know how my mum did it (she even learned how to play the tin whistle to aid our practice) but if it weren't for her drive, passion and care for her children's happiness, I would not have the job I have today, travelling the world, performing music with a lovely bunch of people. The same can be said for my brother Niall, who is an Associate Director of the Irish World Academy in Limerick University and the Director of Undergraduate Studies, responsible for BA Irish Music and Dance, BA Voice and Dance and Certificate in Music and Dance (he's the talented one). So thanks Mum. If I had an ounce of your energy and passion I would be extremely happy.

Baby Elephant

I am often envious of Rachel and Becky when watching them clog dance on stage to the point where I threaten to join their clog group in Newcastle. But then I remember my dance experiences as a kid. I took Irish dancing lessons from the age of five. I was never very good at it but the dancing teachers never really had the heart to tell me that and hoped for improvement. I went to Moira Skehill and John Brooks for the first 8 years. Every week my mum would take my sister and I for lessons. I used to complain bitterly about going but when I was there I enjoyed the lessons very much. My third teacher, Thomas Bracken took me for lessons for 3 years until he finally said to me "Do you enjoy dancing Niopha?" My answer was a typical teenager's

The Thomas Bracken dance school. Just some of the dancers – my sister, second from right. Me at the back with Mr. Bracken

St. Colmcilles ladies and the Abbey Ceilidh Band

CComhaltas Ceoltóirí Éireann is the largest group involved with the preservation and promotion of Irish traditional music around the world. They have branches in many cities and towns worldwide. We have a branch in my hometown of St Albans, which has been going since the early 1970s. My brother, sister and I all went to classes in St Albans. Through our branch of Comhaltas we performed at many concerts and festivals and entered many competitions. This was all down to a man called Pat Judge. He ran our Comhaltas branch for many years and was revered on the Irish music scene.

The highlight of the year was the Fleadh Cheoil na hÉireann, which means feast of music (or as we called t, the All Ireland). It was a weekend festival held in Ireland every August bank holiday weekend. The festival was based around competitions of every variety – tin whistle to marching band competitions. Over 200,000 people would attend from all over the world. The way to qualify for the Fleadh for people from the UK was to enter and be placed first or second in your regional heat, which enabled you to go to the All Britain Fleadh. You then had to be placed first or second at this competition to go to the All Ireland. It was a big deal and the pressure was immense to get a place in the finals. I remember running from competition to competition as I would enter as many as possible – tin whistle, tin whistle slow air, fiddle, fiddle slow air, mandolin, singing, lilting, duet, trio, groupacheoil and ceilidh band – to try to secure a place at the All Ireland on some instrument! I think I even entered into the whistling competition once.

The highlight of the All Ireland weekend was the senior ceilidh band competition. It was the last competition of the weekend held in a huge marquee as none of the town venues were big enough to hold the attendants. My brother was in the Colmcilles Ceilidh band. They often won this coveted prize. I remember being so envious of the band and desperately wanted to be a part of it. I really looked up to the girls in the band. They were the older cool kids that I admired.

Needless to say Britain was well represented at the fleadh. Among those who made the trip were the Abbey Ceili Band, below, from St. Albans.

From the Irish Post Newspaper from 1992

Caroline, Rosemary, Angela Judge, Carmel Dwyer, Bernadette Balantine, Eilish Byrne and Kathleen Murray. They were amazing musicians and often Rosemary, Angela and Carmel gave me music lessons. As we got older some of the fiddle players in the band could not make some of the gigs they had because of other commitments and I was so thrilled when Pat Judge asked me to stand in for them. I was so excited to be able to travel around the country (in our beat up old transit van often referred to as the passion wagon. I never asked why it got that name in fear of the answer)

playing for ceilidhs with this amazing band. I thought I was the bees knees! Not sure how my brother felt about this. He probably thought I was cramping his style. When I was 15, Pat Judge put together a Ceilidh band for the 15–18 age group to enter the fleadhs. We rehearsed every Thursday night, tutored by Pat himself. After just 10 months of forming we were amazed to find ourselves in the All Ireland final. We thought we were amazing. Finally I felt like I was in a cool gang. We were convinced we were going to win… but we were pipped to the post by a band from Manchester. We were heartbroken. Thought it was the end of the world. We came second in the All Ireland! In hindsight I think we were a little hard on ourselves. We had a great time going to the competitions and we did extremely well for a band that had been together for such a short period of time. We were all great friends too. The band was made up of three groups of sisters – Julianne and Mhari-Louise Healy, Maria and Michelle O' Sullivan, Nuala and I – one brother and sister – Karen and Mark Scanlan – and Sinead Keen and Pat Mc Manus. We would all hang out at the competitions and gigs and have a whale of a time, however sadly the band broke up shortly after this photo was taken as a lot of us had pressure with school work and studies. I think its time for a reunion. Look at those band shirts! They were bright green and very shiny. Delightful.

The classical side

I started playing classical music when I was 6 years old. First on recorder (of every kind – I still have my Grade 5 descant and Grade 3 tenor certificates) with piano and violin following shortly after that. I had the same music teacher for all. Her name was Mrs. Mould. She was a very serious and strict teacher, who frankly scared the living daylights out of me but she got great results out of the children she taught and I advanced very quickly on my instruments. She introduced me to the St Albans School of Music where I attended Suzuki and junior orchestra from a young age. I moved up to the Philomusica after getting my Grade 5 violin. Over the years of my classical playing I had many teachers for violin and piano. I enjoyed my lessons but found the stereotypical classical learning system of doing grades and theory tests very stressful. It took the fun out of the lessons as it was always at the back of my mind that in a short period of time I would be, once again, performing grade pieces, playing scales, doing sight reading tests and aural tests in front of a scary examiner. However the Orchestra was a different matter. I made so many friends and loved to be a part of a huge sound, making wonderful classical music pieces come to life. I was a second violinist sitting in the middle of the orchestra. The sheer power of the orchestra and the beauty of the

music we played used to make the hair stand up on the back of my neck. I left the orchestra after giving up music in my late teens and to this day still miss that experience. However when Adrian told us that we were going to have a 10 piece band which would include a string quartet I was thrilled. The chance to play with other classical players again. It is definitely my favorite part of being in the band. Such a treat to play with the wonderful musicians – Kath, Becca and Gemma. I'm very lucky.

Jelly babies

"Hello jelly babies!" would be the cry from my fiddle teacher, Brendan Mulkere, as he walked into the classroom for our Sunday morning lessons. I was always slightly nervous as I so wanted to get my homework done properly and play the pieces of music Brendan had given me the previous week well. He was a real inspiration to me and also to hundreds of musicians he taught in London. I have heard people say "He's taught all the good musicians that have come out of London for the last 30 years." I had never heard the fiddle played so beautifully before and he was an amazing accordion player to boot. He was a hard but fair teacher and he rewarded the children well if they worked hard for him. I have wonderful memories of performing at festivals and concerts from a very young age with Brendan. One concert we did London in particular. It was a huge theatre and it had tables with lamps on for the audience to sit at. I thought it was so posh. Plus I got to sit beside Brendan whilst performing on stage. I thought, "I must be doing alright at this fiddle playing then".

Whilst writing about this memory it has struck me that I was never nervous when performing as a kid. Even when playing with a musician I revered so much, I just got into the music and surroundings. These days I panic and get nervous about playing live with the band. In desperation to back Becky and Rachel's beautiful songs and Adrian and Chris' playing and arrangements sympathetically, I get what is commonly called in the band, 'Goat fiddle'. The nerves take hold and I start shaking uncontrollably. When it's really bad, Chris gives me a sideways glance. In future I think I will try to remember being that fearless kid that just 'dug in' and enjoyed playing her heart out.

The O'Rythmics

When I was eighteen I hit my rebellious stage. A little late, I know. I couldn't cope with the stresses of college and my musical activities but instead of dropping one or a few of my extra curricular activities I dropped all music. Gave up the violin completely. It sat in the corner of my living room gathering dust for at least 5 years. My family and I went to a Christmas party held at St Albans Irish centre where we met a family friend John Devine. John had played Irish music as a child and like me, had given it up many years previously for work and family. He had been asked to pick up his flute and bodhran again to play for a St Patrick's Day gig in his local pub and he asked me if I wanted to be in his scratch band. I was nervous at first but agreed to join in. It was from that gig that we then formed The O'Rythmics. We played lots of local pubs at the weekends and many weddings and corporate events. I loved playing and singing with the band. I had a great social life and it was extra spending money on top of my nursing job at that time.

I don't think I would be playing again today if John had not asked me to do that paddy's day gig. John left his electrician's job behind and has forged himself a great job in music. He is a development officer in Britain for the Irish arts organization, Comhaltas Ceoltóirí Éireann and plays in his family band, Devines, with his wife Caz and son Jo. He also plays in Wild Willy Barrett's French Connection band. Our paths cross quite often on the festival circuit. He came to see The Unthanks perform at Celtic Connections last year. Hopefully we will meet and have a few tunes at Christmas time again.

Bossy Boots

Whilst listening to all my dad's recordings of our family to find a suitable one to go with my air that I wrote him for the Mount The Air album, I found a cassette tape labelled 'Bossy boots'. It was me at 8 years old. I had recorded a whistle lesson for my 5-year-old sister. I was trying to teach her 'Sackows Jig'. "I want you to play it like this Nuala," I said and played the jig at breakneck speed. "Not like this!" And then a burst of comedy whistle playing. "You've got to get it right for our next lesson, OK. Or there will be trouble."

I probably got my teaching style from my brother Niall who was forced on a regular basis to give my sister and me lessons. I remember one lesson in particular when Nuala and I were not focusing on Niall's tutoring at all. I was sat on the sofa giggling and laughing and Niall kicked me! The tin whistle shot into the roof of my mouth and all hell broke loose. Screaming from both Nuala and me, my mum was shouting at my brother and my dad was trying to calm me down and prise the tin whistle out of my hands. Anyway, no death occurred and in the long run I was very pleased as I got out of doing whistle practice for at least a week because of my minor injury! This was an isolated incident and Niall gave us many lessons, taught me many great tunes.

In fact, without Niall I would not be where I am today with my music. Over the years I have always been included in bands that Niall has put together, to do gigs all over the UK, Ireland and in Europe. He has got me many interviews with bands, even travelling with me to Boston, USA for one job. He is the reason why I came up to Newcastle. He introduced me to the Folk Degree and put me forward for the course. Niall and his wife Sandra continue to be a great support with all my musical exploits and I owe them so much for all their help and encouragement. Perhaps Niall still feels guilty about the "Whistle incident"!

My fondest memory of all is playing music with my brother and sister. All family parties and friends' parties we attended would include my brother and I playing music for my sister to dance to. My dad loved a good 'shindig' and would always put on a good spread of grub. He would invite work colleagues, neighbours and friends over and a great time would be had by all. The night would always end with a singing and music and session. Playing in The Unthanks gives me the same wonderful feelings. They are like family to me. It gives me the same sense of unity and I have the same bond with Rachel, Becky, Adrian and Chris. Being in close synchrony with others is such a powerful feeling. I am a very lucky gal.

Mum and Dad

Makeshift ceilidh band for my sister's wedding. (L—R My brother Nia Caz Devine (family friend) Sandra Joyce (sister-in-law), Siobho O'Donahue (family friend) my sister Nuala, moi, John Devine and n Uncle John Gildea.

Look at that fringe!

Nuala and I dancing to the Colmcilles ceilidh band at our Halloween party. My brother is the grim reaper on the left

My brother and I playing at my dad's retirement party circa 1983

A FAN WRITES...

No 1. Phil Weight

I'd been dimly aware of Rachel Unthank & The Winterset from the early days, though not paid too much attention as I had grown up on prog and rock, and was not in any sense a "folkie". But one evening in 2009 watching *Later with Jools* I saw The Unthanks sing 'Lucky Gilchrist'. Something sparked, and I decided I had to go to see them play live. So I did. And I did again, twice. Sometimes you just realise that you "get" a band and what it's creating. Then I met Rachel and Becky for the first time at the Roundhouse after *The Beggars Opera* show. I took a friend to see The Unthanks at Shepherd's Bush, and he was hooked too. They tend to do that to you.

Getting ready for work on 8th December 2010, I was armed with my ticket for the Union Chapel that evening, looking forward to seeing the band play the Anthony & The Johnsons / Robert Wyatt concert. But within an hour I was at the hospital with my daughters, as their mum Maggie had just suffered a catastrophic brain haemorrhage. That evening, as The Unthanks took the stage, we said goodbye to Maggie as the life-support was switched off.

Three months later I was at Shepherd's Bush Empire to see the band play the *Last* tour. Before the show, Niopha was at her regular station on the merchandise desk. I nearly didn't, but I summoned up the courage to speak to her and explained why I'd missed the December gig. Later, deep into the set, Rachel stepped up to the mic to say "This is called Starless. This is for Maggie." Then music.... "Old friend charity, cruel twisted smile, and the smile signals emptiness for me. Starless and bible black." I stood at the front rail and wept hard. A catharsis – the first time I'd really let go since we lost her. That night the band did something for me that I don't think could have happened in any other way. I still can't stop myself from crying whenever the band plays that song.

From that night I felt more personally tied into the songs The Unthanks sing. So much so that, hearing about their group singing weekends, I did something out of character for me, and decided it was time to let go of old fears and inhibitions, and to go and sing. I hadn't sung publicly for over 40 years, since primary school, but these people made me want to –it seemed the right thing to do. So on a cold Friday in November 2011 I walked into a room in Seahouses and was greeted by Rachel and Becky; within hours, through their careful and gentle guidance, I found myself singing glorious songs with other people. For some that's a regular thing. For me, it was like a jigsaw piece that had been missing for years. I sang with a pint in the pub. I sang on a wild beach by the sea. I made new friends. By Sunday morning I was in some way a more complete person. I haven't missed a weekend since. I've learned great songs. I've sung in a castle. I've grown. Last year we sang to, and with, 800 people at the Home Gathering festival; that night we sang as part of The Unthanks stage performance of 'Sea Coal', and together we created something almost transcendent. I'm a lucky man, and I love these people for giving me the chance, and the impetus, to do this.

In the years since 2009 I've met and made friends with the extended Unthanks and McNally families, with Niopha Keegan and Chris Price, and many others, and they have all been unswervingly warm and welcoming and they have collectively widened my understanding of traditional music, the history of songs, the fun of group singing, and of life in general. I no longer see them as "a band", but as friends, and I'm the richer for it. I've seen them launch albums and, deservedly, win awards. Their music and their warmth as people has helped me through pain and hard times, but it's also brought me great fun, and it has broadened my musical knowledge enormously. For all those things I'll be forever grateful. And I'll keep singing.

Pow! Billy Bragg's son defeats Becky at Wychwood Festival.

So let's hear Aperitifs with Mr H read by John Rowe.

Aperitifs with Mr H by Jonathan Trigell read by John Rowe. And Cham is published by Serpent's Tale. ~~Tale~~

Finally let's welcome the wonderful Rachel Unthank and the Winterset; Rachel and her sister Becky come from a hotbed of traditional North East song and dance and craic and tale telling and joke telling and scary things under the stairs and walking down the front at Whitley Bay in your vest in November. In other words, they're the inheritors, curators and gleeful distorters of a body of words and music that go back hundreds of years. The band is completed by Belinda O Hooley and ~~Jackie Oates~~ NIOPHA KEEGAN

1 Why is keeping these old songs alive important to you?

2 Once you've arranged them and sung them, who do they belong to?

3 So when you write a new song, are you trying to write it in that traditional style and how easy is that?

4 In traditional songs the language is spare, the stories are operatic in their grandness - is it possible to write that kind of song today?

Outtakes from The Bairns shoot
by Karen Melvin.

The Winterset at Northern Stage, Newcastle,
Winning a Journal Culture Award.

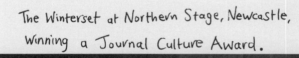

*The*Journal

culture

artsheritagemusictheatrelist... ...umscountrysciencefilmsportar...

Rachel Unthank set for summer

David Essex on love and music

Stockton Festival hits 20

north east
england

AUGUST 07

£1.30

where sold separately

Bonny bairns

Rachel Unthank and the Winterset's new album may be called The Bairns, but it brings a striking maturity to the folk band, as **Tamzin Lewis** discovers.

Rachel and Becky Unthank are recovering from a long night of singing and trampolining. The singing they describe as enforced, while the trampolining was optional at a family party held to celebrate the arrival of an Australian cousin in the North-East.

They apologise for jabbering in a hungover-slept-on-the-floor-last-night kind of way, but having youth on their side, neither looks the worse for wear. Excitement is also taking the edge off a late night, as when I meet the sisters at Rachel's Tyne Valley home, they are post-party but pre-holiday: setting off in the early hours on a girly trip to Crete with their mum Pat.

The trip is well timed, a probable calm before the storm, as they are about to launch their atmospheric second album The Bairns, booked to play at summer festivals across Europe and set to go on an extensive national tour in the autumn.

Rachel Unthank and the Winterset's first album Cruel Sister, released on independent record label RabbleRouser Music, won the group acclaim, a national following and an international licensing agreement with EMI Records. Despite the big record deal The Bairns has been produced by Rachel's partner Adrian McNally, of RabbleRouser, in much the same unpretentious, ad hoc way as Cruel Sister.

You are more likely to discover the band recording in a remote Northumberland cottage with cloth stapled on the walls than in a state-of-the-art studio. Some of Rachel's vocals were recorded under the stairs at home while on one track Becky provides percussion with the heels of her red shoes.

Rather than leaning towards the mainstream, The Bairns takes Rachel Unthank and the Winterset into darker, more personal and more adventurous territory than Cruel

Sister. "We want to do what we do, whether it is commercially successful or not," Rachel, 29, says. "We don't have big expectations, we just take things as they come, but hopefully with EMI we will have the opportunity of reaching a wider audience.

"We are trying to make music which we would like to listen to and if it became boring, we would change it. Our aim is to keep developing and progressing and I hope that we are doing something which isn't predictable."

Like the debut, The Bairns reflects Rachel and Becky's dedication to the living tradition of Northumbrian music, within which they have been immersed since childhood. Their dad, George, is a member of folk band The Keelers and a Rapper Sword dancer, while Pat sings with women's group Werca's Folk.

"We are drawn to good stories," cellist Rachel says. "So our material is quite dark as a lot of the good stories are serious. But we are light-hearted, so we counterbalance the material by having a laugh when we play live."

Becky, 22, continues: "We wanted to counterbalance the album, too, and have used ditties between songs to break it up. We do tend to pick sad songs – not on purpose – we just like them."

The Bairns draws together Northumbrian songs such as Terry Conway's Farewell Regality or The Lad with the Trousers On, with a cover of Sea Song by British drummer/vocalist Robert Wyatt and a snippet of A Minor Place by American singer-songwriter Bonnie 'Prince' Billy.

Rachel says: "Some material was already in our repertoire, but we also looked at new songs. We are proud to have such a rich culture to draw from and I did some research of songbooks, including the Northumbrian Minstrelsy, which has some great tunes. Other traditional songs like I Wish, I Wish, I have been

singing for 10 years or so, but they take a while to come out."

"That's true," Becky says. "There were a few songs which we had been singing around the house and that we both wanted to do, like Blue Bleezing Blind Drunk. We worked out how to do it over a bottle of wine in the house."

There are also two new songs by pianist Belinda O'Hooley: Blackbird, written for Becky whose constant singing reminds her of a song-bird; and Whitethorn, written about her own Irish ancestry.

"Belinda's great grandmother had 15 children, of whom two survived," Rachel says. "Those who were stillborn couldn't be laid to rest in the churchyard and they were buried under a whitethorn tree.

"The tree died recently and Belinda's dad replaced it. She was so moved by the story that she wrote a song. It was such a huge responsibility to sing this song that I was quite

Picture: Karen Melvin

From left: Becky Unthank, Niopha Keegan, Belinda O'Hooley and Rachel Unthank.

scared of it, but I have finally managed to find a way to do it."

Belinda's contribution to the album has also helped develop a more sophisticated and complex sound, as her reflective and virtuoso piano playing ingeniously complements Rachel and Becky's gorgeously lilting and powerful vocals.

Becky says: "With the album there was a process of standing around the piano and trying things out. If they didn't work, we would try something else. The Bairns might not be to everyone's taste. We like it, though."

It is remarkable that such a strong album has come out of a relatively turbulent period this year for Rachel Unthank and the Winterset. Viola player Jackie Oates left the band mid-recording to pursue her own career and the remaining three auditioned extensively

for a replacement while continuing to work on The Bairns. Their new member is fiddle-player Niopha Keegan, a former nurse from St Albans, who studied on the folk and traditional music degree course at Newcastle University. The Winterset's tight schedule meant Niopha had to learn the band's entire repertoire in a couple of days before playing three gigs and starting rehearsals for the album, part of which had to be recorded in overnight sessions.

Rachel says: "Jackie is a great musician who helped define our sound, but it didn't work out. Niopha was recommended to us and she brings a different style to the band and has fitted in really well."

Becky says: "It is lovely to have someone so enthusiastic about being in the band." Her own loyalties have also been torn recently and Becky has deferred her final year at

Manchester University, where she studies history of art and design, to concentrate on touring this year and next. She says: "It's hard studying and committing to the band when you have to be away every weekend. It'll be nice just to be a singer for a year."

Rachel Unthank and the Winterset launched The Bairns at the end of July at the Cambridge Folk Festival where last year the band were voted Live Performance of the Year. In March, the group won Artist of the Year in The Journal Culture Awards, recognition which followed Cruel Sister being named as Mojo Magazine Folk Album of the Year in 2005.

※ The Bairns is released on August 20, www.rachelunthank.com. Rachel Unthank and the Winterset play The Sage Gateshead on September 16. Contact: (0191) 443-4661, www.thesagegateshead.org

At the Arches, Glasgow, now sadly closed down.

A rare performance of full Felton Lonnin arrangeme
with string quintet, RNCM, Manchester.

Becky on stage photographed by Adrian from the sound desk.

Unthankfully

Rachel Unthank & The Winterset have been making great leaps forward and Colin Irwin is impressed!

It's gloomy out. The traffic looks angry, the shops are half empty and Leeds United, once the city's pride and joy, have just plummeted out of the Championship and into administration. The bar of the art deco Queens Hotel offers an oasis of calm until the dull rumble of the appalling James Blunt disturbs the neutrality of the muzak nursing the genteel afternoon G&T brigade.

Suddenly our reverie is shattered. Loud voices. Louder peels of laughter. People running. Noisy banter. High spirits. There *is* life in Leeds. Rachel Unthank & The Winterset have entered the building.

They've been in Durham; Beamish, to be precise, shooting the cover of their new album *The Bairns*. And, still decked out in their Sunday best, they've driven straight down to Leeds, bounding into the hotel bar in various states of exuberance.

Becky Unthank, at 22 the baby of the band, leads them in, generously dispensing hugs, giggles and jokes to anyone in her path. She's followed by the tall, friendly Belinda O'Hooley, queen of the wry one-liner. Then there's Niopha Keegan, the new girl on fiddle, her matey Hertfordshire accent contrasting sharply with Belinda's Yorkshire drollness and Becky's Tyneside lilt. They are joined, more sedately, by Rachel Unthank who, riven by self-doubt ("I still can't believe people actually come to hear us play") rather reluctantly finds her name in lights as the band's nominal leader and focal point.

She shouldn't do. Her earthy, sometimes even harsh singing is a startling antidote to the gentle whimsicality, indeed feyness, that's been one of the prevalent features of many of the artists who've emerged in the name of folk music in recent years. Rachel and her more sultry voiced younger sister may be relatively tender in years, but they carry many of the traits of traditional singers and have a real feel of the roots of the music, particularly that of the North East. Not surprising really given a strong family background in traditional music (their parents are both singers) represented by their willingness to don clogs and kick up the dust whenever the opportunity arises and their fervent desire to uncompromisingly champion the Tyneside music and culture.

"One of the reasons me and Becky sing the way we do is that from a young age our parents would take us to see singers like Sheila Stewart, so we never did want to sing in a nice pretty way," says Rachel. "As a small child I'd be sat under the table in the singarounds and I loved it. Part of it was being in an adult's world, but it was also because you could hear all these stories. My brother was bored stupid but I loved the whole storytelling element of it."

Rachel always wanted to sing but needed strong coaxing before she found the courage to do it. There were various bands and an appearance at the semi-finals of the Young Folk Awards, but it wasn't until Becky had grown big enough to provide moral support and spine-tingling harmonies that the promise started to reach fruition. Performing in local clubs ("The Elliotts of Birtley had a huge impact on us just in the way their club is – a bit of

> ## "We're young women who've had a nice upbringing but… we still feel those songs. We like the grit and we don't want to shy away from it."

craic, some singing and banter"), the sisters built a healthy reputation as unaccompanied performers of songs they'd mostly been raised on in the North East. It all resulted – *eventually* – in their debut album *Cruel Sister*, launched at the 2005 Holmfirth Folk Festival.

Bold and defiantly honest almost to the point of foolhardiness, it took a lot of people by surprise. Long, dark ballads like the harrowing eight-and-a-half minutes or so of the title track; a proud Tyneside identity in *Rap Her To Bank*; a fierce sense of tradition with an outdoor recording of *Greatham Calling On Song*, complete with sword dancers; plenty of local dialect and an intriguing smattering of contemporary songs, including Nick Drake's *Riverman*, Alex Glasgow's *20 Long Weeks* and Cyril Tawney's *Monday Morning*.

One of the first reviews pilloried them for singing the Tawney song on the basis that as young lasses they couldn't possibly know anything about standing in a bus queue on a Monday morning with a hangover. "I don't think he can have contact with many young women these days," laughs Rachel.

Others say they don't have the life experience to tackle songs about pits, betrayed wives and brutal murder. "I understand that but we've been singing those songs for so long they feel a part of us," says Rachel. "We're young women who've had a nice upbringing but… we still *feel* those songs. We like the grit and we don't want to shy away from it."

Cruel Sister divided opinion. Oddly for an album with its roots so strongly in the tradition it was largely overlooked by the folk mainstream – failing to get a sniff at a BBC Folk Award nomination – yet attracted a devoted audience outside after being championed on radio by the likes of Phill Jupitus and Bob Harris.

It was also the launchpad of Rachel Unthank & The Winterset. Still a teenager and about to go off to Manchester University, Becky was unsure about committing herself to music the way Rachel wanted to, so a reluctant Rachel was given top billing. "When we were making the first album I was a bit stressed," says Becky. "I was working behind the bar in a nightclub in Newcastle until 5 in the morning on Fridays and Saturdays and all I really wanted to do was go clubbing with my friends, even though I did love singing. But once I had the option to leave if I wanted, I really got into it and decided I'd done all the night clubbing I wanted to do. Since then I've just loved singing more and more."

One musician drafted in to play on the album was the larger than life Belinda O'Hooley, who in 2001 became a household name for 15 minutes when she won *Stars In Their Eyes* impersonating Annie Lennox. Her next door neighbour in Huddersfield was a certain Adrian McNally, who heard her playing one day and ended up producing and releasing her solo album *Music Is My Silence* on his Rabble Rouser label. Later McNally teamed up with Rachel Unthank and, looking for a pianist to play on a couple of tracks on *Cruel Sister*, invited Belinda. They liked her so much they asked her to join the band. Singer, fiddle and viola player Jackie Oates was also inducted at the tail end of the recording and The Winterset were off on their journey.

Belinda instantly brought a wealth of different experiences to the table. As a child she spent summers in Ireland playing traditional songs with her cousin, the Irish singer Tommy Fleming, but by now she'd developed an indie heart. It also became second nature to her to adapt her music without a second thought after years singing in old people's nursing homes. "That's the best teacher for me because you have to play so many different styles every day. Over the years I've learned so many old songs. I don't use music books or anything, I just learn them from the old folks – it's a bit like folk music in that way. The majority of the chords I bring to the band have come from singing with old people. Music hall, love songs from the '30s, dance tunes, a lot of them you'd never have heard. They've all got their favourites from when they were young."

Rachel wasn't initially sure about all this. "What we do is very traditional and I didn't know if it would mix well, but we had a few goes in Belinda's kitchen – *Fair Rosamund* and *20 Long Weeks* – and I was converted. She has the sensitivity to bring her own background without playing over what you're singing. She's really intuitive and listens to singers and storytellers."

In fact Belinda has become an integral ingredient of the band, both on stage – where her bold keyboards and rampant humour shine gloriously – and in the studio, where her dramatic backdrops are key, taking the new album in a series of weird and wonderful directions. *Bleezing Blind Drunk* is an epic arrangement of the old Sheila Stewart classic that ends in a totally unexpected but utterly thrilling burlesque fury.

"How many times did we try to arrange that?" says Becky. "We were wary about it because we're young and it's about a battered wife, but it's a complex song, we didn't just want to do it sad because it's angry too – it expresses frustration. We like to explore things. If something sounds too predictable or boring we'll have another go."

Late last year, Jackie Oates released her first solo album to great acclaim and as The Winterset started recording their new album *The Bairns*, with a year of touring planned on the back of it, Jackie decided to bale out (she's since replaced Nancy Kerr in Tim Van Eyken's band).

"No, I'm not bitter at all," says Rachel with conviction. "I loved playing with Jackie. She added a lot to our sound. She's very English in her playing and singing and she had a huge part in the success we've had. We're really grateful she was with us for that time."

So you didn't have a huge great row then? "*No!* It was just one of those things. When we first started playing together we weren't doing so much but then it suddenly became a big part of all our lives and she was unsure where her first commitment lay. She wanted to do her solo album and I'm sure she'll do really well. She's a great singer."

Her departure did, however, create the pressing problem of finding a suitable replacement in a hurry. Enter Niopha Keegan.

Despite the Herts accent, Niopha is of strong Irish stock, whose musical upbringing had been almost entirely built around the insular Irish community in St Albans. She'd been playing since she was five ("Frankie Gavin, Martin Hayes, De Dannan, Planxty… that's the music I grew up with") but a surfeit of classical orchestras dulled her enthusiasm and she gave up playing completely in her teens. She was working as a nurse until her brother – the highly regarded Limerick-based flute player Niall Keegan – dragged her off to see Karen Tweed and persuaded her to apply for the Folk & Traditional music degree course in Newcastle.

"It's been a real eye-opener coming to Newcastle learning about different genres," she says. "I hadn't heard any English or Scottish music before. Now I'm playing all sorts. I jumped at the chance of joining the girls. It's so far from what I normally do, it's a real challenge but I'm really enjoying it."

All sorts is right. If Rachel Unthank & The Winterset are breaking down barriers to reach a wholly new audience, they're doing it the hard way. Their approach to traditional song is uncompromisingly hardcore yet the songs are mostly bleak and, despite Belinda O'Hooley's protestations that she's only doing what comes naturally, the arrangements are unorthodox. On stage they've taken to performing *For Today I Am A Boy*, the delicious Antony & The Johnsons song of sexual confusion which takes on a whole new suitcase of suggestion when they perform it. They also do a Bonnie Prince Billy song and the new album includes Robert Wyatt's decidedly left-field *Sea Song*.

"It was on a compilation tape Adrian made for my birthday," says Becky. "I really liked the words. It's so magical. It's about a special bond between two people, but not in a sexual way. It's so melancholy and it has echoes of traditional music. I was so worried how to do that song. I mean, it's so unusual anyway it's not like I could make it any *stranger*. Then I thought 'Well for a start you have a completely different accent and you're a girl!'"

Another track on the new album is *White Thorn*, written by Belinda specifically for Rachel to sing. "It's a story passed down from my dad's family in Ireland," says Belinda. "They lived in a hill farming community about 100 years ago and were desperately poor. My great grandad's wife had 16 children and only two survived. The rest were either stillborn or died not long after birth and they were buried in front of the white thorn. It died recently and he was going to replace it with a new white thorn because to him it was still a graveyard. That's what inspired me to write the song."

Becky is now taking a year out from uni to concentrate on the band, with *The Bairns* set for official release at the Cambridge Folk Festival, where they will bring their unique mix of doom and laughter to the main stage. You won't often get Nick Drake and Robert Wyatt interspersed with clog dancing, and while *The Bairns* may prove even more challenging than *Cruel Sister*, it's an even bet that it'll propel the Unthank name into yet more uncharted territory.

"It's nice to think that people who aren't aware of folk music would like us but I'd never change the style to go on a wider mission to get people interested, I wouldn't know *how* to," says Rachel. "It's a common thing to hear that it's not that great to be English for empirical reasons, so I do have a slight crusade element of showing what a strong culture we have and that it's something we can be proud of. But I don't want to do that at the expense of the tradition itself. I'm also a product of the time and I want to be a musician in today's stratosphere as well."

www.rachelunthank.com

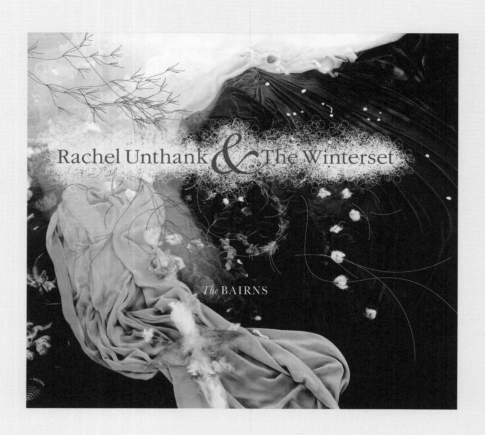

6

THE BAIRNS

ALBUM LAUNCH: Rachel Unthank, left with Niopha Keegan performing at Blakes in Newcastle. Picture: Paul Norris www.ichewcastle.co.uk/buyaphoto ref: 00975086

Rachel launches new album

NORTH folk sensations Rachel Unthank & The Winterset last night launched their critically-acclaimed new album in a distinctly low-key fashion.

The Ryton artist has been attracting universal praise from reviewers for the record, which she chose to showcase at a Newcastle café.

But the band gave the crowd at Blakes, in Grey Street, a real taste of the modern folk that has been described as "magnificently original", "utterly gorgeous" and "quite possibly the folk album of this generation".

A short, intimate performance by *The Journal* Culture Awards' Artist Of The Year, last night marked the release of their album *The Bairns*, ahead of a

gig at The Sage Gateshead on September 16.

Ryton-born Rachel, 29, is joined in the band by sister Becky, 22, pianist Belinda O'Hooley and new fiddle-player Niopha Keegan.

Anyone wanting to listen to track 1, Felton Lonnin, can do so on http://www.myspace.com/rachelunthank

TRANSCENDENT FOLK

Paul Morley
POP

Rachel Unthank and the Winterset
★★★★★

On their magical, discreetly twisted records, the female north-east avant garde folk group Rachel Unthank and the Winterset create a sensationally graceful sound that can be epic and subdued, dreamy and specific, as well as supernaturally ancient and defiantly modern. Their music is extremely serious, and seriously moving, and is respectful, beautifully played traditional music that will please purists. It is abstractly influenced not only by the now traditional gestures and textures of 1960s folk-rock music (Denny, Drake, Pentangle, the Watersons), but also by more daring experimental music – the lush reserve of Eno and Budd, the sensual repetition of Reich and Glass, the infected cabaret of Brecht and Weill, the twilight intensity of Mum and The Field.

It's like hearing a proud, uncompromising 19th-century folk troupe singing impudent and rebellious songs, who are aware of Nico, the Cowboy Junkies, Björk, Nick Cave and Sufjan Stevens. The daughters of a musician, they show on 'The Bairns', their uncanny, genre transcending latest album, that they've got a fine intuitive knack for locating and interpreting wonderful, incident-packed old and new songs, and for writing and arranging appropriately spirited original material.

At the Borderline, modest, slightly awed, occasionally blushing maiden-aliens from a remote, misty north, in front of the increasing number of fans won over by their abrasive gentleness, they reveal a wit and playfulness that's not necessarily absent on their albums, but which lurks only in the shadows. Between bittersweet, menacing songs about death and desolation, lust and loss, revenge and temptation, the relaxed, self-deprecating repartee among the women, especially between untwin singing sisters Rachel and Becky, demonstrates not just their love for each other, but also for the way their music is as entertaining and delightful as it is provocative and unforgiving. Drummerless, mostly using just piano, fiddle and plaintive voice, they perform tragic, enthralling music with exquisite sensitivity, possibly because their comic timing is so perfect, as if to say life is inherently unhappy, but you shouldn't let it get you down. You should see the way they smile at each other when they sing, caught up in the stories and the melodies, still hearing the music for the first surprising time. They even throw in some hearty clog dancing, easily making the idea seem more

Enchantingly fraught Rachel Unthank

+

POP CHOICE

Newton Faulkner
Acoustic upstart with Mick Hucknall looks and the commercial staying power of James Blunt. Exeter University (01392 263518), Thurs; Portsmouth Guildhall (023 9282 4355), Fri; Cambridge Corn Exchange (01223 357851), Sat.

The Cult Goth-metal act from the 1980s. London The Forum (0870 400 0688) Fri, Sat.
Alex Buttle

contemporary and stylish than boys in skinny trousers holding electric guitars like it's 1969.

It's the raw, gorgeous voices of the contrasting, but complementary Unthank sisters that lift the group into greatness. Becky's audacious, blissful performance of two classic liquescent English sad songs, Nick Drake's *Riverman* and Robert Wyatt's *Sea Song*, doesn't overshadow Rachel's own fraught, enchanting singing. Both their voices are lovely and inspired in different ways, and when they sing together the charming, unworldly Unthanks seem positively unearthly. They might not end up being the best-selling British all-girl group of all time, but they're well on their way to being the most charismatic and imaginative.

Rachel Unthank and the Winterset tour details on www.rachelunthank.com

---

"Just beautiful, beautiful music. One day all music will sound like this" *Paul Jupitus, BBC 6 Music*

Forging links between folk worlds old, new and other, 2008 Mercury Music Award nominees **Rachel Unthank and The Winterset** have blown a bracing north-easterly gale through traditional English song, casting it in an endlessly inventive and playful new mould. Subverting the familiar with love and authority and singing in their own lilting Geordie accents, they have been described by poet Ian MacMillan as the "inheriters, curators and gleeful distorters" of Tyneside's traditions. Discreetly provocative arrangements draw on elements of blues, jazz, music hall, burlesque cabaret, classical and leftfield contemporary music, making their interpretation of folk music peerless, fearless and wholeheartedly brave.

Featuring:
Rachel Unthank   *voice, feet and cello*
Becky Unthank   *voice and feet*
Niopha Keegan   *violin, accordion and voice*
Stef Conner   *piano and voice*

Wednesday 4th February, 8.00pm
BALLYMONEY: Ballymoney Town Hall
Tickets £7/£5 conc. from 028 2766 0230
Promoted by Ballymoney Borough Arts Committee

Thursday 5th February, 8.00pm
BANGOR:
North Down Museum, The Castle
Tickets £9/£7 conc. from 028 9127 1200
Promoted by North Down Borough Council

Friday 6th February, 8.00pm
LETTERKENNY:
Regional Cultural Centre
Tickets €15/€12 conc. from 074 91 29186
Promoted by Donegal County Council

Saturday 7th February, Doors: 8.30pm
SLIGO: The Clarence Hotel
Tickets €15 from 071 91 42211
Promoted by Itchy Feet Promotions
www.itchyfeet.ie

Sunday 8th February, Doors: 8.00pm
BELFAST: Black Box, Hill Street
Tickets £12/£8 conc. from Belfast Welcome Centre
028 9024 6609 and online at www.movingonmusic.co.uk
Promoted by Moving on Music

Moving On Music Presents

The Newcastle Latest.

MOVING ON MUSIC

Rachel Unthank & The Winterset

On Tour 4th – 8th February 2009

"Music as tough as it is gentle, as ancient as it is modern and as coldly desolate as it is achingly intimate"
The Observer

www.rachelunthank.com ~ www.myspace.com/rachelunthank
www.movingonmusic.co.uk

DELTA   arts council   arts council   PRS Foundation for new music   The National Lottery

Above left: Adrian McNally remodels the Winterset from the sound desk. Above: A gift from a young fan.

Below: Set lists.
A busy and exciting calendar.

AN ARTIST WRITES...

No 4. Simon Taffe, Founder and Director of End Of The Road Festival

I first discovered The Unthanks in 2008. It was about the time I was getting bored of "Folk Music" or "New Folk", but when I heard their record playing in a record shop in Brighton I was completely floored. The arrangements and harmonies by these two young women from Newcastle stopped me in my tracks. I remember being impatient to play their music and I got in the car and put it on and drove back through the Sussex countryside; it was one of the those rare moments when the whole family agreed with no argument. That album, *The Bairns*, stayed in the player for a good month or so solidly.

You can't really put a label on their music which is what so great about them. They were one of those bands that come along every once in a while which I feel the need to play immediately to all my friends. I have a lot of friends who only really listen to loud garage and punk music and even they were going out to buy Unthanks records, which says something about their uniqueness. They are one of a handful of bands whose next record I eagerly look forward to and they always come up with something that interests me.

Bairns Tour Set Lists

ONE SET

Sandgate
Monday Morning
Blue Bleezing Blind Drunk
Lousy Cutter
Felton Lonnin
Lull
Blackbird
Whitethorn
My Lad's A Canny Lad
Sea Song
Ma Bonny Lad
Can't Stop It Raining
My Donald
I Wish
For Today I Am A Boy
Fareweel Regality

TWO SETS

Sandgate
Blue Bleezing Blind Drunk
Felton Lonnin
Can't Stop It Raining
My Donald
Lull
Blackbird
I Wish
Lousy Cutter

John Dead/My Bonny Lad
White Thorn
For Today I Am A Boy
Fair Ros/Twenty Long Weeks
Sea Song
My Lad's A Canny Lad
Monday Morning
Cold n Stiff
Farewell Regality

AUG

				1	2	3
					THE BIG CHILL Herefordshire	
4	5	6	7 EDINBURGH	8 BELLADRUM Scotland	9 SUMMER SUNDAE Leicester	10
11 THE MALTINGS PROMS SNAPE With Lau	12 London media	13	14	15	16	17
18 London Jazz Cafe	19	20 whitby	21 whitby	22 whitby	23 ROCK N ROOTS FESTIVAL	24 Lakes Pat
25 Lakes Pat	26	27 HOLLAND	28 NORWAY FESTIVAL	29	30 ELECTRIC PICNIC IRELAND	31 MOSELEY FOLK FESTIVAL Birmingham

SEPT

1	2	3	4	5	6	7
				Tunbridge Wells	Tunbridge Wells	
8 Mercurys rehearsals	9 Mercurys Awards	10	11	12	13	14
15	16	17 USA TOUR	18 Cedar Rapids, Iowa	19 Minneapolis	20 Chicago	21 Chicago
22 Ann Arbor	23 Toronto	24	25 Northampton	26 New York	27	28 Philadelphia
29 Vienna	30 Cambridge					

OCT

		1 USA RETURN	2	3 wedding	4 out	5 out
6 Stef Out 10am – 5pm	7 Stef Out 10am – 5pm	8 OXFORD Stef Out 10am – 5pm	9 OXFORD Holywell Music Rooms	10 Stef Out – 1pm	11	12
13 Stef Out 10am – 5pm	14 Stef Out 6pm 10am – 5pm	15 Stef Out 10am – 5pm	16 Stef Out 10am – 5pm	17	18 BBC all day	19 DURHAM GALA THEATRE
20	21	22	23	24	25	26

NCEM YORK	Queens Festival Belfast With Ian McMillan and Alasdair Roberts		Beggars Banquet (filming for BBC 2)	Beggars Banquet (filming for BBC 2)	Band Rehearsals.	
27	28 Stef Out 7pm – 10pm	29 Stef 10	30 2-5pm Stef	31		

NOV

					Stef Band rehearsal. Concert	
3 Band Rehearsal.	4 Rehearsal 7-10pm	5 Stef out	6 Stef out	7	8	9
10	11	12 EUROPE	13 DATES.	14 HOPEFULLY	15 BELGIUM THIS	16 PARIS. WEEK
17 FRANKFURT	18 HAMBURG	19 BERLIN	20 CROSSING BORDERS HOLLAND	21 London gig	22 ST BRIDES CHURCH LIVERPOOL	23 MEMORIAL HALL SHEFFIELD
24	25	26 LANCASTER	27 TAUNTON The Brewhouse	28 PENZANCE Acorn AC	29 GLOUCESTER Ruskin Mill	30 CANTERBURY Gulbenkian Theatre BEN FOLDS LONDON

DEC

1 BEN FOLDS IPSWICH	2 Stef out	3 Stef out	4 Band	5 rehearsal	6	7
8	9	10 Stef out	11 LONDON Union Chapel	12 HEBDEN BRIDGE Trades Club	13 BRISTOL Queen Elizabeth Theatre	14 LICHFIELD Arts Centre
15 CARDIFF St Davids Hall	16 CARDIGAN Theatre Mwldan	17	18	19	20 ADELE! Roundhouse	21
22	23	24	25	26	27	28
29	30	31				

AN ARTIST WRITES...

No 5. Paul Hartnoll, musician (Orbital)

The Unthanks single handedly got me back into listening to music for the simple pleasure of listening itself.

I'd been going through a musical analytical phase, always pulling apart the sounds in my mind and putting it all back together, working out the process rather than listening for joy. Then I heard The Bairns. That was it. It was like musical sorbet. It cleansed my musical palette in one fell swoop. My mind went with the flow and stopped analysing, simply enjoying.

This was music steeped in tradition yet modern and full of air and light. I found it looked both backwards and forwards at the same time. Musically omni-present. From this I went on to discover other contemporary folk like Bella Hardy and Emily Portman, eventually being introduced to Lisa Knapp by The Unthanks over breakfast, during the time we recorded a cover of 'A Forest' by The Cure.

I have, of course, begun to analyse what it is that I hear but it is from a position of pure pleasure. Becky with her voice like smoke —I can never fully tell where silence ends and her voice begins, it just seems to slide in and out of the audio spectrum —more of a presence than a definition. Then, in stark contrast, Rachel strikes up like a bell, with a definition so sharp, it's a voice made of glass. Smooth, clear and sharp. The pleasing combination of the two voices knitting together makes me smile consistently. Such a fine concoction to soothe my ears at the end of my working day at the electronic music coalface.

Paul Hartnoll

Rachel Unthank & The Winterset

The BAIRNS

September Major-City Album Tour 2007

FRI 14 EDINBURGH The Bongo Club
0131 558 7604 / www.thebongoclub.co.uk

SAT 15 GLASGOW The Arches
7pm (early show) · 0870 240 7528 / www.thearches.com

SUN 16 GATESHEAD The Sage Gateshead
0191 443 4661 / www.thesagegateshead.org

THU 20 CARDIFF The Point
029 2016 0873 / www.thepointcardiffbay.com

FRI 21 LONDON The Spitz
020 7392 9032 / www.spitz.co.uk

SAT 22 READING South Street Arts Centre
0118 9606060 / www.readingarts.com

SUN 23 DERBY The Guildhall
01332 255 800 / www.assemblyrooms-derby.co.uk

MON 24 NORWICH Norwich Arts Centre
01603 660352 / www.norwichartscentre.co.uk

TUE 25 LEICESTER The Y Theatre
0116 255 7066 / www.leicesterymca.co.uk

WED 26 LINCOLN Drill Hall
01522 873894 / www.lincolndrillhall.com

THU 27 BRISTOL St Georges Hall
0845 40 24 001 / www.stgeorgesbristol.co.uk

FRI 28 BIRMINGHAM The MAC
0121 440 3838 / www.macarts.co.uk

SAT 29 MANCHESTER Royal Northern
College of Music 0161 907 5555 / www.rncm.ac.uk

SUN 30 LEEDS City Varieties
08456 441 881 / www.cityvarieties.co.uk

"Just beautiful, beautiful music" *PHILL JUPITUS* "I simply can't recommend them enough" *BOB HARRIS*
"Simply gripping..their ambition knows no bounds" *FROOTS*

Rachel Unthank & The Winterset

"Understated, elegant, plaintive brilliance" *The List*
"utterly gorgeous" *The Guardian* "spine tingling" *Mojo*
"beyond tradition to a magical, essentially Geordie place. Breathtaking" *Manchester Evening News*

The BAIRNS Tour Oct - Dec 2007

October

17 DARLINGTON Darlington Arts Centre
01325 486 555 www.darlingtonarts.co.uk

18 HEBDEN BRIDGE Trades Club
01422 815265 www.tradesclub.info

20 CAMBRIDGE The Junction
01223 511511 www.junction.co.uk

25 BUILTH WELLS Wyeside Arts Centre
01982 552555 www.wyeside.co.uk

26 PONTARDAWE Arts Centre
01792 863722 www.npt.gov.uk/theatres

27 LUDLOW Assembly Rooms
01584 878141 www.ludlowassemblyrooms.co.uk

November

01 THE MAGPIES NEST, Islington, London
www.themagpiesnest.co.uk, www.cutashine.co.uk/tickets

02 EXETER The Barnfield Theatre
01392 270891 www.barnfieldtheatre.co.uk

03 FAREHAM Ashcroft Arts Centre
01329 223100 www.ashcroft.org.uk

04 BRIDGWATER Bar 27
0871 2200260 www.midnightmango.co.uk

09 WYCOMBE Swan Theatre
01494 512000 www.wycombeswan.co.uk

10 WILTSHIRE Wiltshire Music Centre
01225 860100 www.wiltshiremusic.org.uk

11 NEWCASTLE South Shields Folk Club
0191 567 1617 www.talus.force9.co.uk/ssfc/

22 WOLVERHAMPTON Little Civic Theatre
0870 3207000 www.wolvescivic.co.uk

24 MILTON KEYNES The Stables
01908 280800 www.stables.org

25 NOTTINGHAM The Maze
0115 947 5650 www.cosmicamerican.com

28 POCKLINGTON Arts Centre
01759 301547 www.pocklingtonartscentre.co.uk

29 BURY The Met
0161 761 2216 www.themet.biz

30 HUDDERSFIELD Lawrence Batley Theatre
01484 430528 www.lbt-uk.org

December

01 DURHAM The Store, Dipton
01207 571177 www.cap-a-pie.co.uk

02 NEWCASTLE The Round
0191 2605605 www.the-round.com

03 COLCHESTER Arts Centre
01206 500 900 www.colchesterartscentre.com

EMI   www.rachelunthank.com   www.myspace.com/rachelunthank   RABBLE ROUSER

shots from the dressing room of
The Cedar Cultural Centre, Minneapolis.

7
STEF CONNER

Having parted ways with Belinda O'Hooley not that long after The Bairns was released, Stef Conner was drafted in to The Winterset to play the album live, so we could tour it around the world as planned, but she became so much more than that. Although she was there to play an album that had already been made, and gone by the time we made our next, Stef's playing came with huge amounts of personality and intensity, taking our stagecraft to the next level. Looking back, she really was thrown in at the deep end, to fill big boots and commit to a hectic tour schedule, and it's uncertain we'd be still at it and going so strong now without her dedication and talents at that time. Plus, she was such fun! It was a show-packed, high-octane, jet-setting whirlwind of a time for the band, during which we lived in each others' pockets and enjoyed the ride together. Here, Stef shares her memories...

was fortunate enough to spend two crazy, exciting, nspiring years performing with the artists formerly known as 'Rachel Unthank & the Winterset' from 2008–2009. Those two years formed one of the most important formative artistic experiences of my life and totally changed the way I think about music. From my very first audition to my final performance at Womad, the musical philosophy I absorbed from them – and tried (not always successfully) to adhere to – was "play ess!" Often, even when I thought my playing was as minimal as it possibly could be, feedback from Adrian (the ever-present Overseeing Ears) would be that there were even more notes that could be left out for the greater good! In Rachel Unthank & the Winterset's music, voices, words and stories were paramount... and although I didn't always get it at the time (I was pretty obsessed with unusual chords and piano techniques) when I listen back to the songs now, it's clear that that

is one of the things that makes them so incredibly special – the stark, raw, almost uncomfortably close focus on Rachel and Becky's voices (and Niopha's when she was dragged to the front of the stage) as they told their amazing stories in song.

I'm very happy to share a few of my enduring memories from those two years. One of the most amazing things about touring with the Winterset was meeting so many other incredible musicians on the road, many of whom I would never have heard otherwise. Devon Sproule, a UK-based American singer-songwriter was one of my favourites – her songs still bring tears to my eyes every time I listen to them. Touring with Ben Folds was another huge highlight. I'm a bit of a super-fan and even played piano in a Ben Folds Five tribute band as a teenager. Consequently, I don't think I managed to say a proper sentence to him the entire time we were on tour in Europe… I just made unintelligible grunting sounds, with my jaw on the floor! Then there was John Smith, one of the most talented singer-songwriters I've ever heard and a total inspiration. And, I remember all of us watching Get the Blessing for the first time at a festival in Bristol — we were completely blown away by their rhythmic feel and crunchy riffs, and so totally thrilled to play a gig with them not long after. And of course there's Lau — compulsory listening, I was informed, when I first joined the Winterset, as they were everybody's favourite band. Rightly so! The list could probably go on forever, from hearing Tibetan monks chanting at Womad New Zealand, to playing at The Roundhouse with Adele… Eek! I must admit I really miss being part of that inspiring musical whirl.

Places as well as people were unforgettable. Playing at Port Fairy Folk Festival in Australia was something I'll never forget, not only because the gig so was incredible, but also because we stayed in a house that had a Shetland pony, a stag and a highland cow living in the garden! I think Becky sang to them every morning we were there. When we played at FMM Sines in Portugal, it wasn't only the brilliant eclectic programme — Swedish death metal followed by Qawwali singing — that we loved, but also the fact that the entire floor was covered with fresh mint! I can't quite believe how many amazing touring experiences we packed into two years — snowy Norway, sunny Spain, German Christmas markets, Dutch audiences clapping in perfect rhythmic unison, staying with Rachel and Becky's lovely family in Australia, dodging huntsman spiders in the loos at Australian festivals and getting lost in endless Iowa corn fields.

It wasn't all meeting musical geniuses, watching sunsets and *growing as an artist* though. Life on the road had its fair share of polystyrene breakfast plates, dinner in service stations, 4am starts, fighting over who sat in the uncomfortable middle seat of the van and leaving important things behind and then crying about it! I remember it was often tricky to find the right balance between getting a manageable amount of sleep and arriving in time for flights. There was more than one occasion when we found ourselves running through airports with arms flailing and Rachel's be-hatted cello puffing and panting in the rear. A rather terrifying incident when I thought I'd lost my passport — before discovering that Rachel had nicked it and left hers at home — springs to mind! And I don't much like to talk about the time I had my visa cancelled and found myself being frog-marched out of US immigration and onto a plane back to the UK. Dark times! Instead of playing with Ben Folds in Las Vegas, I sat in my front room and watched Jeremy Kyle. That was a bad day for me… but

also a terrified Adrian's piano debut — you could sa that everything happens for a reason!

I wonder if the vibe in the band has changed muc since it stopped being a 'girl-band' and let boys in I can't quite imagine a venue doing the hospitabl deed of covering their tiny dressing room with shin pink fabric for The Unthanks now! We were basicall the same as The Pussycat Dolls back then… well… w did once play in a venue that had light bulbs aroun the mirror. And there was clog dancing! Preening wa important too.

You can take the girls out of Newcastle… New York, 2008.

Peer pressure must have been high, because by th time I left the band we were definitely all wearing th same eye shadow. When the time came to perforr at the Mercury Music Awards (ARRRGH!) Niopha Becky and I formed a syndicate in order to purchas our first Chanel red lipstick. I must have pulled on over on the other two because I still have it and I don' think I ever bought them out… it only ran out las week! (RIP Chanel Red, 2009–2016). If wearing tha

Tour madness, Toff in Town, Melbourne.

ipstick isn't "hitting the big time", I don't know what s! Another important way of keeping pretty for the tage was exercising. We did that in our hotel rooms vith Becky's Martine McCutcheon exercise video and hampoo bottles in each hand instead of weights. I hink we managed at least four minutes a day! We lefinitely burned more calories laughing at each other han doing squats. There was no mistaking that the Winterset was a girl-band if you looked into the back of the van when we were on the road — instruments nd other musical paraphernalia languished under a nassive pile of crumpled up dresses and odd shoes (also nown as percussion instruments)… and the cello case vas always well-dressed. Poor Adrian! I think even the atnav was a girl… although we usually called her 'Ted'.

Most of all, I miss playing those fabulous songs, istening to Rachel and Becky sing and accompanying he wonderful Niopha Keegan. What a privilege to have erformed such incredible music.

Below: With The Wilsons, Howard Assembly Rooms, Leeds.

Right: Stef's portrait of the Winterset on dressing room wall of Hugh's Room, Toronto.

Clockwise from top right:
With Rachel; Niagra Falls;
Stef introduced at one of her first
shows, The Borderline, London;
Abbey Road; with Adrian.

A FAN WRITES...

No 2. Alice Bentley

Scraps of Unthanks Thinks

Late 2007, *The Bairns* – one listen I was intrigued and touched, a second listen and I was swallowed whole.

A couple of months later, a cool February evening, and we travelled across town on the 19A to a small room over the Cherry Tree pub by Walkinstown Roundabout, and there heard them in person for the first time: four women on stage and Adrian scurrying around in the dark at the back. Hearing for the first time Becky sing 'River Man', and the legendary hairs stood up, and Rachel delivered 'Blue Bleezing Blind Drunk' with all the raw energy of the story it tells. Afterwards, full of the joys of the experience, thanking them, I blurted out (crazy fan lady) "It feels like I know you". But that is how their songs, their voices, speak: directly to the listener. We feel we are, or we have been the person listening to, the lass dumped

by her canny lad, or left on shore with the babies, while her man battles with whales, whisky, waves, and worse on the salt seas.

The stories may be sad, but they are also stoic. They rarely wallow in "woe is me", but rather relate the grace of the human (and particularly the female) spirit in the face of all the woes that the merciless world bestows upon her people. The sparse knocking of heels on a wooden floor or the wild joyousness of dancing clogs, are the heartbeat of songs that touch the heart.

Playfully complex, and heart stoppingly simple, the interweaving of these contrasting strands of colour continues to surprise and move me with every new exploration. The Unthanks, through their music, have spun a web of connections between people across time and space: between those whose lives are told in the songs and all of us who hear them.

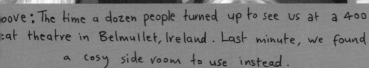

Above: The time a dozen people turned up to see us at a 400 seat theatre in Belmullet, Ireland. Last minute, we found a cosy side room to use instead.

Voices and Clogs From England's Far-North Reaches

YANA PASKOVA FOR THE NEW YORK TIMES

Rachel Unthank and the Winterset *Rachel, left, and Becky Unthank brought clog dances of Northumberland, England, to Joe's Pub.*

Northumbrian clog dancing came to Joe's Pub on Friday night with Rachel Unthank and the Winterset, a four-woman group that put some singular twists on traditionalism.

JON PARELES

MUSIC REVIEW

Rachel Unthank and the Winterset, which also includes Rachel's sister (and fellow clog dancer), Becky Unthank, mostly sings folk and folk-rooted songs that the Unthanks learned close to home in Northumberland, a county in northeastern England. The group's second album, "The Bairns" (Real World), holds tales of cruel husbands, lullabies for beloved children and the laments of women longing for their seafaring men. "The miserable ones are the best," Becky Unthank said with a smile.

Winterset's few instruments are acoustic ones: Stef Conner's piano, Rachel Unthank's cello and Niopha Keegan's violin or accordion. Rachel Unthank's voice has a reedy focus, while Becky's is lower and breathier. Their vocal style sounds homegrown; the Unthank sisters are proud of their Geordie accent and the regional dialect in the lyrics. But what they do with the songs defies folk purism and typical attempts to update. There were no folk-rock guitars, no trendy beats. Instead, there were silences and surprises. The Winterset fearlessly took some songs at glacial speed to linger within their melancholy — like "I Wish, I Wish," about a pregnant woman's suicidal regret, sung over an accordion drone while Ms. Con-

ner plucked inside the piano. It turned others into changeable, asymmetrical reveries.

One sister might start a song only to have the other take over later. Perhaps harmony vocals would float in, suggesting church-choir chords or ancient drones. Piano parts could be like parlor-song chords or something far more sparse: a lone tolling note, a splintered jazz cluster. The fiddle might raise a Celtic-sounding melody or an angular counterpoint.

The song with the clog dancing, "Blue's Gaen Oot O'the Fashion," was a medley of traditional tunes about men being press-ganged, or forced to serve as sailors, and it incorporated a cappella vocal harmonies, a jiglike fiddle tune and a hymnlike singalong chorus into the robust, clattery dancing.

The Winterset takes an almost avant-garde approach to its songs, old and recent. It's as easy to imagine them sharing a bill with Bjork as playing a folk festival. The set included "Sea Song" by Robert Wyatt, a free-associative, proudly amorphous composition that meanders through keys and meters on its way to the conclusion, "Your lunacy fits neatly with my own, my very own/You're not alone." With Becky Unthank singing and Rachel Unthank calmly, steadily stamping one foot, the song moved into a coda of vocal harmony and three circling chords reminiscent of Philip Glass, soon to be joined by Ms. Keegan with shades of old fiddle tunes. It was far from traditional, but close in spirit.

Thank you for being a part of our 10th anniversary celebration. It is through the artistic excellence of artists like you that Joe's Pub has cemented its reputation as New York City's most influential venue. We are honored to call you part of the Joe's Pub family!

Sincerely,

Shanta Thake
Director

Kevin Abb
General M

Staff of Joe's Pub at The Public Theater

Service station shenanigans, America.

Misprint: For one night only

LINBURY STUDIO AT THE ROYAL OPERA HOUSE
*see ticket wallet for Restricted View/Seat Type descriptions
see reverse for conditions*

ROYAL OPERA HOUSE

Thursday
23 July 2009
8:00 PM

Voices Across The World
Rebecca Unthank and The Winterset

Middle Gallery Standing Left   £9.50
                    Standard
MG 20   1
Standing Place   LATECOMERS MAY NOT BE ADMITTED

NAME   COMPANY

AORAN McNALY   Rachel Unthank

EMI Music
UK and Ireland

VISITOR

**TO BE WORN AT ALL TIMES WHILST ON
COMPANY PREMISES.**

VALID ON DAY OF ISSUE ONLY.

PLEASE RETURN THIS PASS TO RECEPTION
WHEN LEAVING PREMISES.

069781

STAGE
WEEKEND

WINTERSET
McNALY

BBC RADIO 2 88-91FM
26, 27, 28 & 29 JULY 2007
CAMBRIDGE
FOLK FESTIVAL

17-26 DE JULHO
FmmSiNEs
FESTIVAL MÚSICAS DO MUNDO 2008

Rachel Unthank
Rachel Unthank & The Winterset
Artistas

UNISON

ARTIST

BERGENFEST 2010 27. APRIL–2. MAI

GLASTONBURY 2008

field of Avalon

**AVALON MAIN STAGE
ARTISTS & GUESTS**

8

AUSTRALIA 2009

Adrian McNally

*The following was found by Adrian in a notebook, written in Heathrow Airport
after the first tour of Australia by Rachel Unthank & The Winterset.*

Thirty-five hours into our return journey from Sydney and we're still not home. A five hour delay in Singapore messed up our connection at Heathrow (co-pilot coughing up blood — a decent excuse I suppose). We're four hours into our wait at Heathrow and I've taken to balancing a bottle of water on my head in order to enforce stillness on myself. I suffer from vertigo (not to be confused with a fear of heights!) which is unfortunate for a touring musician, because it can be triggered by any form of motion, whereby the tools we have to create balance send confusing messages to the brain because there is a feeling of motion without seeing it. So planes, ships, escalators and lifts mean that I have an almost permanent level of nausea on tour, and the vertigo - when a person feels as if they, or the objects around them, are moving when they are not — can continue for weeks or months after coming home.

The bottle balancing seems to be doing the trick and providing small amusement for the stir crazy troops. We seem to have weathered the period of getting on each other's nerves and broken through into a mild hysteria, although that could just be from all the E-numbers in the plane food. We are already recounting as legend the moment, in Singapore airport, when I ask a poor waitress for milk for my coffee. When she finally understands, she points to some sachets of powder labelled 'creamer'. Having established that there is a language barrier, I pick up a sachet, hold it up and helpfully offer the single word 'Disgusting!'. She brings me some milk.

It was terrible behaviour. The long haul insanity that caused my unnecessary animation is now being mimicked back to me with cartoon exaggeration.

Rachel and Becky have been for a free Chanel makeover in duty free, just for something to do, and were given morning cocktails into the bargain, returning both feeling and looking faintly ridiculous. Stef has a plastic bag on her back and is running round the airport pretending it's a parachute, I think. Niopha will kill someone soon if she doesn't get nicotine. I've purchased Horses by Patti Smith (again) and a *Best Of* Ian Dury from HMV, and I buy the new *Mojo* and *Uncut*, both of which contain features on us. We are amused by the somewhat tabloid headline "Take a walk on the

Tyneside". Makes a change from the endless puns on Unthank I suppose… if we see one more article entitled "Unthank you for the music"…

So our Australia adventure is over, for now. Has it been successful? Well, successful enough that we're planning to go back already. Not successful enough for it to break even, but I only take a meagre fee for being manager, agent, label, producer and arranger precisely so that we can put it back in and keep building. You can't be the manager of a band that can't afford to exist or progress. Going to a new territory is very much like starting again. Back to that feeling of wondering whether anyone will show up. We needn't have worried.

Our first Australia ever show was hijacked. By Unthanks. Unthanks and connected family. Rachel and Becky have a lot of family in Australia. They all turn out. And it's not like inviting out your old Auntie Beryl. They're party animals, the lot of them. The girls take the stage to whoops and hollers. The atmosphere at the first show creates a word of mouth that sees us put on two more Sydney shows before we leave Australia 5 weeks later, having also tried our luck in Melbourne, Adelaide, Brisbane, New Zealand (we went to New Zealand, for the weekend! Ridiculous!) and out in the sticks, Yackandandah, a name which allows even someone as hopeless with accents as me to pull off a good Aussie drawl. After the second Sydney show, we deliberate on whether its wise to try a third. It is suggested that if we do, Sarah Blasko might come and do a spot as special guest. We share the same agent and she had been to our second show. She's big news in her home country. She would use the spot to test out some new material and our last show would be boosted by a major star who sells more tickets for one Australian show than we had managed in five weeks!

Despite her credentials, she was apparently impressed enough with us to feel nervous about doing the show

(or maybe she was more nervous about the audience of marauding Unthank family members) so I find myself doing her a deal. I say I will go on and open, so that she isn't the opening act. I tell her truthfully that I have never once performed on a stage on my own before. Not even at an open mic. It's a genuine attempt to put myself in a more nerve-wracking scenario than her, because I can fully appreciate that it's because she's a big star in Sydney that she's nervous, not in spite of it. Doing a tiny little club can feel very exposing if you're used to thousands and all the production values that come with. It works. She agrees. I play songs by Loudon Wainwright III, Tim Hardin, Nick Drake, Bonnie Dobson and Sufjan Stevens. My debut comes and goes to a full house who are more than generous because they know it's my first ever solo effort, and then Sarah is just awesome, captivating. Fantastic presence.

Then Rachel, Becky, Niopha and Stef. It is conducted with the relaxed and connected vibe of a band enriched and elated after such an adventure together. Favourite moments from the tour are shared on stage and Unthank-related family members are thanked and paid tribute to. Having toured the rest of the country in the two weeks since the last show, it has a celebratory, triumphant air of a home return, which is a bizarre and ridiculous feeling on the other side of the world, and crowns the sense that we are very welcome and appreciated here.

Our gate is open. Time to go home.

Adrian McNally, April 2009.

Clockwise from top left: Rachel avoiding iguanas in Woodford; Adrian practicing for Sydney solo set; family in Sydney; family in the Blue Mountains; Airports; Rachel in Port Faivy.

9
JUST A SECOND

Adrian McNally

The following is a blog about the Mercury Music Prize of 2008 that Adrian wrote but which was never published. At this point he was managing, arranging and producing for Rachel Unthank & The Winterset, but he was not yet an onstage member.

I'm sat in the Grosvenor House Hotel on Park Lane, don't you know, waiting for the girls to come out of their visa application interviews at the US embassy, on the 11th of September of all dates (or 9/11 as it's known), for our Stateside tour next week. It's only 8.30am, but already we've had an eventful morning. We got to the train station this morning to discover one band member had forgotten her passport. Luckily we had only travelled 10 minutes from Niopha's parents house. Niopha's mum went back for the passport, only to have to return home again when another band member realised she had forgotten her application forms. Can you see what I'm dealing with here?! But I lost my passport while we were in Holland, so withering disappointed looks and tuts are not my privilege today.

That is a story in itself. I had to get security guards to let me back onto the closed down festival site at 3am to look for the passport. Searching around the spiegeltent we had played the night before in the

darkness, I was just about to give up when I spotted a shadowy figure in the corner. It was a technician who had bunked down in the venue for the night. I took a closer look, expecting I might have to wake her to ask if she had seen my passport, and noticed something familiar under her head, that she had folded up and used as a makeshift pillow. It was my coat. And in it, my passport.

So here I am in the Grosvenor, the 5 star venue of the Nationwide Mercury Prize, with a moment to reflect on an evening in a lifetime, two nights ago now. The heady perfume that they pump into the lobby of the Grosvenor is making me nauseous, so it's difficult to focus, but I can remember emotions including excitement, anxiety, anticipation, happiness even, pride definitely - and then, confusion.

We made the journey south a whole four days before the ceremony, firstly for an Unthank family gathering.

It was the naming ceremony of baby Joshua; the newest and cutest new member of the family, and son of Rachel and Becky's brother and his wife. Then into London for rehearsals and soundchecks on Monday morning. We arrive on time, from four separate destinations, with no incident. Excitement has not caved in to nervousness yet and everyone is chipper. The piano has arrived, we have the lovely Sam to look after our every whim and the cool famous bands who we would normally be intimidated by, are all smiling back because they're all crapping it too.

The Great Room, one of Europe's largest ballrooms, is, well, large. The carpet is a bit Auntie Doris, but no one will see that when the lights go down. It's 11.30am when the girls take the stage for the first soundcheck of the day, and although the piano keys are stiff, because it's new, and Stef's knuckles are throbbing from the impact of those glissandi in 'Blue Bleezing Blind Drunk', everything goes handsomely. The girls do four run-throughs for the TV people, I flit between the sound desk and the BBC van outside, where the TV sound is engineered, and all sounds good. Great even. The ladies do the first of what will be many BBC 6 Music interviews (they have decided to follow us around for the two days) and by midday we're heading off to our hotel with the rest of the day to kill, which is predominantly achieved by shopping and eating. Not drinking though. Definitely not drinking.

Rachel and I wake at 8.10am to a phone call from BBC Radio Newcastle, who want her on air in 15 minutes. BBC Radio Newcastle, which recently cancelled its weekly folk show, which, even though it likes to interview Rachel and Becky, still doesn't regard the music as suitable for airplay, even when the Mercury Music Prize nomination points out that we are not just niche music.

So today is MMP day. We started called it the MMP (pronounced 'm-m-p' in lower case) as a code, when we were told we'd been nominated but weren't allowed to tell anyone. The excitement over the past 6 week about the final has nothing to do with any anticipation of winning. The performance of 'Blue Bleezing Blind Drunk' on the night will be a debut TV performance So for the girls, it's "will we play well, will we sing well what will we wear, will we look good, will we look fat will I just forget how to play it in a sudden fit of nerves will it be good enough to get us on Jools's show?!... "There's no time to worry about winning!

We arrive at Grosvenor House at 1.30pm for a TV interview with our local news team back in the North East. Then we are taken in for the afternoon's run-through rehearsal. This is the first time that ever other person we see is famous. There's Alex from th Arctics, Laura Marling and her band, Lauren Lavern being surprisingly tall, a super cool lady we take to b Estelle, Adele (rhymes with Estelle), and isn't that Jool Holland underneath the flat cap? We lie low with ou new friends the Portico Quartet. Typical for the nich genre bands to cling together.

Things are running late. By the time we finally get ou turn, the girls are super-late for make-up. Havin waited around for half the day, the girls come off stag and within the hour they're spruced up and on the red carpet. Fortunately, they had all decided in advance what to wear, so getting ready is quick, but considerabl anxieties abound concerning the use of a make-u artist; they had wanted the time to be able to take it of if they didn't like it! Fortunately they liked it!

5.30pm. We walk out of one door in the building, ge in a car and travel 30 metres at the most, for the red carpet experience. We open the car doors, only to fine that some previous arrivals are still hogging the rug, so the chauffeur closes our doors again and we have to si and wait our turn! The girls experienced the paparazz bombardment of camera flashes for the first time a

...he first Mercury press conference 6 weeks ago, and so ...opefully this time they will know what to expect and ...on't look so startled. I have to say — because it's true — ...hey look fabulous.

...have a moment when we hit the red carpet; I suddenly ...ealise I haven't worked out what I'm going to do ...nyself. Well, that's not true. I was planning on just ...anging back, but it turns out that there is no 'back' ...o hang in. Our approach to the red carpet is from the ...ide of it, rather than down it, so there is nowhere to ...ide. I step far enough away from the band so as not to ...e in the photos, but I fear I end up looking like their ...ecurity person. I smile towards the girls. A security ...erson wouldn't smile like I'm smiling. But I still feel ...aft. Then I remember my camera and take my own ...ocu-photos of them being photographed. I find my ...ole.

...After half an hour on the carpet, doing interviews with ...he BBC, Sky, ITV, NME etc... what do we do? We ...o straight back to our room! The red carpet arrival is ...one early. The event doesn't start for another hour. ...o Stef goes back to make-up for more titivation, I get ...ack on the computer to further advance our continued ...isa saga for the States, and Becky nibbles chocolates to ...heck which ones Rachel can have (Rachel's allergic to ...azelnuts).

When we finally take the stairs down to the ballroom, we're all still surprisingly calm. The room looks fabulous. Over 100 dining tables glistening with cutlery, champagne buckets, a near-360 degree black backdrop adorned with twinkly lights, 3 stages down one side of the room, and chandeliers catching state of the art stage lighting. We are shown to our table, which is on the front row, right in front of Jools Holland's podium. But we're performing in 15 minutes, so we don't stay at the table. We head backstage and immediately bump into Alison Krauss. She is very taken with Rachel's dress, which makes Rachel's year.

The Last Shadow Puppets open up in dramatic, Scott Walker-esque fashion, quickly followed by the highly entertaining Neon Neon. Before we know it, I'm dashing to the sound desk and the girls are on stage, standing by. The introduction by Jools is flattering and they're on. Thank fuck for that. Becky opens up beautifully. Sometimes her nerves manifest physically, making her voice quiver in a way she cannot control. If this had happened, she would never have gotten over it, so it's a relief, to say the least, and I'm unspeakably happy for her. I'm concentrating on my sound engineering, which is a lottery because I'm only mixing their monitors and they're so far away from me that I can't even make out their faces, so I don't really know how it goes, but what I do note is that the audience are pin-drop silent in a way they were not for the first two acts.

When I return backstage, it's a relief that no band member seems paranoid about playing or singing badly, and they're already receiving compliments from passers by. Jools says that Rachel Unthank & The Winterset should win because they played such a lovely waltz. Does he mean this, or is he just letting everyone know that he knows it was a waltz? Jools says "sounded great" to me as I'm passing, and I say "cheers mate". Cheers mate?! You don't say "cheers mate" to Jools Holland! Damn it.

The girls are desperate for champagne and a front row seat but are whisked off again for more interviews. I go and sit down with our EMI chaps and Becky's boyfriend. My lord this is glamorous. Jools's podium is five yards away, so we're bound to be on the telly, Robert Plant is to my left shoulder and isn't that two of Radiohead at the next table? I normally leave the over-excitement to the girls. I'm largely unmoved and not intimidated by showbiz. I'd rather be at home making music or a white wine sauce, but even I am a bit stirred.

British Sea Power are awesome. Then the girls join us, followed by cameras, which stay in our faces until the end. Blimey.

The performances are rattled through in the space of an hour. Estelle's performance cracks with the high musical and physical energy of her smiling band, Adele goes for a bit of show-stopping with a solo performance, Laura Marling and the Portico Quartet are all the way over on a stage we can only just see, Plant, Krauss and the Radiohead boys sit with the rest of us to watch videos of themselves. Elbow sound big and Guy Garvey's voice is on superb form. Have I missed anyone? Oh, Burial of course; the favourite. Nowhere to be seen. But it is a happy experience that all the performances are really good.

In the break, we are congratulated by all sorts of industry bods, including none other than the man who bought EMI recently, which kind of feels like meeting the grim reaper! He's nice though. We hear that in the TV coverage someone has said nice things on the telly about the production on *The Bairns*, so I'm chuffed, and Adele tells the girls they were the highlight of her night and invites us to a party that we resolve to attend but when we arrive later it is all over. The girls are torn away to go on the Radio 2 Radcliffe and Maconie show. Whenever they've been on before, Mark Radcliffe has always been away, so the girls have been looking forward to meeting him. They're both very charming to us all. On air, Stuart says that our album is perhaps the first Mercury nominated album from the 'token gesture' genres of folk, jazz and classical to actually be in contention for the first prize. I've been very content with the notion that, though I don't think we will win, I do think we will be in contention, so I am delighted to hear Stuart agree. But secretly I know that *The Bairns* would not be the first folk album to nearly win, because I was once told that Norma Waterson nearly won in the mid-nineties when Pulp won. Shame that. Nowt wrong with Pulp mind.

I'm speaking to the very nice head of Beggars Banquet,

and when I confess I'm not sure whether to have a fa[n] moment with Ed from Radiohead, without consultin[g] me for approval, he comes straight over and introduce[s] me, thankfully as Rachel's producer and not just a[s] some dumb, geeky Radiohead fan, which would hav[e] also been accurate. We talk for around 20 minute[s], me about how great *In Rainbows* is and he about ho[w] great Rachel & co. are, and because we both hav[e] considered reasons why we think so, it doesn't feel a[t] all sycophantic or luvvie. Surely *In Rainbows* is going t[o] win. They've made out and out rock albums, then the[y] have more albums with greater electronic leanings, an[d] *In Rainbows* sounds like the first complete Radiohea[d] album, like the rest was just all leading to this poin[t]. Every Radiohead album to me has sounded like a[n] enthralling part of a bigger journey, and In Rainbow[s] sounds like the destination. It sounds contemporar[y] and cutting edge, but it also seriously rocks! I imagin[e] it's perhaps the first album that every member of th[e] band has been completely happy with. Ed confirms m[y] thoughts. They say that music unites different culture[s] across the world. Tonight it bridged the great chasr[n] between middle class Oxford education and a Sout[h] Yorkshire pit village!

Jools returns to the podium for the announcement an[d] it takes a while for everyone to settle down. I feel sick[.] We haven't had any serious notions about winning, bu[t] everyone keeps telling us that they think we're going t[o] win and the thought has pushed its way past the self[-] preserving doubts and planted the seed of a possibilit[y] in our imaginations. There is no drawn-out reality[-] show type drama hyping. He just comes straight ou[t] with it. Elbow.

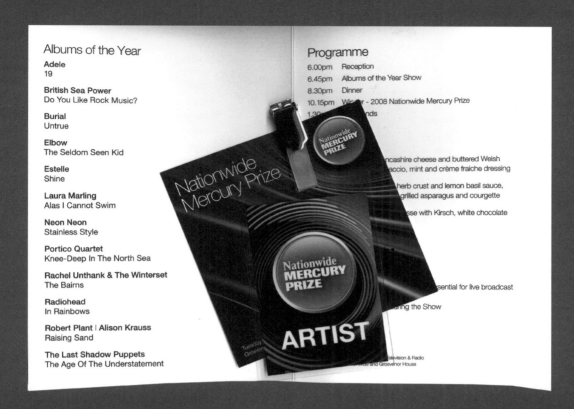

Albums of the Year

Adele
19

British Sea Power
Do You Like Rock Music?

Burial
Untrue

Elbow
The Seldom Seen Kid

Estelle
Shine

Laura Marling
Alas I Cannot Swim

Neon Neon
Stainless Style

Portico Quartet
Knee-Deep In The North Sea

Rachel Unthank & The Winterset
The Bairns

Radiohead
In Rainbows

Robert Plant | Alison Krauss
Raising Sand

The Last Shadow Puppets
The Age Of The Understatement

Programme

6.00pm   Reception
6.45pm   Albums of the Year Show
8.30pm   Dinner
10.15pm   Winner - 2008 Nationwide Mercury Prize
1.30 ...   ...nds

...ncashire cheese and buttered Welsh
...accio, mint and crème fraiche dressing

...herb crust and lemon basil sauce,
...grilled asparagus and courgette

...sse with Kirsch, white chocolate

...sential for live broadcast

...ing the Show

...Television & Radio
...nwide and Grosvenor House

We tried our best with the smiles, but our parents have told us that they could see our disappointment on the elly. Hopefully it's just because they know us so well nd no one else could tell. But the disappointment ades away almost immediately. It really was only a seed f a possibility in my imagination, and I really didn't hink that Jools had an 'R' on tip of his tongue before e opened that envelope.

We enjoy the rest of our evening in good spirits, meeting ore great and good, and sharing happy retrospective houghts with our EMI team about how far we've come n the past year.

ate into the night, our revelry took a twist when two ifferent judges independently tell us that the debate or first prize had come down to a tight contest between lbow and ourselves. I think they thought we would be appy to hear that we had come second. But with the MMP, there is no second! Once upon a time, in years one by, head judge Simon Frith would announce he winner and often reveal how close it had been nd who between. But that doesn't happen anymore. Only the winner is announced. If there was a silver or ronze, we'd have been ecstatic with either, but there sn't. So it is quite a puzzle to the brain to know how o feel about coming second when there is no second. he only thing to do is to return to the glow of pride nd surprise we felt on discovering we were nominated n the first place. For that we will always be happy nd grateful.

We're all back at home now. The journey back to Northumberland was not pleasant. The van broke down at Hemel Hempstead and we had to wait around until rush hour started and do the rest in a courtesy hire car. Long day. We texted in to Radcliffe and Maconie on the journey home to tell them of our woes, and caused some confusion and amusement by telling them our 'bongo' had broken down, which is the model of our van, but we didn't tell them that bit. We thought they'd have fun with the notion of a bongo breaking down, and how only a folk band would travel in a bongo, and they did.

So we'll watch it with the rest of you on TV tonight.

Most awards are a load of rubbish aren't they? But the Mercurys are a bit special, and judged by a different, independent panel every year. How the bookies expect to make a prediction, I don't know, and I'm not sure they ever successfully have. So I do feel proud. Which is to say that I'm allowing myself a proud feeling just this once. Proud of the people I manage and produce; of their talent and personality; but mainly of their character, their strength, resilience, aptitude, patience, grace and balls! It's a privilege to serve them. Tuesday was certainly a landmark, but we've only just begun.

Adrian McNally, 11/09/2008

10
BIRTHDAYS ON TOUR

Señor Becky

We have spent a lot of time away from home in the last ten years, and had some fantastic experiences. We've had some brilliant times touring in the UK and Ireland, we've played America and Australia two or three times each, gone on a five-week tour of Europe that covered eleven different countries... leaving us with loads of great memories and experiences for which I am eternally grateful.

One down side to being away, though, is missing out on important occasions with friends and family year after year. It can make the pang for home strong, so we like to distract people when it comes to birthdays, do something silly or fun, to be a gang, a band, a family. Just for that time, what we have is each other. Those experiences we've shared together bond us, whether it's the exhilaration of a fantastic gig, exploring a new city, or piling into a corner of a bar or a tour bus with pints or cuppas. It was our time; we only had each other so we made the most of it.

When it comes to the silliness one or two birthday stand out in my mind. We had a good one for Adrian in Tulsa, Oklahoma, when we were on an America tour supporting Ben Folds! Back then we were sti Rachel Unthank & The Winterset, and were just abou to become The Unthanks. Stef Connor, our pian player, was leaving to do a Masters in Composition We had been in the studio making our first Unthank album, *Here's the Tender Coming*, with Adrian taking ove from Stef on piano. The America tour with Ben Fold was one of the last tours we had planned with Stef, s it's a shame she never made it across the America border. Something about a lost passport, and the nev passport not having the correct visa in it, meant tha after three hours of Stef and Adrian being interrogate separately in isolation, Adrian ended up in the righ part of Detroit airport with Rachel, Niopha and me but unfortunately Stef was deported!

There were tears, there was confusion, what were w to do? We couldn't afford to fly home! Also, it wa

n opportunity of a lifetime just to get the chance to atch Ben Folds and his band play night after night cross America, never mind the fact we would be etting our music out there to new ears. "You do it, drian," I suggested. "Yes!" Niopha and Rachel agreed. ut we hadn't performed as a band yet. The album asn't finished and there had been no rehearsals. But was our only real option—for us to scrape something ogether in the 24 hours we had before the first show nd for Adrian's first performance as an onstage ember of The Unthanks to be in The House of Blues n Las Vegas in front of his piano hero Ben Folds. lthough he was due in any case to take over the piano tool a few months later, Adrian was reticent about ecoming an onstage member at all, let alone with a ay's notice and preparation. His doubts about his own bility had prevented him from putting himself on the iano stool in the first place, having paired us up with elinda O'Hooley. And now here we were.

If my lack of piano practice as a child could come ack and haunt me in a real nightmare," Adrian has een heard to say, "it might well be this, with a day's otice to come up with a show in front of 2000 eople in Las Vegas with Ben Folds in the wings." On ne night, Ben was chuckling in the wings, or was he miling encouragingly? Either way, he knew Adrian's redicament and nerves, and gave Adrian just the right alance of praise and stick about it. The day of intense reparation paid off, more or less, but that wasn't the

end of it. We had done enough to survive our thirty minute support slot with Ben, but halfway through this tour, we were to do three shows of our own, for which we would need a ninety minute set. So the new plan was hatched, which meant we spent every day after that rehearsing in cheap motel rooms and doing four-piece versions of songs like 'Felton Lonnin' and 'Because He Was a Bonny Lad'. I even had a small piano role on 'Close the Coalhouse Door'! Outside, the sun shone on cities like LA and San Diego. We hope one day to return and actually see them! It was an all or nothing sort of effort. Tense but exciting! Poor old Stef spent her plane journey home frantically writing the piano parts out to send to Adrian to aid his predicament.

Halfway through the tour it was Adrian's birthday, so naturally we bought him some Elton John inspired plastic glasses and some beads with a coffin on (look, we had limited shopping options that morning). These were his birthday gifts, which he wore proudly on the long drive through America's mid-west. At a petrol station en route, the friendly woman behind the counter almost screamed, she was so thrilled to meet Rachel, Niopha and me, but not because we were in a band. Having heard our accents she was simply excited to meet someone from a different country, whilst taking a cautious sideways glance at Adrian's ridiculous accessorising every now and again. Middle America. Of all the places to be forced to stand out and look ridiculous on your birthday.

By the time we got to Tulsa, we were ready to let off some steam! After our performance in an old cowboy dance hall, complete with sprung dance floor, we joined the crowds and united in their passion for Ben's brilliant music. We danced, we whooped, we sang along to our favourite songs. The bar staff had clocked the fact that we were the penniless support act and kindly poured us very large measures. We were high as kites! High on life and on music, with a little help from the bar. Adrian even got a birthday song from the band — his favourite Ben Folds song, 'Alice Childress'.

We still wonder (argue!) to this day whether or not there was a man lying on a bed of nails in the bar we went to afterwards. Or what happened to the artwork some mysterious guy randomly gave to us in the bar, or where my missing stick on moustache ended up, or how we managed to get home. Actually Niopha Keegan took charge of us that night, thank goodness. According to her, Adrian instantly fell asleep in the taxi and started snoring loudly, Rachel talked incessantly and sang to the driver all the way back to the hotel, barely pausing for breath. Her repertoire included 'Uptown Girl', 'Oklahoma' and '24 Hours From Tulsa'. We arrived at the hotel, I apparently fell in a bush and that was that. Birthday night out done.

After that, the false moustache has become a bit of a tradition for birthdays on tour. Here's a selection of photos as evidence.

Moustaches are so passé! Adrian's birthday, a Tuesday afternoon in Marsden, W. Yorks.

ben folds
way to europe
2008

BEN FOLDS WAY TO NORMAL

LL ACCESS

CUBEPASSES.COM

BEN FOLDS 2009

ALL ACCESS

	VENUE	
eryone travels to Amsterdam,..arrives thu, 20		
en stays in Amsterdam…Others stay in The H		
e Hague, NETH	CROSSING BORDER	
ssen, GERMANY	ROCK PALAST FEST	
euven, BELGIUM	HET DEPOT EDEN	
aris, FRANCE	LE TRABENDO	
OFF night…Frankfurt		
rankfurt, GERMANY	KUNSTLERHAUS MOU	
Berlin, GERMANY	KESSELHAUS	
OFF night… London		
OFF night… London		
London, UK	SHEPHERD'S BUSH EMPIRE	1900
all return to USA…		

NTHANK is Special Guest in Leuven, Paris, Frankfurt, Berlin & London

Right: The Unthanks and Ben Folds

RACHEL UNTHANK
CE SOIR EN PREMIÈR

Rachel Unthank & The Winterset

NE PAS JETER SUR LA VOIE PUBLIQUE

"LA PLUS TROUBLANTE DES APPARITIONS DU REVIVAL BRITISH FOLK" - VOLUME
"SPINE-TINGLING.. DEEPLY ATMOSPHERIC.. CONSTANTLY SURPRISING ****" - MOJO
"A MAGICAL ALBUM...A WORK OF TOWERING QUALITY" - THE TELEGRAPH

NOUVEL ALBUM
THE BAIRNS

ROUGH TRADE

Top left: Emergency rehearsal in Las Vegas as Adrian steps in.
Top right and centre: Cocktails in Hooters.
Centre left: Tapioca milkshake in China town, New York.
Bottom right: Rachel and Adrian in central park, New York.

2008. Clockwise from top left:
Stef on stage;
Good times at The Big Chill;
High flying on the Isle of Mull;
Glastonbury.

A FAN WRITES...

No 3. Gary Dearlove & Jools Ampadu

We first saw the Unthanks at the Howard Assembly Rooms in Leeds which is a lovely, intimate venue. We had heard the music on record (yes, we still refer to recorded music in all its formats as 'records'!) so we knew that the music had an emotional power that you don't really get in too many places. But seeing the band live that first time was like a wave of calm, a rush of peace (if that makes any sense?), which has never changed in all the many times we have seen the band perform in many line-ups since. There was a lot going on in our lives at that time and that first live experience took us away from everything and, hopefully without going too over the top, confirmed that all is still in good in the world! The Unthanks always fill us with hope – and the experience of sharing real music with real human beings (both on stage and in the audience) is something that we will cherish to the end of our days.

Womad, 2009 - Stef waves goodbye
at the final Winterset gig.

II
NURSERY CRYMES
Chris Price & Adrian McNally

Chris and Adrian lived a childhood four doors apart, in a small pit village near Barnsley. They met at 18 months, when new to the village, the McNallys were invited up to the Prices' for a neighbourly Christmas drink. The boys were introduced, Chris gave Adrian a whack round the head, and they've been brothers ever since – the sort of brothers that barely spoke or acknowledged each other at school, but who shared an almost private (from their peers) love of music, of tinkering about with cassette decks, recording make–believe radio stations and making up stupid songs. Here they share a few thoughts..

Chris: Noise was always pounding out of the detached house at the end of our street via means of either the stereo or the piano in the hallway. This was the McNally residence.

By the age of around 10, you would often find Adrian and myself sat - no *placed* - on the sofa, centrally between two huge, homemade speakers. The albums that Adrian's dad, Max, would present to us to were like nothing *I* had heard before: *Close To The Edge* by Yes, *In The Court Of The Crimson King* by King Crimson, *Tarkus* by ELP and *Foxtrot* by Genesis to name but a few. We loved to play the Pink Floyd experimental piece from their album *Ummagumma*, entitled 'Several Species Of Small Furry Animals Gathered Together In A Cave And Grooving With A Pict' at high volume, with the lights off. There were a further two speakers behind us, set up for quadraphonic sound, which picked out lots more detail in the music, so we'd be jumping out of our skin every other second. Terrifying for a 10-year-

old but totally captivating. Certainly a far cry from the glam-pop sounds of Kajagoogoo and Howard Jones, from our own day.

Adrian: Ah yes Chris. All that clever music, mostly from the four or five years that preceded our birth, for better or worse made the supposedly theatrical and over the top pop music of our own day sound pretty dull eh? Still, we managed to find time for Adam and the Ants, and then finally some parent rebellion with a craze for Iron Maiden's *Live After Death*.

As I remember it though (and I might be wrong) some of that placing-us-in-the-right-place-between-the-speakers came once we'd started to show our own interest in my dad's records. Until then, the prog-assault was just drifting into my noggin while I was constructing football stadia from Lego.

Its my recollection that we discovered 'Supper's Ready'

on *Foxtrot* by Genesis partially by ourselves. Or at least, it was of our own accord that we started repeat listening to it. I recall us sitting in a single armchair together (not between the speakers — my dad would have had a fit), poring over the lyrics and the artwork in the gatefold sleeve. "Winston Churchill dressed in drag", "butterflies, flutter-bys and gutter flies", and then later on from *Selling England By The Pound*, the likes of "Liquid Len", "Harold Demure, from Art Literature" and "Mick the Prick, fresh out the nick"…

You and I are referred to as the proggie, muso element in The Unthanks, but now I think of it, lots of the music we were first transfixed by was largely because of the words, the storytelling, the childlike, folk-like, nursery rhymes of Peter Gabriel. Ok, so turning the lights off when our folks were out and running round the room to '21st Century Schizoid Man' or 'Close To The Edge' until we bumped into each other, was definitely about a love for thrilling chaos and complexity in music, but with early Genesis, with War of the Worlds, with Peter and the Wolf (the rock version of Prokofiev's masterpiece of course, with Keith Tippett, Viv Stanshall, Bill Bruford, Phil Collins, Julie Driscoll, Stéphane Grappelli, Cozy Powell, Manfred Mann, with animated gatefold artwork aplenty)… We were essentially listening to music that was there to serve the stories, to paint musical pictures, and in that sense, is it any wonder that we've ended up doing what we do?

The one time I hit him back and how pleased I look.
You can just see Chris crying up the road behind my right shoulder.

Guitar Hero

The first time I heard Don McLean on the radio singing the song 'Vincent' it really impressed me to think that someone would cover one of my dad's songs and have it played on the radio. He played guitar and sang to me a fair bit as a child so more often than not his versions were my first experiences of those songs.

At a young age he taught me the chords D major, A major and E major. You can play literally hundreds of songs armed with these three chords and the one I liked to play most was my dad's - no sorry - Tim Hardin's song 'If I Were A Carpenter'.

Was this before or after you put your head through the back of your dad's acoustic guitar mate?

I loved hearing your dad sing, which was a much rarer treat for me. There was so much music in our house but no one sang. The sweet timbre of his voice, and earnestness of his sentiment, even when pissed as a fart. 'Suite: Judy Blue Eyes' by Crosby Stills and Nash, 'You've Got A Friend' on that balcony late at night in Spain with your mum bawling her eyes out, and all those soulful American folk albums that countered the angular English music down at our house. What owe our parents for so much of the pleasure we have experienced in our lives, don't we, let alone the career we've fallen into. For the career, we can blame them, but the pleasure cannot be over-estimated. It will be my first love, and… etc.

Dancing

Adrian and I didn't dance to music back then but for some reason would often chase each other around my folks' coffee table to The Doobie Brothers track 'Without You', or sometimes if we fancied a change 'Good Lovin' Gone Bad' by Bad Company. We would collapse on the sofa feeling sick at the end of the song. Then get up and do it again.

You definitely couldn't call it dancing. Or chasing really. Just an odd little ritual, like that seemed the most natural thing to want to do in response to those particular pieces of music. I used to run on the spot in response to 'I Robot' by the Alan Parsons Project. Hmm. Maybe that is an admission too far. Ritual dance then. Another early sign of folk tendencies perhaps?

Religion (Or Not)

Sometimes it's fun to close your eyes and pick out at random a record from the cabinet and pop it on. I found a few gems in my dad's collection by using this method. Between you and I we managed to learn

...ust about all of the words to the *Jesus Christ Superstar* ...oundtrack. Although we only lived four doors apart ...e still had sleepovers and at night in bed we would ...ing the album from beginning to end. One night you ...ould be Jesus and I'd be Judas and then we'd swap on ...he next sleepover.

...his thread is starting to sound a bit homoerotic mate. ...We were just children, folks. Try to remember that). ...Maybe you heard it before I did, but the first time I ...emember hearing *Jesus Christ Superstar* was at school, in ...he slot at the end of term when we were normally asked ...o bring in games, but one Easter they sat us down in ...ront of the film. I think we were eleven. Naturally the ...ajority of the class thought it was tedious, while we ...hought it was amazing, went home, and found it in ...our dad's record collection, and within a week or two ...e knew every word.

...gain, I think this is another example of us being drawn ...rst and foremost to musical storytelling. Neither of

us are religious, but we were being told the greatest story on earth all the same, using scaffolding, sexy dancing and the soul and funk of the late Sixties. The amazing, convincing storytellers - the performances of Ted Neeley and Carl Anderson in the original motion film soundtrack once wowed me as a kid and now as an adult make me cry, which makes me realise I wasn't wrong as a kid to be so drawn to them, just as we've become drawn as adults to the truth and beauty in the performances of Robert Wyatt and Nick Drake. Wyatt in particular, with his and Alfie Benge's greater attention to the human, social and political content in their songwriting, gave me the emotional intelligence to reject some of the more lyrically vacuous music I had grown up with as indulgent and meaningless. We might have grown up with technically clever music, but we were always destined for a life in folk, is what I think I'm saying. My sister however, who had to sit on her bed and put up with our mimed performances as Jesus and Judas, might beg to differ.

HERE'S THE TENDER COMING

A FAN WRITES...

No 4. Susannah Gent

Since the political devolution process in the late 90s Northern Ireland, Wales and Scotland have enjoyed a more independent encouragement via the establishment of their culture, and their folk music has benefited from this. England hasn't enjoyed the same encouragement sadly, which is where The Unthanks, along with some other bands, have helped to redress the balance, which is very brave, hugely respected and has put modern English folk music back on the map which is folktastic! :-)

A FAN WRITES...

No 5. Lee Ingram, Leicester

A while ago, 'Here's The Tender Coming' inspired a lunch-time game for some of the Primary aged children I worked with. Dressed in improvised blanket-skirts and aprons (from the dressing up box) and hauling football nets or collecting sea-coal stones, peace was broken by the shout of "Here's the tender coming". At this point, the lassies ran to hide the boys away, while others attempted to capture and escort the laddies back to their picnic-bench frigate. The children loved using language from the song, which sounded quite exotic to them. For a short while, hinny and bonny lassie became frequent calls across our rural Devonshire playground.

The making of Here's the Tender Coming.

Clockwise from top left: Members of the Northern Sinfonia recording
At First She Starts with Becky in the booth; Rachel working hard on
song research, not playing solitaire; Chris playing the dulcitone in
Annachie Gordon; Adrian doing something he doesn't quite know how
to do, as usual; Engineer Adam finds the lava lamp more distracting
than Adrian's playing.

Opposite: Neil Harland (bass) and Julian Sutton (melodeon) both of
whom have appeared on several Unthank albums; Adrian tell's Rachel
and Becky they don't have to sing today; Becky's best mate Shelley
singing on the title track; he likes what he sees!; the boys rehearsing at
home; old cymbal head (Adrian).

The UNTHANKS

plus special guests
Jonny Kearney
and Lucy Farrell

HERE'S THE TENDER COMING

OCTOBER

10 LEICESTER DeMontfort Hall 0116 2333111
11 CARDIFF The Glee Club 0871 4720400

12 LONDON Shepherds Bush Empire
   0844 4772000 www.ticketweb.co.uk

13 OXFORD The North Wall 01865 319450
14 NORWICH Arts Centre 01603 660352
15 NOTTINGHAM Arts Theatre 0115 9476096
16 BUXTON Opera House 0845 1272190
17 WHITCHURCH Leisure Centre 01948 660660
18 EXETER Phoenix 01392 667080
19 MANCHESTER Band on the Wall 0161 8321111
20 MANCHESTER Band on the Wall 0161 8321111
21 CAMBRIDGE The Junction 01223 511511
22 GATESHEAD The Sage Gateshead 0191 4434661
24 HALIFAX Parish Church www.ticketweb.co.uk
25 GLASGOW Oran Mor 0141 3576200
26 EDINBURGH Voodoo Rooms 0131 5567060
27 ABERDEEN The Lemon Tree 01224 641122
28 YORK The Duchess 01904 641413
29 WARWICK Arts Centre 0247 6524524
30 READING Concert Hall 0118 9606060

NOVEMBER

01 BRISTOL Old Vic Theatre Royal 0117 9877877
02 BRIGHTON Komedia 0845 2938480
19 CHICHESTER Minerva Theatre 01243 781312
20 HEREFORD The Freedom Centre 01432 340555
21 LIVERPOOL St Brides Church wegottickets.com
24 DERBY Assembly Rooms 01322 255800
25 LINCOLN Theatre Royal 01522 519999
26 BURY The Met 0161 7612216
27 BERWICK The Maltings 01289 330999
28 STOCKTON The Arc 01642 525199

DECEMBER

01 SHEFFIELD Memorial Hall 0114 2789789
02 LEEDS Howard Assembly Rooms 0844 848 2727
03 KENDAL The Brewery 01539 725133
05 HEBDEN BRIDGE Trades Club 01422 845265
06 HEBDEN BRIDGE Trades Club 01422 845265
07 WOLVERHAMPTON Wulfren Hall 0870 3207000
08 MILTON KEYNES The Stables 01908 280800
09 ALDERSHOT West End Centre 01252 330040
10 BRIDGEWATER Arts Centre 01278 422700
11 EAST GRINSTEAD Arts Centre 01342 302000

A new 9-piece extended line-up featuring piano, drums, double bass, string quartet and brass.
www.the-unthanks.com

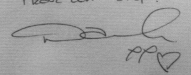

DAWN FRENCH

13.8.10

Dear Unthanks people,
                    I HAD to write to tell
you I think you are utterly bloody fantastic.
I have listened to your album for 2
weeks now, to the exclusion of all other
favourite music, and I hear a new and
wonderful, different thing each time. Its
funny and silly and heartbreaking and
shocking and everything....
          Thank goodness you're here!!

          Much big love to you,
              plus buckets of respec.
          Please don't stop!

A FAN WRITES...

No 6. Steve Brown

Our first live encounter with The Unthanks, of which there
have been many subsequently, happened at The Trades Club in
Hebden Bridge in 2009. With unquenchable appetites for live
music across all styles, my wife Julie first picked up on the band
which then fell sweetly with their visit to Hebden, so tickets were
snapped up hurriedly. On the night of the show, babysitting arrangements delayed our departure from home and we finally arrived at The Trades Club to find it packed, with no sign of a seat
anywhere. We stood at the back of the room unsure what to do
when I was grabbed by the hand by a cheery, purposeful woman
who guided us through the tightly packed tables to the 2 remaining seats that we had been unable to see from the back and which
were at the very stage edge, slightly right of centre.
We just couldn't believe our luck.

After a brilliant set by support act Johnny and Lucy, The
Unthanks arrived on stage where we immediately recognised
our "usherette" to be none other than Rachel Unthank herself.
Needless to say, the show was one of the best we have ever been
to, and we witnessed it from a perfect vantage point.

A FAN WRITES...

No 7. Chris Brookes

Humility and harmony

I can't remember where we first heard The Unthanks on record,
however I do remember when we first met Rachel. She was
running a singing session for the young'uns (not the group –
I mean under 11s) at Coldham's Common family campsite at
Cambridge. The year was 2009. A friend had told me that the
Unthanks had played the Royal Opera House, so I was expecting
a big star. I wasn't disappointed, her singing was fantastic and
even better was the way she got kids of all ages joining in and
finding out that singing together is one of life's biggest thrills.
Even more amazing, and just typical of the family, was that
before the singing started she cleaned up old chips and wrappings
left over from the previous night's gatherings, so the kids would
have a lovely space to sing. They are collectively the most down
to earth, uplifting singers I have met. They bring together both
humility and harmony – now there's an album title.

CONTRO CANTO

quartaedizione_duemiladieci

Comune
Castelfidardo
ProLoco
Castelfidardo

arci

Provincia
Ancona

THE UNTHANKS
Jonny Kearney & Lucy Farrell supporter
from UK • ingresso libero

"Semplicità contagiosa, voce irresistibile" – La Repubblica
"E' così che si scrivono i grandi dischi" – Rolling Stone
"Disco e gruppo pressoché unici" - Rumore
"Colpiti al cuore, di nuovo" – Il Mucchio Selvaggio
*"Un pizzico di creatività che lo fa brillare
per originalità e personalità poetica"* - Buscadero

giovedì
29
aprile

CASTELFIDARDO
Auditorium San Francesco ore 21

infoline 071.203045 / 339.6733590 www.contro-canto.org

ROSSINI
PIANOFORTI
www.rossinipianoforti.it • Tel. 071.7820189

The Unthanks first live band rehearsal, Chorlton, Manchester.

Here's the Tender Coming tour pics.
Bottom left: Jo Silverston and Hannah Peel
"Er, what do we do with these again?"

Hannah Peel

hausdermusik
das klangmuseum

THE UNTHANKS
25. APRIL 2010
20:00 UHR

LIVE ON STAGE SPECIAL.

PLAGUE

TREMBLING BELLS · HURRAY FOR THE RIFF RAFF
WALSH & POUND · OLIVIA CHANEY · THE UNTHANKS
SAM LEE · SHIRLEY COLLINS · JACKIE OATES
THE BELLES OF LONDON CITY · MICHAEL TYACK

ISSUE ZERO

The magical Jonny Kearney and Lucy Farrell,
who were special guests during the Tender tour.

AN INTIMATE EVENING WITH

The UNTHANKS

WITH SUPPORT FROM
JONNY KEARNEY AND LUCY FARRELL

A TOUR OF SMALL, INTIMATE
VENUES WITH THE UNTHANKS
CLOSE-UP AND PAIRED DOWN, IN
THE GUISE OF THEIR CORE
CREATIVE QUINTET.

WED 11TH APRIL 2012
NEWBROUGH TOWN HALL, NORTHUMBERLAND
01434 674 162 - WWW.THE-UNTHANKS.COM

THU 12TH APRIL 2012
HIGH HOUSE FARM BREWERY, MATFEN, NORTHUMBERLAND
TICKETS FROM THE BREWERY OR ON-LINE FROM WWW.THE-UNTHANKS.COM

FRI 13TH APRIL 2012
ALNWICK PLAYHOUSE
01665 510 785 - WWW.ALNWICKPLAYHOUSE.CO.UK

WED 9TH MAY 2012
GREAT HALL, DISCOVERY MUSEUM, NEWCASTLE
TICKETS ON-LINE FROM WWW.THE-UNTHANKS.COM

TICKET DETAILS FROM WWW.THE-UNTHANKS.COM
SUPPORT FROM WWW.JONNYANDLUCY.COM

VISIT WWW.THE-UNTHANKS.COM FOR DETAILS OF SUMMER
SHOWS WITH BRIGHOUSE AND RASTRICK BRASS BAND

RABBLE ROUSER

THE UNTHANKS

LIVE IN THE UK

TOUR DATES:

3rd May   Oxfordshire | Wood Festival
4th May   Brighton | St Georges Church
5th May   Southampton | The Brook
6th May   Leeds | Brudenell Social Club
8th May   Manchester | The Lowry
9th May   Barnsley | Civic Hall
0th May   Newcastle | Evolution Festival
1st May   Leigh on Sea | Wesley Methodist Church
st June   London | Union Chapel
nd June   Bath International Festival | Komedia
rd June   Aberdeen | Lemon Tree
th June   Edinburgh | Queens Hall
th June   Newcastle | Live Theatre
th June   Newcastle | Live Theatre [Afternoon]
th June   Newcastle | Live Theatre

FURTHER INFORMATION:

ww.the-unthanks.com
ww.myspace.com/rachelunthank
ww.twitter.com/theunthanks

esigned by Owen Davey for
nd of the Road

"Absolutely exquisite. A real work of art. I will be playing it at least forever." *Paul Morley*

"Even more satisfying, compelling, and varied than the Mercury-nominated The Bairns. Haunting, original and magnificent." *The Guardian*

★★★★

'HERE'S THE TENDER COMING', THE ALBUM IS OUT NOW.

The UNTHANKS
HERE'S THE TENDER COMING

No 6. Colin Firth, Actor

Hearing The Unthanks up close is one of the best things that has happened to me. I couldn't believe my good fortune when they agreed to join The People Speak. They were very high on my wishlist and I'd been going round muttering, "We'll never get them."I'd fallen in love with their voices. There are a lot of great voices around, but this ability to hit the emotional spot is a bit of a mystery. Perhaps it's the way they can tell a story. It feels like they're confiding something.

They exceeded expectations, and 'The Testimony Of Patience Kershaw'has rung in my mind ever since. Everyone who was present was blown away. I got comments for weeks from people who wanted to know more about The Unthanks, people who knew them already and wanted me to know that they knew them already –and people, myself included, who wanted to know about Patience Kershaw. It was a passionate response all round –and I'll be forever grateful to them.

It was a bonus that they turned out to be lovely people too. And what a great name.

Adrian singing Shipbuilding at The People Speak book launch, The Tabernacle, London

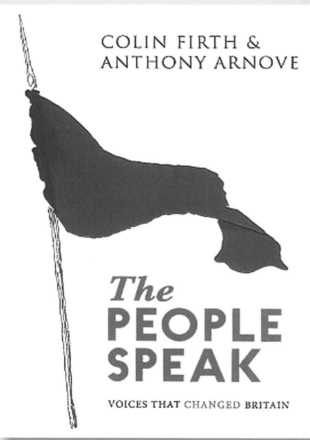

COLIN FIRTH &
ANTHONY ARNOVE

The
PEOPLE
SPEAK

VOICES THAT CHANGED BRITAIN

Adrian: On the 19th September 2010, we found ourselves in the Green Room of a West End theatre with Sir Ben Kingsley, Keira Knightley, Sir Ian McKellen, Kelly Macdonald, Laura Marling, Joss Stone, Omad Djalili, Colin Salmon, Celia Imrie and Saffron Burrows, wondering what on earth we were doing there. We had been invited by Colin Firth to take part in the British leg of a project that started in America, inspired by historian Howard Zinn. The People Speak is a 2009 American documentary feature film that uses dramatic and musical performances (including by Bob Dylan and Bruce Springsteen) of the letters, diaries, and speeches of everyday Americans. The film gives voice to those who, by insisting on equality and justice, spoke up for social change throughout US history and also illustrates the relevance of this to today's society. We were asked by Colin Firth to perform 'The Testimony of Patience Kershaw'. It was a very inspiring afternoon. We left the Prince of Wales Theatre with stories that would leave us in colossal namedropping territory. Handy then that it was such a worthy event! A film of the show was aired on The History Channel, and we played again for Colin at The Tabernacle, London for the launch of the book The People Speak: Voices That Changed Britain, where I also sang 'Shipbuilding'.

MARCH 2010 No. 321   THE ESSENTIAL FOLK, ROOTS & WORLD MUSIC GUIDE   £4.20

fROOTS

31st ANNIVERSARY YEAR 1979 - 2010

Local Music From Out There

the sisters of spookyfolk
the unthanks

The Unthanks are the Marmite of English folk music, attracting adulatory praise and fierce vitriol in equal measure. Colin Irwin opens the doors to Unthankland: photos by Judith Burrows.

I feared carnage. The ten members of The Unthanks touring band had driven to London through the night after last night's gig in the frozen northern climes of Stockton-on-Tees and, nearing the end of an intimidatingly intensive 40-date British tour, I was half-expecting to find Rachel and Becky Unthank in vintage Gallagher brothers mode, knocking ten bells out of one another while the rest of the band mechanically go through the motions in hostile silence as a carefully worded press release is constructed to announce their impending split.

But hey, lots of people get lots of things wrong about The Unthanks and here's Niopha Keegan waiting in the foyer with a huge smile and a big hug to allay those fears. Well, there was the scary night in Edinburgh when they had to manhandle a piano up three flights of stairs to the gig, but apart from that everything has gone swimmingly and they're having the time of their lives. "It's like having a big pyjama party," says Rachel of life on the Unthank tour bus. "I don't want it to end," affirms Becky. "We're going to become nomads and stay on the road *forever*," announces Niopha decisively.

Artists from the folk and roots worlds have impinged on the mainstream in varying styles and degrees of success down the years but, almost uniquely, The Unthanks have done it without a conscious thought of commercial consideration. Indeed, the first suggestion of a crossover breakthrough with the stark debut album *Cruel Sister* in 2005 provoked them not into capitalising with a chirpier, more obviously populist follow-up, but instead to ever more unyieldingly bleak emotions with *The Bairns*. Yet, far from frightening the supposedly limited vision and deadened sensibilities of real people in the real Cowell-brainwashed world, *The Bairns* took them several leaps forward. It earned them a licensing deal with EMI, got lots of airplay in places you wouldn't expect to hear traditional song, was shortlisted for the Mercury Music Prize (and nearly winning it), captured hearts right across the musical divide and sold at a rate that still makes Rachel Unthank gulp with astonishment.

Then, suddenly burdened with a high profile, the pressure of expectation and very large question marks about whether they could survive the departure of their hugely popular and influential pianist Belinda O'Hooley, they dared to dare again on their third album *Here's The Tender Coming*. A grander affair entirely with brass, strings, drums, electric guitars and everything, it still resolutely eschewed populist gambits and, in terms of material and the vocal performances of its two main protagonists, stuck close to their core traditional music values. The folk song traditions of the North East which shaped their whole psyche from childhood clearly still burn right through them. It's not on any of their albums, but one of the strongest songs in their live act is *Tar Barrel In Dale*, written by their dad George (of The Keelers) about the amazing annual New Year's Eve ritual where villagers dress in a variety of colourful costumes to parade through the Northumberland village of Allendale with flaming whiskey barrels on their heads filled with tar, before igniting a huge bonfire with them on the stroke of midnight.

Their widely contrasting vocal styles – Rachel sounds raw and vulnerable, while Becky's voice is creamy and sensual – evolved largely from close encounters with the mostly unaccompanied singers they heard at festivals, folk clubs and singarounds, and even a cursory conversation with them leaves you in no doubt that their first love is and will always be traditional song. Their warm and often very funny stage presentation – itself something of a paradox given the doomy weight of so much of the material they favour – comes with a smattering of close harmony, unaccompanied vocals and displays of clog dancing and their joy at being involved with it is palpable. At last summer's Cambridge Folk Festival they'd arrive on site first thing in the mornings to run vocal workshops and spend the rest of the time absorbing in wonder every drop of music on offer. However weird and wonderful the arrangements that materialise around them, the Unthank creed is driven by one thing and one thing only – the power of the song.

And yet… while reviewers seem to love them unconditionally, opinions in the folk world that fuelled them appear sharply divided. It's *de rigeur*, of course, for anyone associated with a specialist genre to be vilified by the denizens of that genre once they achieve broader popularity whether they deserve it or not, but The Unthanks have been subjected to a particularly vitriolic barrage. "We do seem to be like Marmite – you either love us or hate us," observes Rachel wryly, recalling the catalogue of criticisms hurled against them, from the frocks they wear on stage to accusations that they're the puppets of an evil svengali to charges that they can't actually sing. Most people I've interviewed recently have complained bitterly about messageboard terrorists and The Unthanks know in their hearts they shouldn't fret about the demented rants of a handful of obsessives – especially when they've been going out each night getting standing ovations from full houses – but the remarks still hurt.

"Maybe I do sing out of tune sometimes," says Rachel with a twinkle in her eye, "but we've never claimed to be great singers. I mean, I love Kate Rusby's voice but I can't sing like that – I just sing like I do. I don't get up on stage so that everyone goes 'Oooh what a lovely voice you've got', I get up on stage because I love these stories and I want to sing them to people. Communicating a story is what it's always been about for me. I was quite affected early on by people like The Keelers and The Wilsons, who are fabulous male singers who sing very loudly and early on I suppose I was trying to sing like my dad. I wasn't trying to be a lovely singer, I was trying to be like these big burly shanty singers."

The man answering the 'svengali' charges is Adrian McNally, opinionated band manager, producer, arranger, driver, pianist and Rachel's husband. I interview him separately to Rachel, but his sentiments are the same. "We've had so much nonsense thrown at us, so many ignorant rumours," he says, "but because we've largely tried to adopt a position of silent dignity rather than getting involved, we continue to be ranted at. Because we don't respond, people think we're thick-skinned and not bothered about it, but nothing could be further from the truth. We're very determined and passionate people but we're not thick-skinned at all. It doesn't upset us if people don't like our music, that's fine, but the nonsense that's been written about us on messageboards is awful and has threatened on numerous occasions our desire to continue at all."

Adrian McNally was managing Last Night's Fun when he first set eyes on Rachel Unthank at Whitby Folk Festival. "It was love at first sight," he says, all misty-eyed. "Well, it was for *me*… it wasn't for her." They kept bumping into one another at different festivals and eventually became romantically attached at Warwick Festival around 2002. It was still a long time, however, before they embarked on a professional relationship ("Jeezus, couples have enough to argue about without worrying about business arrangements").

Originally from a pit village near Barnsley, he grew up with a piano in the house and played in numerous bands of different musical hues on the pub/ working men's club circuit, though the only one that paid any serious bills was a Robbie Williams tribute band. A fund of anecdotes swiftly accompany this revelation. "We were doing these big tours, playing five nights a week, ladies' nights to 2,000 women in big hotels and it was weird – we were treated like the real thing. None of us were into Robbie at all, but I've probably never had so much fun as a musician in my life."

"We were set up by five every night and we didn't go on stage until about 10, so wherever we were I'd get my *Good Beer Guide* out and hit the best pubs. I was writing a book about it all. It was meant to be a tour diary but it ended up more as a 'state of England' thing because every single town we went to was exactly the same, completely crippled by its 1960s ring road. So there'd be this little place that couldn't grow any more because of the ring road and instead of sorting it out the council would end up selling a load of land to retailers. Then the guitarist got into real ale and started coming with me and that was the end of the book."

He attributes his interest in traditional song to a prepubescent love of Genesis. The band not the Bible. "For Rachel and Becky, growing up was all about storytelling and in a way it was the same for us. Genesis's *Supper's Ready* from *Foxtrot* is all about the storytelling. Peter Gabriel's words were like nursery rhymes and as kids we were hooked on these fables and characters. In middle school one boring Easter they put on *Jesus Christ Superstar* and I thought it was amazing. Within a week I knew every word. I'd not been to a musical before or since but the storytelling was very much the thing that shone through. Now if I get the choice to go out and listen to some folk music I'd rather go and listen to some old boys and girls in a room above a pub singing unaccompanied. Same as Rachel and Becky. That's how I like my folk music. But if it is going to be accompanied then it has to be there for the story. If it's not then it's in the way and it shouldn't be there."

Recognising that Rachel Unthank was blessed with a natural talent but didn't have a clue about business, Adrian decided her career needed a guiding hand. "Being brought up with the music and wanting to be a folk singer, it had been so much her destiny she was completely paralysed by fear about making her first move and her head was so far in the sand she was never gonna get to a point where she thought practically and logistically, 'Right, so what am I gonna do about this?'. So I had to drag her kicking and screaming through the first couple of years. Even writing something like 'Rachel Unthank is good' on a press release sounded too self-assured for her and getting her to collaborate with other musicians was painful. It was really awful and tested us as much as two people as it did artistically. They were tough times but once Rachel and Becky saw what was there for them and that the people in front of them really were interested in what they were playing, they couldn't get enough of it."

He insists that even in those difficult early days he saw their potential and formulated a plan to help them realise it. "There's so much you have to teach a performer but Rachel and Becky had all the stuff you can't teach. There was so much naivety and vulnerability and rawness to them initially – what you can't teach is the commitment to the music they wanted to sing, the relationship they have with that music and the way they put it across to an audience. That's the bit you can't teach and I attribute it entirely to their parents and their upbringing in folk circles, the way they've seen people perform around them with commitment and without vanity. People who don't get up on stage for themselves but to share an experience, a human experience. And I wanted to work with them."

Recruited to play on the debut album *Cruel Sister*, Jackie Oates and Belinda O'Hooley stayed with Rachel and Becky to complete the Rachel Unthank & The Winterset line-up, quickly winning over audiences with their charm, humour and quality. The way I remember it, non-specialist radio stations and magazines championed the album, while the folk world largely cold-shouldered it, though Adrian disputes this. "Anybody who mattered to us in the North East, people whose music we respect, like The Wilsons and Voice Squad in Ireland and Nic Jones, who came to see us in York, they liked us. The small minority of dissenting voices were predictable and we never felt ostracised by the folk world at all. There was a core of people who understood what we were doing. The way Rachel and Becky were singing was true to their roots so we weren't dented by any criticism at the time. People who gave it proper consideration liked it rather than those who just saw pretty girls with young voices and assumed it was namby-pamby. Anyone who scratched underneath the surface always got it and the criticisms came from those who hadn't paid it much attention."

The sudden departure of Jackie Oates as The Winterset were set to record second album *The Bairns* clouded the issue and it's a topic they're still not keen to discuss for fear that anything they say may be misinterpreted and stir up friction where they insist none exists. "We've kind of made a decision not to talk about the ins and outs of Jackie and Belinda [O'Hooley] leaving because we've been so misrepresented. Being in a band is a bit like being in a family, it has its ups and downs and it's very complicated."

Into the band in Jackie's place came Niopha Keegan, the splendidly chummy Hertfordshire-Irish fiddle player and a fine singer in her own right, whose role has recently further expanded into a growing involvement with the arrangements. Her brother, the highly-rated flautist Niall Keegan, has been trying to coax her to Ireland to record a solo album – and one day she might just do that – but suggestions that she might feel like an outsider within The Unthanks are met with snorts of derision.

"I'm considered an honorary Unthank by the whole family and the girls are so loving and giving I consider them my best friends. We get on brilliantly and they've helped me through a lot of personal issues and problems that only my mother has helped me with in the past so I owe a lot to them. I've grown personally, professionally and musically and I wouldn't have done that if I hadn't met them."

Jackie Oates seemed a bit frustrated by her role in the band, Niopha… "There you go, that's where we differ. I'm loving what I'm doing with the guys, ok? Jackie is obviously a very driven young lady who wants to do her own music and hopefully I will some time, but I'm enjoying what I'm doing so much at the moment it's just not that time for me. It's a confidence thing. If someone put me in a room and said pick some songs and write some arrangements I'd be petrified, but being in a band has been a progression for me and I'm a far more confident player now."

So you're not planning on leaving any time soon? "Noooooooooooo. No way! I'm really enjoying it. The big band experience has been amazing and we've got a new album coming up and I'm really looking forward to that."

The departure of Bonnie Tyler-loving pianist, former Annie Lennox *Stars In Their Eyes* winner and Yorkshire's queen

of the droll one-liner Belinda O'Hooley, in the midst of the snowballing interest in *The Bairns*, caused another upheaval. "It was really weird," concedes Becky. "Apart from the two of us singing together as a duo, she'd always been there when we started the band and it was quite a shock when she left."

O'Hooley played such a key role in *The Bairns* – including writing two original songs for it – that many wondered if they'd cope without her. Even the other band members may have had their doubts, though abandoning ship was never an option. "The passion in this band for traditional music comes from us," says Rachel. "We love singing and we love traditional songs and that's never going to go away." Becky takes up the point: "It doesn't matter how many people come to see us. We just want to keep doing what we're doing."

The first person they interviewed for the piano stool was Stef Conner, and the way Becky tells it, the moment they heard her they knew there *was* life after Belinda O'Hooley. However, Stef – who was studying for a PhD in music at the time and is a classical musician at heart – was always going to be a stopgap. "She writes operas in Chinese for gamelan orchestras!" says Niopha in wonder. "And she was trying to do that in the back of the van on her computer while touring with us and as soon as we came off stage she'd rush to her hotel room to start writing again. She's one of these people who thrives on being busy and getting challenged, but it reached a point when she realised that she needed to give that her full attention."

The way things work, the selection of material is left entirely to Rachel and Becky and once they've settled on which songs they want to record, the others pitch in with arrangements. McNally had long had a sound in his head involving brass and strings and, even before Belinda O'Hooley's departure, decided the next album would be far less concentrated on piano. They still needed a pianist, however, and the way they tell it, Rachel and Becky ganged up on McNally to bully him into taking on the job.

Becky: "We said to him, instead of trying to explain what you mean to another pianist, 'why not just do it yourself'. We love his instinct and his ideas and I think he gets the best out of us so we dragged him on stage with us."

It meant, of course, relinquishing their all-female status… "Well we never deliberately set out to be an all-girl band," says Rachel. "You have to stay true to yourself and it would have been stupid to look for a girl when the person we wanted on stage with us was a guy. We're still very girl-heavy with seven girls and three guys. We have a boy corner of the stage at the moment."

In for a penny, McNally also recruited his oldest friend, guitarist Chris Price, who'd started off with him in no-hoper bands way back in their teenage years in Yorkshire. Now living in Hitchin, Price had a day job working for HMV in London's Oxford Circus when Adrian took him out for a pint and invited him to give it all up for life on the road with The Unthanks (to which they decided to amend the name to give Becky equal billing and take the pressure off Rachel). "I was already a massive fan of the band so I couldn't turn it down," says Price. "It's brilliant. First time I've played on a proper album and the first time I've toured and I *love* it. It's a far cry from HMV…"

Apart from his dad's broad collection of American folk music, Price's strongest early influences were prog rockers like King Crimson, Genesis and Yes, with Frank Zappa, Led Zeppelin and Robert Wyatt also dipping into the equation. Part of McNally's thinking in asking him to join was the same as his reasoning for previously bringing Belinda O'Hooley into the band – neither of them were imbued with traditional music and therefore weren't hidebound by established ways of playing it. "They aren't from folk backgrounds and don't know what a folk cliché is so they don't play one. They don't play in the genre, they play more by intuition in response to the song rather than the genre and hopefully we serve each song more truthfully as a result."

The songs Rachel and Becky came up with for the *Here's The Tender Coming* album last year seem to represent a who's who of the British folk world's most iconic

figures. There's a terrific arrangement of *Annachie Gordon* from the singing of Nic Jones, Ewan MacColl's *Nobody Knew She Was There*, Anne Briggs' *Living By The Water* and Lal Waterson's *At First She Starts*, while Frank Higgins' heartbreaking *The Testimony Of Patience Kershaw* and the evocative title track *Here's The Tender Coming* – a subtle colossus when they play it live – are both big songs previously tackled by some of the folk revival's big names.

"It wasn't deliberate," says Becky. "We just look for songs that speak to us and stimulate us. I've loved *Annachie Gordon* since I was a little kid but I never dared sing it because it seemed too long and too big and too high and too low. But I loved it so much I thought I'd learn it anyway."

"When Becky sang it round the house I kept crying every time she sang it and I thought 'We can't put this on the album, I'll be in tears every time we do it live,'" says Rachel. Niopha had a similar reaction when they brought MacColl's *Nobody Knew She Was There* (or *The Cleaner's Song*, as Niopha calls it) to the table. Niopha's not the only one… especially when you hear Rachel's back story about it.

"We dedicated *The Bairns* to our Auntie June, who died while we were making it. When she was very ill and finding it difficult to communicate, we started talking about that song and she said 'Do you want me to teach you a bit of it?' And she taught me the song and made me sing every line back to her to make sure I'd got it right. It made her forget she was ill and she just shone when she was teaching it to me, so the song means so much to our family. It just so happens it was written by Ewan MacColl."

The late Auntie June, who died on Becky's birthday, also used to sing *The Testimony Of Patience Kershaw*. "We'd go into the hospice and sing to her and we'd say 'We'd better stop, the nurse is coming' and she'd say 'Not until you finish the song'."

Becky: "She died before *The Bairns* came out but we sang her the whole album before it happened. She was a big inspiration to us. Her ashes are scattered in Whitby and we go to the flower bed and sing songs to her and scatter lucky heather."

"I think," adds Rachel, "it encapsulates our and a lot of other people's relationships with music. There's something within us all where people define themselves by the music they listen to, and for our family, music is the way we communicate and celebrate and commiserate."

Similarly close to their hearts is *Lucky Gilchrist*, Adrian McNally's poptastic tribute to Rachel's old uni friend from Glasgow, Gary Gilchrist, who died suddenly from a hereditary heart disease in Singapore. "He was very camp but so heterosexual at the same time – it was a strange dichotomy. He was a skinny lad into drama, very innovative and creative and a larger than life character. We wanted to reflect that in the music, as well as influences like Sufjan Stevens. The first time he ever saw me clog dancing he couldn't believe what was going on. He just watched me with his mouth open and when I finished he said 'How do you make your feet go so *fast*?'" Which is why we see them breaking into a frenetic bout of 7/8 time clog dancing when they perform it on stage.

There are no left-field contemporary songs by the likes of Nick Drake, Robert Wyatt, Bonnie Prince Billy, The Beatles or Antony & The Johnsons on *Here's The Ten-*

der Coming, but that's not deliberate either. They draw no distinction between the sources of their material. "For us music is music, we don't put it in genres," says Becky. "If a song speaks to us and we love it, we'll do it. When I first heard *Sea Song* I didn't know much about Robert Wyatt and if I had I'd have been scared to sing it. Same with *River Man*. I got it free on a CD on the front of *Q* magazine and I didn't have a clue who Nick Drake was."

Having recorded *Here's The Tender Coming* to Adrian McNally's grand design, they had little choice but to assemble a big band to do it justice on stage. It's quite a sight and – when they hit the mark – it's quite a sound too, with brass and strings applying different layers and textures. At one point Rachel even pops up playing drums.

"People probably think we must have loads of money to make an album like that," she says, "but we don't. In fact we don't have any more money than we ever did – less probably. But this is what we wanted to do and where we wanted to go with music so we just said 'let's do it'. We know it's not sustainable but while we've got the opportunity to work with these great musicians we'll do it."

The wheels have obviously been oiled by their association with EMI, but while distribution and profile have been raised as a result, EMI have no creative input or say in their music at all and only came on board after the band had started creating their own success. So how *did* a band playing primarily traditional songs in such a relatively esoteric fashion manage to connect so well with the mainstream?

Becky: "It's the same reason we like the songs in the first place – they're really great songs that speak to people about everyday life. But then why don't they listen to Belle Stewart? It's a mystery."

Rachel: "Sometimes people from the folk world think the mainstream want something nice and polished but I don't think they always do – they want something real and authentic. The comment we always get from people who don't know about folk music is that they're surprised we sing in our own accents and our response is 'Well, why *wouldn't* we?'. I think people connect with honesty."

Becky: "My boyfriend was in a punk band when I met him and I tried to get him into folk music and played him all these things I thought of as crossover stuff and he hated it all. But when I played him my dad's stuff and Belle Stewart and took him to see The Wilsons he was blown away. I almost insulted him by playing him the other stuff first."

N eedless to say Adrian McNally has plenty of theories, too, about why The Unthanks can appear on a big TV show like *Later…* and play *Here's The Tender Coming*, a deeply moving but morose and decidedly non-populist song about press gangs littered with North Eastern dialect. Even some of their supporters felt they should have gone for something more upbeat and less depressing, but they didn't get where they are by faint-heartedly diluting the message or patronising audiences by bowing to popular perceptions of short attention spans. Their appearance on *Later…* that night had a huge impact on a non-folkie audience.

"Robert Wyatt once said of his own music, 'It's not me that's great, it's just that 90% of rock music is rubbish and it makes what I do sound interesting and eclectic and original'. I don't mean to associate us with the great man or even mean there's a lot of poor folk music around, I just think there's been a lot of misguided attempts to court the mainstream. The narrative of this nu folk thing is, you put all the bits and pieces of authenticity and rootsiness and acousticness into one pot and it feels more earnest, which is what people seem to be craving at the moment. The whole Bon Iver thing – that story of him going up into the snowy mountains and locking himself in a cabin for a week to record his album on primitive equipment… people buy into this whole idea."

"Yet the folk world from the other side of the tracks, i.e. people from a traditional background looking for a bit of mainstream success, is diluted in pop sensibilities and a nice bit of reverb and anyone from the mainstream or left-field music listening can smell the ambition a mile off. It stinks of ambition. It's not honest, it's not authentic and there's nothing real about it at all. That's where I feel the folk world has totally missed its opportunity. All the old guys – the Waterson:Carthys and Dick Gaughans of this world – are still hammering it out as real and raw as ever and the old stuff that's not supposed to be cool is totally cool as far as I'm concerned. But a lot of the young acts are too sanitised and clean."

With a new album being plotted as we speak and other ventures under consideration – ranging from an unaccompanied album to a special concert performance of Robert Wyatt and Antony & The Johnsons songs – Unthank world is far from sanitised and clean, but right now it's flying.

www.the-unthanks.com

13
LUCY'S BIRTHDAY
Becky Unthank & Adrian McNally

It was spring 2010 when we all clambered onto a tour bus — seven Unthanks plus Jonny Kearney and Lucy Farrell, to tour eleven European countries in five weeks, starting in Norway and finishing in Portugal. Jonny and Lucy had been touring the UK with us a lot in the past six month. Our audiences were as captured by their music and company as we were.

ADRIAN: With a couple of weeks to go, I remember thinking about the empty beds there would be on the bus. We couldn't afford to take any more of our ten-piece ensemble but it was a shame to have empty beds on a five-week tour of Europe. I think we gave Jonny and Lucy about a week's notice. We knew they'd survive without a fee, on CD sales alone, as they had been averaging sixty a night on our UK shows, outselling us every night!

The bus pulled up in Corbridge with Amy Macdonald's ten foot face plastered on the side. The bus company hadn't had time to take it off. Little did we know how popular she was in Europe, and how much attention it would generate. Once or twice, one of the number of brunettes on board would don sunglasses and, from the safety and murky interior of the bus, wave to an excitable throng outside.

BECKY: We had some amazing gigs and experiences together on the Europe tour. I remember waking up one day while we were still travelling, so I climbed out of my bunk to see where we were. We were driving through the mountains in Austria. It was a breathtaking sight, and one I won't forget. That same day, Dean, our

curly-haired Liverpudlian double bass player decide to go for a swim in the deepest, coldest lake in Austria only to find that his legs went numb mid-swim. It wa lucky that we had our Geordie hero Jonny Kearney o hand to drag him out. Some local pine schnapps wa the medicine that night for Dean, recommended b the promoter.

Recommended? It was forcibly imposed on him as remember, despite being teetotal, by locals who wer not amused and insisted on it being compulsory afte being so reckless! It wasn't Dean's only faux pas on th tour, but we'll get to that.

We celebrated a couple of birthdays on the tour - ther was a boozy night in Portugal with the usual moustache for cellist Jo Silverston's birthday. By the time we go to Copenhagen it was Lucy's turn. Her 25th birthday We had worn out the fake moustaches so we neede to come up with a new plan. "You choose, Lucy," w said. "We'll do anything you like, we promise." So Luc explored that vivid and sometimes wicked imaginatio of hers and suggested, "Well we could dress the boys u as girls?"

I am beginning to realise that a lot of these birthday stories involve us girls getting the boys to do something ridiculous. I don't know what this tells you about our characters. Hopefully just that the boys are open minded and fun, not that we girls are pushy and domineering!

So we were each assigned a boy, and hit the charity shops of Copenhagen to find suitable outfits. Then came the make up, and we had Daz the bus driver as the judge. I talk excitely about our wonderful tour around Europe, but admittedly not every gig was packed full. That night's gig was a little rock venue; a black hole with a scattering of people..

It was the poorest attended show of the tour by far, which made Dean's timing for his next prank all the more questionable! There was a song in Jonny and Lucy's support set on which Rachel and I sang backing vocals, and on which Dean played double bass. Rachel and I headed down to stage side at the right point in their set, to find Dean there already in his dress. The dress bought for him to wear later at Lucy's party, of course.

"Dean. What you doing?"
"I'm gonna go on in me dress!"

He thought it was going to be the prank of the year, until he registered the look of disbelief on our faces, and slowly it dawned on him that it wasn't going to work, that he's made a monumental error of judgement. But it was too late and he knew it. "Oh God!"

We were on. Jonny and Lucy did the introductions and we trundled into view. Now Jonny and Lucy are pure magic. It almost became a sport amongst The Unthanks to find new ways, night after night, to articulate just how special each performance was. As people though, they are shy and unassuming in public. In response

to the sight of Dean, they were speechless. Silence filled the air. There may as well have been tumbleweed rolling across the venue. Had we been in the UK, in front of a home crowd, this might have been a funny sight and Jonny and Lucy would have dealt with it just fine; in front of a couple of dozen strangers on our first visit to Denmark, the audience maybe didn't even know who we were, let alone Jonny and Lucy.

After the initial disbelief, Jonny makes an attempt to start the song. It quickly breaks down in embarrassed laughter. He tries again a couple more times. The last time he gets a bit further into the song and it looks like we might make it... but no. He just stops. "Sorry, I can't do this." That's it. The three of us trundle backstage, without playing or singing a single note, having completely wrecked their set.

Later on, when all five boys were in full make-up and glad rags, we were barely any less incongruous than Dean was earlier. The upstairs bar we strode confidently into was a picture of urbane Scandinavia, full of languid hipsters playing board games. Chris and I looked like menacing crazies. Jonny and Dean were downright pretty. It confused the clientele, who decided not to react in any way to us, as if they were being sensitive and modern in case we were some new minority expressing our recently discovered sexuality. We played table football. We had the manic, unsettling air of the Python team when they dressed as old women.

Just the place for a load of English people to act ridiculous and embarrass themselves. There is something very freeing about being on tour though. It can get repetitive and emotionally draining but it can also be so nourishing. It's wonderful having a new experience everyday. Everything is temporary, each experience a one off. So we threw ourselves into the evening. Johnny won the prize for best dressed. It was the resemblance to Liza Minnelli that did it, and another birthday had been celebrated.

Singing workshop! Cáceres, Spain.

"And another thing" - Adrian and Lucy

It's cold in Stockholm

Beautiful Gent, Belgium.

Trust.

Hee hee hee.

"Hmm" Jonny and Lucy.

Oslo gang.

Lucy Farrell and Becky, Castelfidardo, Italy.

Husband and wife.

Bezzies - Dean Ravera and Adi.

Murder on the tour bus?

On the set of Later With Jools Holland.
Below: With Mark Radcliffe, Stuart Macownie
and their producer Lizzie Hoskin at
Matfen Hall, Northumberland, during their
Hadrian's Wall trip.

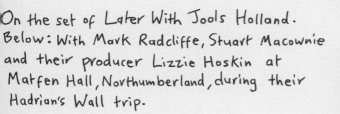

Live Theatre presents

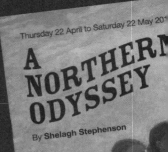

Thursday 22 April to Saturday 22 May 201

A NORTHERN ODYSSEY
By Shelagh Stephenson

A NORTHERN ODYSSEY

By Shelagh Stephenson
The action of the play takes place in Cullercoats from the spring
of 1881 to the autumn of 1882.

Cast (in order of appearance)

Helen French Maggie
Zita Frith Belle
Catherine MacCabe Sally
Ron Cook Winslow Homer
Amy McAllister Fanny
Lizzy McInnerny Rosaleen
Philip Correia Joe
Deka Walmsley Frank

Creative & Production

Shelagh Stephenson Writer
Max Roberts Director
Gary McCann Set & Costume Design
Charles Balfour Lighting Design
Dave Flynn Sound Design
Lee Proud Choreographer
Owen Evans AV Design
Paul Aziz AV Design
Louise Duffy Costume Supervisor
Chris Carr Hair & Make-Up
Drummond Orr Production Manager
Paul Aziz Stage Manager
Heather Robertson Deputy Stage Manag
Dave Flynn Technical Manager
Claire Gerrens Senior Technician
Mark Tolan Technician

Musical arrangements provided courtesy of Mercury Music Prize
nominees **The Unthanks**

Thanks to:
Tyne & Wear Archives & Museums, Newcastle Library Service, North Tyneside
Council, Susan Johnson, Mr & Mrs McCheyne and members of the Northumbria
Basketry Group, especially Ruth Thompson, Liz Balfour and Alan Winlow
www.northumbrianbasketgroup.co.uk

The Unthanks

It has been a real privilege working with Shelagh, Max and Live Theatre, and also getting to know the space ahead of our own shows at Live Theatre in June. I've never written/arranged for theatre before, but it felt quite natural, probably because when I'm arranging for The Unthanks, I tend to wander off on musical tangents when exploring how a song might be accompanied. Shelagh and Max were looking for the music to be loosely based on the musical themes of *Ma Bonny Lad*, and my interpretations usually are, quite loose! I didn't really get my hands on *Ma Bonny Lad* when we put it on *The Bairns*, because the girls arranged it unaccompanied. This time, I had some grand designs for using lots of instruments but in practice, I kept returning to my original piano sketches, which I've tried not to embellish too much. A central theme of the play seems to me to be loneliness/isolation, which I hope is echoed in the sparsity of the music.

Rachel, Becky and Niopha's vocal arrangements have been adapted by the actresses in the play and Rachel and I had some fun sessions with them, de-training the vibrato from their voices and encouraging them to sing in their local accents. We are so under qualified to be coaching singers with infinitely superior technique, but they were good sports and very open to input. Niopha and Chris bashed the tunes out for the dancing and we got in accordion whiz Shona Kipling to add some extra zip. We'll be on tour in Europe by the time the play opens, but we hope to see it when we get back in mid May.

We've been asked by a big London theatre company to arrange the music for a production next year… maybe this will be the start of a new thread to our bow! Thank you Live Theatre.

Adrian McNally
Pianist, Arranger and Producer for The Unthanks

Live Music

Saturday 5, 8pm & Sunday 6 June, 3pm & 8pm
The Unthanks + Support
Tickets: £16; £14 concs. Sun 3pm show: £5 under 16s
Not many bands can count Radiohead, Portishead, Elvis Costello, Robert Wyatt, Ben Folds and Nick Hornby amongst their admirers, but The Unthanks occupy a unique place in music. Sisters Rachel and Becky Unthank are storytellers outside of time, forging links between folk worlds old, new and other, nominated for the Mercury Music Prize, and featured in the Best Albums of the Decade (worldwide, all genres) in The Guardian and Uncut.

What Did You Think?

At Live Theatre it is important to us to find out what visitors really think. Please take a couple of minutes to complete a feedback card or visit **www.live.org.uk/reviews** to let us know what you thought so we can monitor and improve the Live Theatre experience. Thank you.

THE UNTHANKS

Known for their timeless, unsentimental and quietly subversive tales of loss, fear, booze, brawls, abuse and sorrow, siblings Rachel and Becky Unthank are honest, young storytellers outside of time, forging links between folk worlds old, new and other. It's hard to imagine a British folk band with fans like Radiohead, Portishead, Robert Wyatt, Ben Folds, Elvis Costello, Damon Albarn, Ewan McGregor and Nick Hornby, but The Unthanks occupy a unique place in music.

"My favorite county record of 2009. The county of Northumberland, that is. The supernatural singing from Rachel and Becky Unthank and the lovely arrangements are three reasons to hear this wonderful album." - Elvis Costello

The Unthanks Rough Trade debut, "Here's The Tender Coming" is out on March 23rd.

http://www.myspace.com/rachelunthank

Adrian McNally, manager/producer turned pianist for The Unthanks, didn't expect his first performance in the band to be as a chef.

I never thought my debut performance with Rachel and Becky would be as a cook. I've been manager of The Unthanks (and formerly Rachel Unthank & The Winterset) from the beginning, and I also run our label RabbleRouser Music, I'm our UK agent, I produce our albums, arrange and write some of the music. But I was always an invisible off-stage member until recently, when I played all the piano and percussion on our lastest album Here's The Tender Coming, so now I'm an on stage member. But back in the summer of last year, the girls were invited to perform at the world music festival Womad. When the organisers found out that I had cooked for 100 people when Rachel Unthank and I got married last year, they insisted that I take part in their Taste The World sessions - a stage dedicated to bands from all over the world cooking traditional dishes from their own country. So before I'd ever played a note on stage with The Unthanks, I found myself doing a celebrity chef turn, with a little head-set mic, and a big audience. I cooked a posh version of a Scottish soup called Cullen Skink, and added Craster kippers to give it a taste of Northumbria, where the Unthank sisters are from. I had a great timely, and realised in the process that I was much more confident cooking in front of people than I was sat at the piano. I've definitely taken a wrong turn somewhere! Rachel and Becky sang sea songs while I cooked, and an 80 year old man told me he'd been coming to Taste The World for 20 years and my soup was the best food he'd tasted there. Good enough for me. I came away with a scalded hand for a memento - the potato in the soup wasn't cooking quickly enough and so had to keep breaking it down with a masher, while all the steam from the soup turned my first red raw. But I smiled sweetly throughout, through gritted teeth. The TV chef Jamie Oliver's magazine people were there, and asked me if they could publish the recipe.

Posh Cullen Skink with a Northumbrian twist
I thought I'd invented this myself, when I essentially added fish to a leek and potato soup, spruced up with white wine and plenty of butter and herbs. I served it up to some friends, one of who said "oh, you mean Cullen Skink". Cullen Skink is a Scottish dish from the North East town of Cullen in Moray. Skink is often taken to mean 'soup' in Scots, but it's actually derived from the Middle Dutch word 'schenke', meaning shin or hough. A Scottish soup made from a shin or hough of beef came to be known as a Skink.
I've given my own version of Cullen Skink a Northumbrian twist by using the celebrated smoked Craster kipper, almost in the same way you might use bacon with seafood in order to give it a tasty, salty kick. You can order smoked Craster kippers on line from a number of outlets.

Ingredients
1 haddock loin fillet skinned and cubed
1 smoked haddock loin fillet,, undyed if possible, skinned and cubed
1 smoked Craster kipper fillet, small cubes (optional)
1-2 leeks sliced finely
2 shallots, sliced finely
3-4 medium sized potatoes (something floury, like kind edward, maris piper,
or some smaller ones, but nothing waxy like a desree), peeled and sliced VERY finely into 1-2mll thin rounds.
375ml of white wine (about a glass)
Half a pint of boiling water
Half a pint of milk
Half a pint of single cream
A quarter of a block of salted butter
Good dash of fish sauce
One fish stock cube
Half a veggie stock cube
One lemon
Teaspoon of sugar
A really good bunch each of fresh, flat leaf parsley and chives
Salt and pepper

Method
- Saute the shallots and leeks in a small amount of the butter for a few minutes.
- Add the stock cubes and sugar and allow a small amount of caramelisation for a few minutes
- Add the sliced potatoes and mix together for a minute
- Add the boiling water, wine, juice from the lemon and fish sauce. Gently simmer for 12-15 minutes, occasionally squashing the potato with a masher to encourage it to break up. The aim is for some of the potato to break down and thicken the consistency of the soup, and for some of it to stay in small bits, so that you get a soup that is thicker than broth, but that doesn't have that horrible pureed consistency of blended soups. It's soup, not baby food! If there isn't enough liquid to cover the potato, add some of the milk.
- When the potato is all but soft and cooked enough to eat, add the milk and cream, bring back to the boil, then add the fish (apart from the kipper), simmer for a couple of minutes, add the parsley, chives and butter, and season. Serve using the kipper almost like croutons, garnish with a little more parsley and black pepper.

THE UNTHANKS
& SXSW

Weds: Rough Trade Showcase @ Emo's Jr, 603 Red River   ON STAGE: 9PM

Thurs: All Music Is World Music @ Momo's, 618 W 6th St   ON STAGE: 11PM

Fri: Looking For A New England @ St Davids Bethell Church, 301 E 8th St.
                                                          ON STAGE: MIDNIGHT

Sat: SXSW Bootleg BBQ with Mojo Magazine @ Mean Eyed Cat, 1621 West 5th
                                                          ON STAGE: 1.40PM

The
UNTHANKS
Here's the Tender Coming

www.the-unthanks.com

Texas. Tea-total veggie Dean goes on the whisky and steak so as not to offend.

Was it a dream? No, here's the proof. Rachel drums live at SXSW.

The coldest gig ever, Texas.

Pennsylvania

Adi and Dean on Independence Day Indiana, Pennsylvania.

Niopha and Jo salute you.

SXSW Bootleg BBQ with Mojo Magazine at the Mean Eyed Cat.

Two butch boys eating Texas steak.

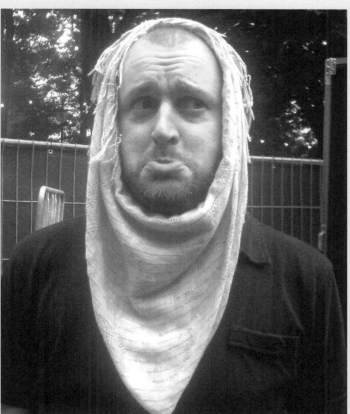

We like to torture Adrian.

Man, wife and best mate.

Touring America can be hard.

Vancouver Island Festival.

Long haul - the relentlessly cheerful Chris.

14
LAST

The Unthanks UK Album Tour 2011
With special guests Trembling Bells

Sat 19/03 **Exeter Phoenix Arts Centre**
Sun 20/03 **Bexhill De La Warr Pavilion**
Mon 21/03 **Bristol Arnolfini**
Tue 22/03 **Cardiff St David Hall/ Main Hall**
Wed 23/03 **Eastleigh The Point**
Thu 24/03 **Oxford Regal**
Fri 25/03 **Leeds Howard Assembly Room**
Sat 26/03 **Leeds Howard Assembly Room**
Sun 27/03 **Nottingham Glee Club**
Wed 30/03 **Manchester Cathedral**
Thur 31/03 **Milton Keynes The Stables**
Fri 1/04 **London O₂ Shepherd's Bush Empire**
Sat 2/04 **Cambridge St Paul's Church**
Mon 4/04 **Norwich Arts Centre**

Tues 5/04 **Bury St Edmonds The Apex C**
Wed 6/04 **Birmingham Town Hall**
Thur 7/04 **Liverpool Stanley Theatre**
Sat 9/04 **Dublin Vicar St**
Sun 10/04 **Cork School of Music**
Mon 11/04 **Limerick Dolans**
Tue 12/04 **Galway The Roisin Dubh**
Wed 13/04 **Kildare The Riverbank Theatre**
Thu 14/04 **Belfast The Empire**
Fri 15/04 **Edinburgh Queen Hall**
Sat 16/04 **Aberdeen The Lemon Tree**
Sun 17/04 **Glasgow The Arches**
Mon 18/04 **Newcastle Tyne Theatre**
Tues 19/04 **Hebden Bridge Picture House**

THE NEW ALBUM FROM THE UNTHANKS

OUT 14.03.11

EMI   www.the-unthanks.com   RABBLE ROUSER

Qu Junktions presents

The UNTHANKS
+ TREMBLING BELLS

'They are like the morning dew that hasn't steamed off yet, they are fresh and new and I really don't think they know how good they are' ~ Robert Wyatt

MONDAY 21st MARCH
Arnolfini, Bristol

Advance Tickets: £15 standing, £17 seated | Doors: 7.30pm
www.arnolfini.org.uk | 0117 9172300

New Album 'Last' out 14th March

THE UNTHANKS

Last RABBLE ROUSER/EMI

★★★★

The Northumbrian five-piece shatter folk's borders, as this expansive yet austere fourth proves, *says Graeme Thomson*

THE UNTHANKS SEEM to regard folk music the same way Miles Davis regarded jazz: as a launchpad for exploring the wider possibilities. Their fourth album, *Last*, certainly proves the Northumbrian quintet have little in common with the more accessible strand of roots music currently popularised by the corporation of Mumfords, Marling & co.

The Unthanks harness the wilder, more elemental part of English folk music and crack it open, creating a powerful, widescreen sound that incorporates elements of jazz, classical, pop and avant-garde minimalism. Since the success of 2009's wonderful *Here's The Tender Coming* they have continued expanding their frame of reference. 2010 saw them collaborate with everyone from Damon Albarn's Africa Express to classical conductor Charles Hazlewood, none of which seems particularly incongruous.

They have previously taken on songs by Robert Wyatt and Bonnie 'Prince' Billy, and among *Last*'s judicious mix of traditional material are three contemporary covers: Tom Waits' stark "No One Knows I'm Gone", King Crimson's "Starless", and Jon Redfern's "Give Away Your Heart", a performance as bereft and beautiful as anything they've ever recorded. All three fit snugly into the wider picture. With The Unthanks it's not a question of either folking up rock material or consciously modernising traditional songs; everything they touch is shaped, quite ,

naturally, to suit their own distinct sound.

Last travels beyond borders. Recorded primarily at home in Northumbria, the dominant instrument is Adrian McNally's piano, around which strings, horns, pipes and guitars add subtle shade. The arrangements are bold and beautifully recorded, but as ever the vocals of Rachel Unthank and her younger sibling Becky provide the heartstone.

Rachel's voice is hard and crisp, like frost on a winter morning. She sings mournful opener "Gan To The Kye" like some 19th century literary heroine, stately and composed on the surface, simmering with passion underneath. Becky's breathy tone is quite different, hanging over songs like a fine mist. On "The Gallowgate Lad" it's so close you can touch it; on "Give Away Your Heart" it has the smoky sensuality of an alto saxophone.

This is a bleakly beautiful record which unfolds slowly. "My Laddie Sits Ower Late Up", perhaps the most traditionally framed song here, is relatively spritely, as is "Canny Hobbie

Elliot", all skipping piano, bright pipes and horns, but otherwise *Last* beds down beneath unforgiving skies. Their towering take on Alex Glasgow's "Close The Coalhouse Door" (*"There's blood inside"*) is genuinely confrontational, a kind of modernist meditation built on an insistent piano sequence that recalls Satie and Steve Reich.

The other dramatic centrepiece is the seven-minute title track. Written by McNally, it's an indictment of our failure to progress as we evolve (*"Man should be the sum of history"*) which sweeps over the past and the future.

It's a sad call to arms which encapsulates the record's mood. *Last* is rooted in the rigours of real life, but seeks to transcend them. And while there's a tendency for the songs to merge into one indistinct flow, it seems self-defeating to try to unpick the individual strands of this LP: its strength lies in holding a distinct – and chilly – atmosphere throughout.

In person The Unthanks seem jocular, unstuffy, playful. Their music, however, is haunting, austere, relentless. You wonder where this overpowering melancholy comes from. Is it simply a reflection of the North East's hard beauty, or the heavy weight of industrial history pressing down on the music? Or does it stem from somewhere even closer to hand? Hard to say. But if they keep making albums as compelling as *Last*, no one should be in any hurry for the answer.

Q&A Rachel Unthank

Last year seemed frantic. Was it a struggle to find the time and space to make the LP?
We enjoyed our colourful 2010 but it's good to get back to what we do. We set ourselves a crazy deadline and we did have to work out of our skins to make it.

The sound is more widescreen this time.
We made *Tender* in a pro studio, but we like home best. We tried different spaces, recording the piano in Snape Maltings, a Victorian

maltings converted into a concert hall, and the strings in our local village hall, which made our string quartet sound like an orchestra!

You draw from a wide frame of reference.
We try to find stories that we might find our own way of telling. "Starless" by King Crimson belongs to a genre beleaguered by a reputation for pompous excess. We want to break down subconscious prejudices to find the beauty within all forms of music. INTERVIEW: GRAEME THOMSON ➤

A FAN WRITES...

No 8. Peter Chick

Amoeba Records in San Francisco, 2011, one of the great music shops on the planet. As I was looking round, something very familiar (but completely out of place) – they were playing *Last* from beginning to end!.

The Unthanks keep folk real and push its boundaries. Mark Edwards talks to them about mining songs and prog rock

I t's the day before their tour starts and the Unthanks are rehearsing in the Letchworth Rugby Club bar. The Unthanks — as anyone who has heard sisters Rachel and Becky sing could tell you — are not from round here. They hail from Northumbria. But other band members are based just north of London, and the tour starts all the way down in Exeter, so this is a good place for a final run-through of the sisters' harmonies. It's not a good place for catering, though, so we drive into the town centre and end up tucking into a roast dinner at the local carvery. This is worth noting because, for 20 years, Adrian McNally — the band's pianist, arranger and producer, and Mr Rachel Unthank — was a vegetarian. He came off the meat-free wagon only recently, when Rachel became pregnant.

"I had a craving for vegetarian sausage rolls, so I sent him out for some," Rachel remembers, "and, when he came back, he'd also brought some proper sausages, 'in case that's what I was really craving'. I said no, I just wanted the vegetarian sausage rolls, and he said, 'Well, I'll just cook these anyway. Maybe the smell will make you realise that this is what you really want.' So he cooked them... and ate them all."

McNally abstained from making music for a similar length of time, after giving up piano lessons when, as a timid 11-year-old, he was terrified of his piano teacher's two large dogs. He resumed keyboard duties when the sisters got fed up with losing a succession of piano players. "Adrian was always the best person to explain to musicians what we wanted," Becky says. "So we said, 'Why don't you just do it yourself?' And we were right."

They certainly were, because together the Unthank sisters and McNally form an extraordinary musical merger. On the one hand, listen to the traditional songs they sing, and to the broad northern dialect they use, and they couldn't possibly be more folk — uncompromising upholders of the tradition. On the other hand, glance at the cover versions they perform on record and live —

No resting on laurels

songs by King Crimson, Tom Waits, Robert Wyatt, Antony and the Johnsons — and listen to the decidedly un-folk arrangements on their new album, Last, and you'd have to conclude that they're not a folk band at all.

Or take the cover of Last. It's a drawing by an American artist, Winslow Homer. Homer lived for a while in the northeast of England, and painted the local fishing lasses. Clearly, this is ripe subject matter for a Northumbrian folk band's cover art. Yet they've chosen instead a drawing of some posh military types waltzing with their fair maidens at a vast, glamorous ball. None of them look as if they've done an honest day's work in their lives.

"The album's got a lot of 3/4 and 6/8 time signatures — quite waltzy — so the picture seemed appropriate," McNally says. "But the other reason we chose it was that it's a depiction of the past, and shows the function of human contact that we don't have so much of any more, that sense of community and social occasion. These days, we spend more time staring into computer screens than into other people's eyes. This is what appeals

to us about folk music. We're much more interested in the content of folk music, being an alternative history, a people's history, than in the vernacular of folk music as a genre — the idea that it should sound a certain way.

"To say that folk should have acoustic guitars or violins, or should be sung in this way or that way, is ridiculous," McNally adds. "Folk follows function. People sang unaccompanied because they sang in the workplace, where there was no accompaniment available. Other tunes were played fast because they were for dancing."

Folk

Such devoted sisters: Rachel, left, and Becky Unthank

The Unthanks are clearly amused that the vernacular of folk music has been co-opted by many of the newer bands, such as Mumford & Sons. "That's all about style, and it'll go away at some point. We want to still be here when all that goes away," McNally says. "So we ignore the stylings of folk and concentrate on the content."

The story, then, is everything. "We don't sing because we think we're great singers," Becky says. "We sing to tell a story. If we have a strong emotional response to a story, and we feel we can tell the story, then that's the song for us."

The band believe that the most honest way for them to tell these stories is to use their own musical vocabulary — and, if that happens to extend well beyond traditional folk styles, then so be it.

The most glaring example of the band's wider musical vocabulary on Last is a cover of King Crimson's Starless, a choice that clearly dates back to McNally's teenage love of the prog-rock band. A sumptuous string arrangement that weaves and flows around the vocal turns what was once an angular, spiky and very male piece of music into something softer, rounder and, crucially, much more welcoming. That's part of the Unthank sisters' storytelling skill: even when, in reality, you're flummoxed by the exact meaning of some of the dialect words they're singing, you feel that you are invited into the song and somehow totally understand what they're telling you.

Often, what they're telling you isn't exactly a barrel of laughs. Starless is followed on the album by Close the Coalhouse Door, a song written by Alex Glasgow for a musical he created with Alan

Plater in the 1970s about the northeast mining industry. The song begins: "Close the coalhouse door, lad/There's blood inside/Blood from broken hands and feet/Blood that's dried on pit-black meat/Blood from hearts that know no beat." It's typical of the brutal nature of many of the folk songs they sing.

"If you've grown up hearing songs like that, you maybe don't think quite how brutal they are," Rachel says. "Or, anyway, you're not frightened of singing about subjects like that. You're not going to shy away from these topics. But perhaps what you don't realise is that other people aren't used to hearing lyrics like that."

"We performed it in Australia on our recent tour there," Becky adds, "and sometimes we'd finish singing it — and, whoa!" She shudders at the memory of the unsettling effect the song had on audiences. "We'd think, 'Why did we just sing that?'"

"There's a lot of northeast mining songs," Rachel says, "and there's no northeast mining any more, so we begin to think of the songs as historical documents. But the New Zealand mining disaster was fresh on everyone's minds. Events like that and what happened in Chile make you realise this is still going on all around the world, and songs like this are still very relevant."

Their subject matter makes it clear that drawing on traditional songs is not simply a celebration of the past; and the album's title, Last, also points to an ambivalent attitude to our history. "The word is meant in a positive sense — endure. It's a call to arms to make sure we do," says McNally, who wrote the song, the only original on the album. "It's not meant to be a glorification of the past, because in many ways the past was bloody awful, but it is a warning that we don't seem to be learning from it, we don't seem to have a combined wisdom to draw on from the past — and now we're in a culture that's so obsessed with the new, that's unlikely to change."

"I just hope we haven't jinxed ourselves with this title, and it turns out to be our last album," Rachel adds, smiling.

As long as they can continue to bring traditional songs (and the odd prog number) to life with gorgeous harmonies and eclectic musical invention, there should be plenty more albums to come.

The Unthanks play Norwich Arts Centre tomorrow; their tour continues until April 19. Last is out now on Rabble Rouser/EMI

PHOTOGRAPH BY PIP

29

Lizzie Jones with Becky.

Dean and Adrian, Union Chapel.

Secret santa and the "Last" supper at the family home of Unthank viola player Becca Spencer, 2011.

The girls.

Expecting.

Rachel with George, Sunderland Minster.

113

NEW COMMISSION
IF Album:
Harbour of Songs

Inspired by The Lone Twin Boat Project and the stories behind the wood donated to build it, a new album has been commissioned for IF: 2012 by The Stables, and produced by the Festival's Artist-in-Residence Adrian McNally – the pianist, arranger and producer for contemporary folk band The Unthanks.

The album – Harbour of Songs – brings together artists including Ivor Novello award-winning and Mercury nominated Villagers, Ivor Novello-nominated Nick Hemming (The Leisure Society), Australian singer-songwriter Sarah Blasko (big in her own country and now making waves here in Europe), rising stars Alasdair Roberts, Hannah Moulette and Raevennan Husbandes, folk legends Ralph McTell and Steve Tilston, internationally successful novelist/writer Nick Hornby, 'The Bard of Barnsley' poet Ian McMillan, American singer-songwriting legend Janis Ian, BBC Folk Award nominees Jonny Kearney and Lucy Farrell, and Guy Chambers – probably Britain's most successful modern songwriter, best known for his work with Robbie Williams – and of course, The Unthanks.

Harbour of Songs is released on Proper Records and available from www.propermusic.com, www.amazon.co.uk, www.play.com and Festival merchandise points. Adrian McNally will be taking part in a talk about the album, and performing with The Unthanks + Guests on Monday 23 July in The Stables Spiegeltent, see page 40.

The Lone Twin Boat Project is featured on page 7.

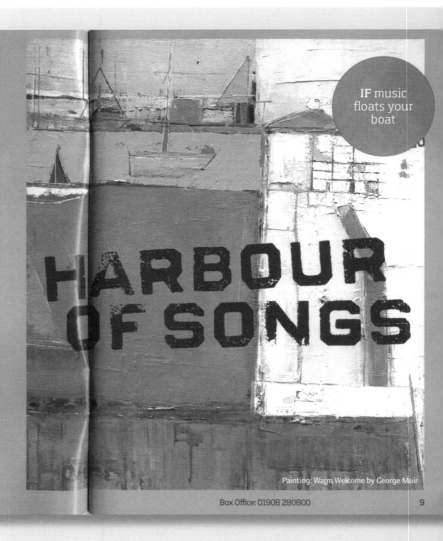

IF music floats your boat

Painting: Warm Welcome by George Muir

8   www.ifmiltonkeynes.org   Box Office: 01908 280800   9

My Rola Bola - Alasdair Roberts.

Recording with Raevennan Husbandes, Annie Whitehead and Lizzie Jones, London.

The Unthanks, appearing 30th May

FRIDAY 30TH MAY

THE UNTHANKS with
MARTIN HAYES AND DENNIS CAHILL
AND THE VOICE SQUAD

Hall One, 7.30pm

The Unthanks are back on home soil, collaborating with two of their biggest influences. Master American guitarist Dennis Cahill with musical partner, perhaps the most revered fiddler that Ireland has ever produced, Martin Hayes. The show will represent the first UK Voice Squad concert appearance of the Irish harmony group since returning from a 20 year hiatus.

TICKETS: £19.50

FRIDAY 30TH MAY

FRED FRITH with
MICHAEL CHAPMAN

Northern Rock Foundation Hall, 8pm

Experimental musicians are essential; their love of finding something new, archaeologists of noise, discovering music people have never encountered

FRIDAY 30TH MAY

SESSION

The Central, Half Moon Lane, 9.30pm - late

Traditional music session led by some of the North-East's finest musicians.

FREE

SATURDAY 31ST MAY

A MORNING SING WITH
THE UNTHANKS

Music Education Centre, 10.30-11.30am

Rachel, Becky and Niopha lead a reviving sing to blow away your Saturday morning cobwebs and set you up for a full day of music.

TICKETS: £10

SATURDAY 31ST MAY

SONIC THINKING: CONVERSATION WITH
FRED FRITH AND ADRIAN UTLEY

Hall Two, 12-1.30pm

Legendary guitarists and sonic sculptors Adrian Utley (Portishead) and Fred Frith talk with each other about their approach to music making, focusing specifically on their approach to finding new sounds, followed by audience Q&A session

TICK

SATURDAY 31ST MAY

JOHN CARTY: IRISH TUNES WORKSHOP

Music Education Centre, 12-1.30pm

Ahead of his concert later in the afternoon, come and learn Irish tunes with fidde and banjo master John Carty. Open to all instruments.

TICKETS: £10

SATURDAY 31ST MAY

LAU-LAND BIG FAMILY
SING & DANCE

Northern Rock Foundation Hall,
12-1pm & 2.30-3.30pm

Come and join us for a special helping of fun, song and dance led by musicians from Sage Gateshead's Learning and Participation team with some special material capturing the musical excitement of Lau-Land. This whole family celebration includes songs and rhythms from around the world especially chosen for children aged 7+. Parents must attend with their children.

TICKETS: £4.50

SATURDAY 31ST MAY

SIMON THOUMIRE: IMPROVISING IN
TRADITIONAL MUSIC WORKSHOP

Music Education Centre, 2.30-4pm

Simon's free-thinking approach to traditional

AN ARTIST WRITES...

No 7. Martin Hayes, fiddle player, Ireland

The Unthanks make music that is without pretence, it is straight, honest and filled with feeling. They treat songs in a way that breaks down the walls of genre and makes them accessible to music lovers of all kinds. Their sophisticated and sensitive arrangements give the songs new relevance and breathes new life into them. The honest and heartfelt way in which they deliver their music is a true inspiration to me.

Sage Gateshead

DATE 29-30/05/14

EVENT Lau-Land

ACCESS AAA

Sage Gateshead

LAU
WELCOME TO LAU-LAND
PATRON: "WHISPERING" BOB HARRIS

29TH - 31ST MAY 2014

LAU-LAND, SAGE GATESHEAD

AN INVITATION TO ENTER INTO LAU'S MUSICAL WORLD

15
HEROES AND INFLUENCES
(PART 1): FOLK HEROES

Becky: What we all need and want from life varies, doesn't it? What I do have, and have always had, is a lot of love and encouragement. These invaluable gifts come from family and friends but mainly from our mam and dad, Pat and George Unthank. They always encouraged us to try new things, to open up our eyes and minds, so that we could work out who we wanted to be. We felt safe and free. I always felt I was lucky, but as the years go on and I meet people who were not as lucky to have had these free and safe foundations, I find myself reflecting on how important it is to me. So first and foremost, before this list of heroes and influences, the biggest influence on us by a country mile is our parents...

Rachel: Our parents have a lot to answer for. Their love of family and of folk music makes us who we are. As kids we were exposed to so much music, singing and dance. It has never felt like a conscious choice to take part, more a way of life. You have to have a song for a family party, and we were wearing clogs before we had noticed that none of our peers were. They have always been so encouraging and we are very grateful.
Warm and sociable, feisty and strong, our sparkling mam has a big heart. She loves to sing in a choir and is a big advocate of the uplifting nourishing power that this brings.

Our jovial, gentle, sociable and magical dad is a free spirit who is always armed with a hug and a philosophical

meandering. Most of all in life, he loves to sing, and sing some more, and then encourage others to do so too.

Becky: Rachel, me and my brother Matthew are all very sociable creatures. This may just be our nature, but it certainly was nurtured. Many people in the folk scene will relate to this I imagine. There is a real sense of togetherness and tolerance. People of all ages, listening to music, ceilidh dancing together... it breaks down those sometimes difficult barriers between age groups. We were allowed to exist in an adult world. We were not at home with a babysitter whilst our mam and dad went to the concert, we were watching the concert, we were dancing at the ceilidhs or we were asleep in a pram in the corner. As well as being lots of fun it was a kind of education. The people we talk about in this part of the book are often the people we were with, and have been really influential to us.

Without them, we wouldn't sing the way that we do or look at folk music or life the way that we do. I purchased a Roy Bailey record at Tynemouth market the other day, I got home and put it on. It was a bit like having a flashback to my childhood. It dawned on me that the stories told through those songs had important humanitarian hearts to them. I thought to myself "Oh Mam and Dad, you are clever, you were teaching us," but maybe they didn't even intend to teach us. Maybe they were just enjoying it themselves.

am not a religious person, but I do believe in us. Us humans. I believe in listening to each other. I believe in the seasons, in traditions and customs. They are the stepping stones that guide us through the year. Many of these ideas are explored in stories and songs, tall or true. They can be safe places for us to explore our imaginations, and to decide which parts of reality are important to us. I didn't need Christianity to teach me about right and wrong because I had my parents, folk songs, stories and all of these heroes and influences we talk about here.

The criteria for this list was for it to feature people or institutions who may be well known and respected in the folk world, or within one part of the world or another, but who may not be so well known beyond that. If you're relatively new to folk music and have arrived at it perhaps through us or maybe a handful of other acts, you'll hopefully enjoy this list as an illustration of our background, how we arrived at the music we play, and maybe you will want to further investigate some of these people too.

It doesn't include artists such as Robert Wyatt, Nick Drake or Antony Hegarty because their histories and influence are well documented throughout popular culture, unlike the people on our list, who are perhaps known only in certain circles. You may still be interested, however, in the influences on us beyond folk music, and they're important to recognise, so these are dealt with by Adrian in 'Heroes and Influences Part 2)'.

There is one person on the list who is not necessarily on it for further investigation, and is therefore the exception to these criteria. Let's start with her...

Auntie June

We Unthanks love a family party. Actually, to be actually correct, it's not just Unthanks but Wintons and Irwins and Sissons and Daglishes too. Cousins, uncles and aunties, grannies, kids, stepkids, newborn babies, boyfriends and girlfriends. Like most families, we don't need to have spent a lot of time together throughout the year to feel at ease in each other's

company. They are almost all from Yorkshire, all like a drink and a song and a chat, and noise. We all make a lot of noise. I remember taking a boyfriend home for Christmas dinner one year. He was astounded at the sheer noise level at the dinner table. Everyone interrupting each other, full of joy, passion and opinion, this was our way of enjoying being together as a family. We were connecting.

I must credit my Uncle Gordon (Winton) and cousin Julie (Irwin) for hosting the most recent and brilliant family Christmas parties (not dinner) in Redcar. They carry the torch well for Auntie June (Gordon's wife, Julie's mum) who was one hell of a host. Everyone has to do a turn at the party, a song or a dance or a tune, and you don't have to be a folkie to join in. Over the years there have been folk songs, jazz dancing, an Eminem rap, electric guitar solos, tricks, always something by Ewan MacColl and always something by Auntie June, or since she died, something for her.

June was my dad's sister and so encouraging of everyone in her family singing and performing. I remember that she loved it when I sang 'River Man' by Nick Drake. Sometimes when I am on stage I think to myself, "I wonder what Auntie June would think of all of this?" I know Rachel feels the same. At Whitby Folk Week years ago, me and Rachel did a gig as an unaccompanied duo, and Auntie June was so proud that she got Rachel in a headlock! It started as a hug but that wasn't quite enough physicality to show us just how proud she was!

She sang 'The King of Rome', 'The Bonsai Tree', 'Nobody Knew She Was There'. She sang the Fred Small song 'Everything Possible' with the lyrics "you can be anybody you want to be" to her grandchildren when they were little, and Rachel has recently started singing it to her two boys. She was a whirlwind of energy, and a generous, positive spirit, in life and in death. We were all devastated when she passed away in 2007. It is no exaggeration to say that we all adored her, her big warm heart. She died on the 9th of January, on my birthday. As well as sadness, I find great strength and comfort in memories of her. Something I will never forget is one of June's most defining characteristics — her AMAZING laugh, as loud and hilarious as my Uncle Gordon's laugh. Infectious and brilliant. *Becky*

The Keelers

This powerful quartet of singers is comprised of Jim Mageean, Alan Fitzsimmons, Peter Wood, and our dad, George. They sing shanties, songs of the sea and of the local area. They have been such a big influence on us, from their love and knowledge of their material to their obvious joy of singing. We learnt to sing harmonies from listening to them, and you may recognise a few song titles from their back catalogue, as they have been extremely generous in teaching us songs and encouraging us to sing. They all bring their own unique qualities— Jim with his passion and encyclopaedic knowledge of songs, and his melodious, rich and rhythmic voice, Alan's spine tingling harmonies, Peter's bass of gravitas and Dad's infectious joyfulness. All four of them sing with passion and gusto, and the skill of great storytellers. We always look forward to hearing them sing. *Rachel*

Johnny Handle

As well as being a person of extraordinary energy, ability and unpredictability (in a good way), Johnny is also an integral figure in the North East folk scene. He took a primary role in the North East's folk revival movement and is an important and brilliant songwriter, his songs seamlessly integrating into the local tradition, such are their quality and relevance. He is also extremely generous in the way he shares his knowledge and songs, and seems to have a thirst to share. I remember working with him in a school once, where his impish humour was infectious. You never knew when you might turn up in the middle of one of his songs or stories. On the journey back home we covered everything from instructions on how to make makeshift instruments for schools to advice on property prices. He is now often seen singing with his

wife Christine Hendry, a beautiful Scots singer wh has also been very encouraging to us. We love to sin his song 'Guard Yer Man Weel', a beautiful, tende mining song from a women's perspective. *Rachel*

Sandra and Nancy Kerr

For as long as I can remember I have been listening t Sandra Kerr and her daughter Nancy sing. As well a being folkie family friends, our mam has been singin in choirs led by Sandra for years, most recently he all-women's choir, Werca's Folk. The glorious, unifie sound that Werca's Folk make can be partly credited t the amount of years they have been singing togethe But it is their passionate, talented leader and arrange Sandra who has brought this group of women togethe to sound like one voice. When I was a kid, my mum an Sandra would go on weekends away with another choir Caedmon. I used to tag along, too young to be left home. Beautiful wild walks, cooking and singing unt the early hour. Hmmm, reminds me of our Unthank singing weekends! Thanks to Folkworks, we went t loads of singing and music workshops when we wer growing up. Nancy's workshops were my favourite. Sh always had such a natural way of being and when sh sang, it was like a bird singing. I think maybe at that ag when people wanted to be Kylie, I wanted to be Nanc Kerr. And Rachel Unthank. Haha! *Becky*

I really enjoyed being in Sandra's Caedmon Choi along with my mam, as a teenager, and she greatl encouraged me to sing more, suggesting that I shoul enter the BBC Radio 2's precursor to the Young Fol Awards, previously called the Young Tradition. Sandr was also the voice of Madeline and the mice on th wonderful children's TV show, *Bagpuss*. Her voice i now a constant accompaniment on all car journeys, a my kids love listening to the *Bagpuss* CD that she kindl gave them. *Rachel*

Folkworks

Folkworks is an arts and education organisation that was set up in the North East in 1988 by Ros Rigby and Alastair Anderson. I was 3 in 1988, Rachel was 10, Matthew was 9 and Folkworks were very much a part of our youth. They put on loads of great concerts bringing artists like Chris Wood, Flook and Swap to the North East. We went to their workshop days to learn songs and instruments, and we did a lot of ceilidh dancing. Connection and friendships were formed at the summer school, singing all day, every day for a week with like-minded kids. It was such a treat. I would arrive home to my parents tired and over sugared but bubbling with enthusiasm and songs. Folkworks are still going strong, now as part of The Sage Gateshead. They are responsible for starting the folk degree (as it's known, thought it probably has a fancier official name) here, bringing a surge of young folkies to the North East. They still run the youth and adult summer schools in Durham every summer and programme great concerts at The Sage Gateshead. Thank you Folkworks. We love you. *Becky*

The Voice Squad

The mellifluous beauty of Gerry Cullen, Phil Callery and Fran McPhail singing together in harmony never ceases to lift our souls to higher places. This traditional Irish trio are all fabulous singers in their own right. Harmony singing is not really part of the Irish tradition, yet these three come together to sing in exquisite harmony. We have been lucky enough to have worked with them, a real treat as we grew up loving their music, and were very happy to discover their warmth and generosity as people. When working with them it inspired us to finish off our vocal arrangement of 'Magpie'. *Rachel*

Joyce McLeod

Joyce is a friend of our family, and is a gutsy, fearless singer. I first heard 'The Testimony Of Patience Kershaw' in a folk club sang by Joyce and was captivated by her powerful, tender and uncompromising performance. For me, Joyce revealed the brutality, beauty and humility of the song, which later made me want to sing it. I have always admired how when Joyce sings, you feel like she means every word, she is totally committed to the song. *Rachel*

Taffy Thomas

The first time I met Taffy, I was about 4 or 5, and I remember it vividly. I was sat cross-legged on the floor amongst a sea of kindred spirits - other folkie kids whose parents had taken them to festivals every summer, where singing, dancing and listening were the events of each day.

Taffy is a storyteller, and on this particular day he was telling the tale of the gingerbread man. It's a small world, the English folk scene, and after finding a lifelong friend in Taffy's daughter Rosie, despite living miles apart, our families and lives became intertwined.

Taffy's past was in street performance— he was a fabulous Salami brother! This involved a bed of nails, fire eating and other dangerously entertaining things. But after having a stroke at the age of 36, Taffy had to learn how to walk and talk again and to live life in a different way. He used traditional tales as speech therapy, using many of the stories he'd previously brought to life in his theatre group Magic Lantern.

I have always known him as a storyteller, very generous with his time and spirit and always so encouraging of our singing. Stories have always been a strong draw to folk music for Rachel and me. Whether it be real life stories or magical tales. Stories of love, of the sea, of the land in which we live or long to find, of the industry that has shaped our communities. Hearing and sharing stories helps us to reflect on our own lives, giving us some context and helping us to make some sense of it all. *Becky*

Sheila Stewart

Sheila was a singer and storyteller whose Scottish travelling roots were key in defining her no-nonsense and otherworldly singing and performance style. We were lucky enough to hear Sheila sing live many times at Whitby Folk Week over the years. We were struck hard by her honest and passionate delivery — things that have become integral to us as both performers and listeners. We heard her sing the song 'Blue Bleezing Blind Drunk' many times, which we recorded on our album *The Bairns*. *Becky*

Tommy Armstrong

Known as the 'Pitman Poet,' Tommy Armstrong lived and worked in County Durham from 1848 until 1920. He wrote many great songs and poems inspired by the people and lives that surrounded him. Some are hilarious like 'Hedgehog Pie' and 'Marla Hill Ducks', and become almost surreal in their humour— the two protagonists in the former growing 'proggles' where there should have been hair, after eating the pie. Tommy also wrote songs for charitable causes and mining disasters, selling broadsheets to raise money for the widows of the miners killed, of which 'Trimdon Grange Explosion' is a truly moving example, and one we love to sing. *Rachel*

The Elliotts of Birtley

The Elliotts are the North East's folk royalty. A family of miners, singers and socialists, they have been a big influence on us. We were taken to their family folk club, which like many clubs, was run in an egalitarian fashion, taking your turn around the circle, anybody who wanted to could sing. A big part of the night would be the crack; the jokes and lighthearted banter, which created a warm, friendly atmosphere. Doreen and her husband Brian Henderson were the last custodians of the Elliott Club, and they still sing with so much passion and warmth, humour, truth and beauty. We learnt many great songs from this family, and were also given a fine example of how to be decent human beings. *Rachel*

The Wilson Family

Along with The Keelers, The Wilsons are the sound of our childhood. Huge, powerful North East voices singing in glorious harmony. They come from Teesside like our mam and dad, and they have that no nonsense, straightforward integrity about them with big warm hearts to match. When I think of The Wilsons, a familiar scene appears in my head. It's all of us Unthanks —Mam, Dad, me, Rachel and our brother Matthew in the pub on Boxing Day. We've got leftover Christmas dinner sandwiches and we are surrounded by singing. All my mum and dad's friends are there and we're all packed tightly in the pub. There is a buzz in the air, as we all wish each other Happy Christmas but we are here for the singing. "Better than Christmas," we say. Then, this brilliant, unmistakable sound comes from one part of the pub. With a huge mass of wild ginger hair (Chris Wilson wins the hair prize) and pint in hand, five brothers— Tom, Chris, Steve, Mike, Ken and sometimes sister Pat— singing with such power and

oul, it blows your socks off. As well as feeling blown
way, it makes us want to join in, and we can and we
o. We were little, with small voices. We could sing to
ur hearts content without any consequence. Trying
ut harmonies and just emitting pure joy at being a
art of this celebratory noise. We still go to Greatham
very Boxing Day. That feeling is yet to wear off. *Becky*

Graeme Miles

raeme was a songwriter, poet and artist who wrote
undreds of songs about Teesside and Cleveland. They
epict the industry, river, people and landscape of
ne area, the grim hardships, and also the beauty of
ne North Yorkshire Moors. I particularly enjoy the
lemental aspect of his work, drawing on the seasons
nd weather which help give his work such a strong
ense of place. Although we grew up on the banks of
ne Tyne, our family are from Teesside so these songs
ave great resonance, and we grew up hearing the
kes of The Wilsons singing his songs. Kevin Hall,
n old family friend, works tirelessly documenting
nd promoting Graeme's work. We helped set up a
ursary in conjunction with Kevin, the English Folk
Dance and Song Society and others, supporting young
eesside talent in honour of Graeme. *Rachel*

Vin Garbutt

his Teesside troubadour is a truly great live performer.
Ie can have you in tears of laughter one moment,
nd tears of anger or sorrow the next. His songs are
ften extremely moving, political and of substance. I
dmire his grit, which is so perfectly balanced against
is maverick onstage humour and all round sparkle.
And he is my fairy Godmothers' cousin! *Rachel*

Alex Glasgow

We find ourselves continually coming back to and
drawing on Alex Glasgow's songs, as they portray aspects
of the North East so eloquently, full of heartache and
humour. Born in Gateshead in 1935, he lived and
worked here until he emigrated to Australia, where
he died in 2001. Of the many things he wrote, which
included pieces for television, our favourite are the
songs for a play called Close the *Coal House Door*, written
by Alan Plater. They are so powerfully moving and
thought provoking. We also drew on his songs for our
shipbuilding project, as songs like 'All In A Day Willy'
capture the complexities of emotions and situations so
perfectly. *Rachel*

Addison Rapper and Clog Dance Team

Formed in 1977, the same year that Rachel was born
(that's how they remember how long they've been
going), our dad helped form this rapper and clog
dance team. They are responsible for those bursts of
percussion that punctuate our performances. Our
tapping toes guided by Auntie Kathleen, we have
shared so many formative times with these lovely
people. Enduring rainy Lakeland campsites together,
and enjoying sunny festival parades, many packets of
crisps and glasses of pop outside dance tour pubs, and
the legendary Christmas Ceilidhs. They instilled a love
of dance, and being part of a team. *Rachel*

16
HEROES AND INFLUENCES
(PART 2): THE OTHER SIDE
Adrian McNally

If you asked Rachel and Becky to do a Top Ten Albums piece, which is a request we get from the press from time to time, it wouldn't tell you much. Their list of heroes shows how the arenas of live performance and participation have been the focus of their musical education. Mine took place between speakers, and for me, the geeky world of top ten lists is one I can pass a little time in quite happily.

This however, is less a list of favourite albums of all time, and more a selection of those which can be said to have influenced the sound, the atmospheres and arrangements of The Unthanks.

Rachel and Becky's vernacular is unaccompanied singing. Also in their vernacular is accent, dialect, a lack of vibrato… many things characterise their voices on a technical level, but most defining of all, for me, in terms of when they are at their best and most natural, most at one with the singing tradition of the North East, is when they're singing unaccompanied. Largely, I prefer to hear folk song this way.

But where would we be, had we never ventured further than unaccompanied singing? Of course, the points at which we use it in our performances now can be very effective, but it is more effective because it almost literally stops the show. The musical colours we us[e] as a band freeze momentarily, and we all experienc[e] together, sometimes off-mic even, that there i[s] nothing more affecting and direct than the huma[n] voice. It is within the context of all our musical colour[s] that this device is so powerful. Now we have a health[y] audience who trust us, we could — and will at som[e] point — undertake an entirely unaccompanied phase o[f] project, and I'm pretty sure that our audience will b[e] delighted. But had we started that way and continue[d] no further, its doubtful we would have turned so man[y] heads beyond the folk world, and created the audienc[e] we have for the songs we love.

So we use music. And because Rachel and Becky['s] true vernacular is that of the unaccompanied singer[,] if there is to be accompaniment, it may as well com[e] from anywhere. In fact, the more distant the style o[f] accompaniment is from anything we might regard a[s] folk, the more pronounced and unfettered Rache[l] and Becky's vernacular remains. I predominantly us[e] musicians from a non-folk background, but that's no[t] because I'm looking to change things. On the contrary[,] I'm looking to leave the power and authority of Rache[l] and Becky's folk vernacular unchanged. Using fol[k] musicians to make folky noises around them would b[e] either adding to or diluting their true form. I want t[o] neither. I prefer to see the music as an atmosphere separate from the singing, as an alter-discourse to the song. This may be something dreamlike and otherly, or something austere and dispassionate to counter and highlight the passion of the vocal performance.

Due to the quasi-orchestral element of much of our music, it could be assumed that I have an appreciation or knowledge of classical music, but I don't. I know a few bits, but no more or even less than the average music listener. It's a journey I'm still looking forward to going on one day. I think it's more accurate to say that I've been stimulated by rock, jazz and folk artists who have been inspired by classical music. Most of them absorbed the influence but ditched the orchestral instruments for modern ones. In being informed by these artists, I must have unwittingly absorbed the classical influence in their popular music, because I've been inspired to put the orchestral instruments back in!

In much the same way as Rachel and Becky have acknowledged the influence of their parents above all others, it is no issue for me either, to recognise and celebrate that I owe my love of music to my mum and

A young (and silly) Max McNally

dad, Queenie and Max. My dad is a music nut and continues to badger all of us with his new discoveries, most of which aren't up to much, because his thirst for the new is so strong that he'll give anything a chance. But I can always tell when there's that extra glint in his eye, when the new discovery really is worth investigation. Some of my favourite childhood memories are ones with my parents, when their love for music became animated late at night, and their desire to play me an old Moody Blues or Joni Mitchell album became stronger than their responsibility to put me to bed. I remember one time late on, my mum telling Max to play me 'Close To The Edge' by Yes and my dad sucking in air and saying he thought I was too young. I was about 11, I think. "Gerrit on!" said the mother. Blew my socks off, so it did.

Thanks Mum and Dad.

Just as we hope you might investigate some of the names on Rachel and Becky's list that are new to you, so we hope you will enjoy searching out the records here that you don't already know.

Islands - King Crimson

The title track to *Islands* is the reason that trumpet features heavily in our music. Not Miles Davis. Not brass bands. In many ways, *Islands* is a bit of a shambles. A bit sixth-form, lyrically, you might say, and the music and production, though beautiful and original, has a folksy, indie naivety. I'm convinced there is even an out-and-out mistake by pianist Keith Tippett at one point. It could be said that my arrangement of Crimson's 'Starless', a track they released in their heaviest, rocky period, was influenced by Crimson's own sound circa *Islands*. The only person ever to identify and point this out to me was my dad's best school days mate, no surprise. The killer moment is a stark, very real, cracked and emotional trumpet solo in the middle. Actually its cornet! As much as what it taught me about the emotion of brass, the whole piece has been very influential on me, even though I went 25 years without hearing it at all. It was just a hazy childhood memory, an earworm that got me obsessed with the musical vertigo created by an atmospheric soundscape suddenly being splintered by something close up and raw. It has subconsciously taught me everything I hold dear about juxtaposing scale and space in music and production to create emotional surprises and counterpoints. I suffer a lot from actual vertigo and the threat of it, which I think is partly what draws me to play with musical equivalents. This device is at the core of arrangements like 'Felton Lonnin' and 'Madam', in which small parlour arrangements of songs with innocent, nursery rhyme words are suddenly juxtaposed without warning with the creeping, foreboding presence of an austere, large orchestra, that you didn't know was there until that point, evoking I hope, the eerie atmospheres of the vast, ancient lands of Northumberland, and the unsettling sense of its peaceful present, undermined by a bloody past.

Sketches of Spain - Miles Davis

I came to jazz late, in my mid-twenties. The proper stuff — Davis, Coltrane, Dolphy, Mingus etc. It would sound conceited to say that I enjoy being confused, as if to suggest that I rarely am, but I'm at my happiest with music when its just beyond my understanding. I feel this with jazz, and when I hear Irish or Pakistani music played at pace. Its slightly too much for my brain to process, and so the response to it is pure. I let it in, give up to it, let it take over me.

Sketches Of Spain is an altogether different experience, however, and it goes without saying, an influence on the title track of *Mount The Air*. While the obvious influence may be the use of trumpet and certain stylistic elements, the broader connection is in the kinship I feel towards the love that arranger Gil Evans and Davis clearly had for the tune. To give that much attention and space to someone else's work — in their case, the themes in Joaquin Rodrigo's *Concierto de Aranjuez*, and in mine the basis of the tune from the traditional song 'I'll Mount The Air On Swallows Wings' you really have to love the work. Davis thought the concerto's adagio melody was "so strong" that "the softer you play it, the stronger it gets". *Sketches Of Spain* presents the melody in many ways, soft and strong. It is a love letter, not to Davis's fans, not to Davis himself, but to the music, to the melody, to the emotion in the melody. Davis yields to it, and offers it to us from as many different

perspectives as he can, so that we might hear and love in the way that he does. I cannot allude or aspire to the heights of Miles, but I know that I love the tune from Mount The Air as he did that melody, and my attempt to create that love for it in others is the reason why our version is ten minutes long, and why the first draft was seventeen minutes long. Those moments that arrive when you realise just how beautiful music can be, are few and far between.

I'd also like to make a connection between the trumpet and the voice. In order to have trumpet play a folk tune like 'Mount The Air', it has to be deconstructed so it can be played in phrases. That's a beautiful thing about wind instruments — because of the need to breath (unless you're Evan Parker!) the music comes out in phrases, statements, sentences. The player has to decide what to say in each phrase, which really focuses the player on what they express. As folk artists primarily focused on storytelling, why wouldn't we use the trumpet?

Miles often played with little vibrato, in much the same way that Rachel and Becky don't sing with much vibrato. Perhaps because vibrato is associated with grandiose, over accomplished, mannered performance, I think we're more inclined to hear honesty and truth in tones that are delivered without it. Again like Rachel and Becky, Miles flirts with tuning, using the outer reaches of a note's pitch to convey emotion and to suggest vulnerability. Rachel and Becky perhaps don't do this as consciously as Miles might have done, but the effect on the ear and the heart is the same.

Music For 18 Musicians - Steve Reich

If you ever get chance to see this performed live, drop everything. The minimalism of Steve Reich is about as far away as you can get from folk music, yet because of the modal structure of some folk music, there are musical elements in common which make it easy and natural to combine the two. In layman's terms, it would not be unusual to find a folk artist using a harmonium of some sort to create a drone, without rhythm, with no or few tonal changes, over which to sing. Reed instruments like melodeons and harmoniums allow the folk performer to create a stillness, to sing an air o, perhaps. If you're using percussive instruments however, such as guitar or piano, you do not have this facility to create constant uninterrupted sound. In the neoclassical world, Reich and others like John Adams, use quick, repetitive figures, or patterns if you like, to sort of create the same hypnosis. When the pattern changes at all, it is only gradually, and perhaps combined with another similar pattern that subtly masks the movement, so that changes in harmony and tone occur slowly and imperceptibly.

The repetitive patterns in Unthanks pieces like 'Annachie Gordon', 'Last Lullaby', 'Close The Coalhouse Door' and so on, are my drones. I'm not the first by any means to apply this principle of neoclassical minimalism in modal folk music. Chris Wood has been at it for years, like on 1999's *Knock John* with Andy Cutting for instance. I only discovered this to be the case recently. Quite depressing, when you think you've had an original idea, to find someone beat you to it. But also, in another way, quite reassuring, that you're not alone, not mad. Marrying two musical worlds together is a dangerous business of course. The very word 'fusion' strikes fear. To stand any chance of success, the fuser has to love and understand both worlds, and above anything, has to love the music/song it is being applied to. The fusion must not be the point. For me, this particular fusion is merely a device that allows the music to stay out of the way, to avoid drawing attention to itself, by being as consistent as possible in both tone and rhythm, allowing the vocal performance and storytelling to shine.

Spirit of Eden - Talk Talk

Having eschewed their rock stadium career, *Spirit of Eden* is Talk Talk's masterclass in timing and space, in revealing new textures, in creating atmospheres. When I was younger, I used to listen to it on an average Tuesday evening, in a determination to turn the telly off and do some studying or just read a book. I soon realised it wasn't the background music I initially thought it was.

Millions Now Living Will Never Die - Tortoise

Tortoise were at the forefront of the early 90s post-rock and electro-acoustic movements. I first saw them support Stereolab in around 91 and it changed my whole thinking about music. Or rather, by totally ignoring or deconstructing the conventional forms of rock music, they validated and articulated a whole load of feelings I had about form. Minimalism and deconstruction in popular music is commonplace now, and acts like Radiohead and Cinematic Orchestra will juxtapose electronic and acoustic sounds as if things have always been that way, but without the likes of Tortoise and also Gastr Del Sol, I'm not sure things would have been.

The Lonesome Touch - Martin Hayes and Dennis Cahill

Here are two other musicians that understand Miles's sentiment above, that "the softer you play it, the stronger it gets". In terms of my own listening history, before there was Miles, there was Hayes and Cahill. Their approach teaches the young, full-blooded musician that less is more, that strength is beauty. That giving the listener more time, as well as the musician, allows the listener to fully appreciate the beauty and meaning in music, or even to appreciate it where it was previously not apparent at all, in a tune that perhaps was only previously thought of as cheery and simple. Chris Wood has done much the same with the English tradition, slowing down and finding the beauty in tunes that were previously only thought fit for dancing, not considered listening. Dennis Cahill is also pivotal to my understanding of how using different chords under the same tune can radically alter the emotion in that tune, especially the use of relative minor chords under tunes in major keys. It is, I admit, my number one weapon!

Tindersticks II - Tindersticks

Dickon Hinchliffe's string arrangements, and the ensemble format of the band were a huge influence on me, particularly on our very first string arrangement, 'Felton Lonnin'. It's an incredibly intimate and beautiful record.

Anglicana - Eliza Carthy

While June Tabor's use of piano with English folk music might be the more obvious reference point, Eliza's 'In London So Fair' from *Anglicana* was more the inspiration for me putting together Rachel and Becky with a pianist. In turn, I suspect Eliza's accompaniment, although on piano, was itself influenced by her dad's guitar style, so it might be truer to say that the predominant influence for initial accompaniment style in the Winterset was both Eliza and Martin Carthy.

Shleep - Robert Wyatt

Everyone knows we love Robert. There is no truer British musical artist, in my opinion. And Alfie of course. Where would he be without Alfie? It would be more obvious for me to go for *Rock Bottom*, containing

perhaps my favourite recordings ever, in 'Sea Song' and 'Alifib/Alife'. But *Rock Bottom* is so singular, I couldn't possibly be influenced by its arrangements (that said, the simplicity of Wyatt's post-accident woodblock percussion probably did inspire our use of high heel percussion, as separate from clogs). His arrangements are bonkers, almost always. When someone deploys such unique imagination, it doesn't even feel possible to borrow from them, because frequently his music sounds so spontaneous that it's clear he means to be and perform this way just once. Just like a jazz musician. When we arranged 'Alifib/Alifie' (it appears on *Archive Treasures*) I deliberately gave this vocal line to strings, rather than have Rachel and Becky attempt them, because they are so clearly improvised, it would be absurd for anyone else to sing them ad verbatim.

I've chosen *Shleep*, partly because of the song 'Maryan' which you will hear clearly influences our arrangement of 'Living By The Water', and partly because it illustrates my belief that Wyatt is perhaps the only prog-leaning musician of his generation who has gone through his life making better and better music, or at least as good. This I believe is because he's not really from the prog stable at all. He has the musical intelligence and vocabulary to be, but first and foremost, he and Alfie are storytelling, socio-political humans. If there's always point to the music, you're only going to make better ones as you get older.

Come On Feel The Illinoise - Sufjan Stevens

Artists like Sufjan and Anohni are individuals who like us, have largely favoured an ensemble approach to music making. We each make music that sounds democratic but isn't! That is the anomaly — if one person devises the music, the parts are handed out fairly. Well, it's not about fairness of course. A single auteur is more interested in the whole, and not just in his part. So out go the flashy guitar solos, the bassists who really want to be guitarists and the unnecessary drum fills. Each player plays his or her part, and no part on its own makes much sense. Jigsaw music, perfected perhaps by Penguin Cafe Orchestra.

Prog has largely been a male dominated sphere. The queue for toilets at gigs is always for the men's (my mother is usually amongst the few making use of the women's). Stevens makes complicated ideas sound graceful, fluid and sensual; ideas that in the hands of others have largely sounded angular, aggressive and difficult. He makes music that is more accessible than his leftfield influences. Commercialism is a compromise. Accessibility is not, because being understood is the ultimate goal! Our music is more accessible than my influences, and I'm proud of that. I'm happy to listen to obtuse music, but if one person in the room doesn't get what we do, I feel like I've failed.

Now you know why I'm so miserable. Ha!

———————

I'm tempted to add *Foxtrot* by Genesis, *A Little Man And A House And The Whole World Window* by Cardiacs, *Aja* by Steely Dan, *Innervisions* by Stevie Wonder, *Hats* by The Blue Nile and *Dry* by PJ Harvey — they were all moments of awakening for me. But while they're probably in our music somewhere, I can't define them as having an overt impact on our sound. Pink Floyd ought to be in there too, but no one record quite defines the influence.

Plus the list as it stands, has lots of neat interconnections. Crimson were influenced by both Reich and Davis, with Davis an influence on Reich. *Islands* itself was apparently influenced by *Sketches of Spain*, as clearly was Talk Talk's *Spirit of Eden*, which in turn was an influence on Tortoise, while *Music For 18 Musicians* is clearly an influence on Sufjan Stevens. I don't have delusions of being part of this lineage, but its a source of joy and confidence that musicians that I love, also love each other.

Influence is at its most exciting and healthy when a musical principle understood by osmosis through listening is then applied to a completely different set of musical circumstances. If you simply want to be like the artist you are influenced by, that will show. If you are merely appropriating a musical principle, its like coming up with a seven, and then finding a three and realising it's what you need to make ten. Help yourself to a three. It doesn't belong to anyone, and it was you alone who had the idea of adding three to the seven. Perhaps my most obscure example might be to reveal that our sombre reading of Graeme Miles's 'Sad February' is influenced by perhaps the most uplifting piece of white pop music there has ever been - Bruce Springsteen's 'Born To Run'. I look forward to the day when someone spots it and tells me what the connection is. Answers on a postcard!

AN ARTIST WRITES...

No 8. Esther Swift, Harpist, Twelfth Day

Last year I was lucky enough to meet Adrian, Becky and Rachel, and play some very carefully chosen moments on the harp for their album, Mount The Air. This was a particular pleasure and joy for me, having grown up listening to The Unthanks and hearing how they have changed and sculpted their music and style over the years. They're insight into traditional music has been a huge influence in the way I think about music myself, combining lots of old and new sounds and genres, whilst still maintaining deep roots in the tradition. Their music is ever careful, ever unexpected, ever exploratory, ever more undefinable, which is what music should be, and what I strive for myself. These things are what make them totally unique and pioneers of both the tradition and the music scene that we share today. It is more difficult than ever to maintain authenticity within our demanding and expanding music industry, but The Unthanks achieve this with a rare and beautiful grace and delicacy.

LIVE AT THE IVEAGH GARDENS

DUBLIN, 18 - 21 JULY 2012
★★★★★

the Waterboys

SPECIAL GUESTS:
THE UNTHANKS
& KATIE KIM

FRI 20 JULY 2012

WWW.AIKENPROMOTIONS.COM

Stage Saturday

Unthanks
Adrian McNally

Cambridge
Folk Festival
26, 27, 28, 29

Adrian McNally
Artist Pass
The Unthanks

Booking Line 0843 208 6000
Book Online www.thelowry.com

THE LOWRY

Lowry, Pier 8, Salford Quays, M50 3AZ

BBC Radio 2 Folk Awards 2012

Theatre **Stalls** **L4**

8 Feb 2012 7:15 PM

Order Numb

g Fee £0.00

GlasgowLife

Main Auditorium
Glasgow Royal Concert Hall, 2 Sauchiehall Street, Glasgow

Booking Ref: 748943
BBC Radio 2 Folk Awards
Main Auditorium
Wednesday
30-January-2013
Cabaret m...

Celtic Connections 2013
Presents

BBC RADIO 2 FOLK AWARDS

Wednesday
30-January-2013
Venue Opens 6:15 pm
Show Start 7:15 pm

Door 3
Cabaret Tables
TABLE33   7
£ 0.00

141 353 8000
w.glasc

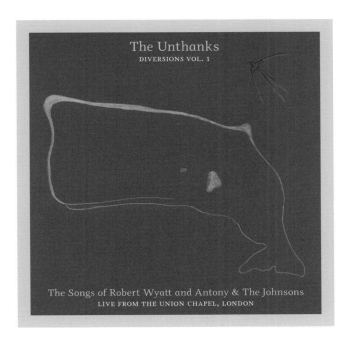

The Unthanks
DIVERSIONS VOL. 1

The Songs of Robert Wyatt and Antony & The Johnsons
LIVE FROM THE UNION CHAPEL, LONDON

17
BAD RIDE HOME

Chris Price

Rob, our sound engineer is sat on the bench seat, squashed in the middle wearing a monkey onesie. The five of us are taking it in turns to be the "warm penguins" in the centre of the huddle but my whole body is still numb. It's around 1am, midwinter and below freezing. We've raided our suitcases for clothes. I've got three layers of everything and I can't physically get any more on. Niopha has needed the loo since the show. The plan was to stop at the next services but we never made it. Now she may not make it.

I'd seen the needle just touching the top of the red as we chugged down the sliproad somewhere near Staines in search of a petrol station. We'd only made it to the roundabout before the vehicle gave up. After around 30 minutes our knight in shining Astra came to our aid...

"Mate! Is this the A30?"

"Yes! Think so".

Window goes up and he's off. B*$t*%d!
So I called out a "man who could," but turns out he couldn't, or wouldn't. Things were not looking good.

Only a couple of hours before, we were coming off stage at Brighton Dome after a triumphant last ever performance of the "Bob and Tony tour / TUPTSORWAA&TJ", more commonly known as

"The Unthanks Perform The Songs of Robert Wyatt and Antony & The Johnsons". The whole tour had been a fantastic experience for all of us in the band and to finish off at Brighton Dome's Concert Hall was the icing on the cake. Euphoria was in the air!

By 3am, I'm banging my head against the steering wheel. We're trying to find a funny side to our situation, a "something-to-tell-the-kids-when-they're-older" sort of thing. We are failing. By 4am, we're laughing, not sure what about, but at least real help is on its way. By 5:30am, I'm having a slight altercation with the fuming mechanic from the van hire company. "Yeah" he says, "when it gets to the top of the red it runs out of fuel!" So what's the point of the bloody red then?" grumbles I. I'm starting to feel less guilty now and more angry. At least he's fixed it and put in enough diesel to take us a few miles to refuel. We pull into a 24hour petrol station less than half a mile up the road from where we'd broken down. Damn, damn and absolute damn (possibly not the exact words I used at the time). Niopha goes for a wee!

It's a quiet ride back to St Albans. With our collective sense of humour thrown out of the window a long time ago, not even a white, ginger, dreadlocked sound engineer in a monkey onesie can raise so much as a half smile now. It's 6:30am. We've arrived at our warm comfy beds at Niopha's mum's, a mere 7hours after leaving Brighton.

"If I had to take a single summary of what Alfie and I have being doing over the years to the proverbial desert island, I wouldn't take one of our own records. I'd take the crystal clear interpretations of The Unthanks."

Robert Wyatt

The premier of Divs. Vol.1, Union Chapel.

This leads to a conversation about Palmer and William Blake (and I'd add writer John Cowper Powys), in which Robert talks about the romantic local sensibility of Britain. "You don't have to go to Italy for romance," he says. "It was here all along. I feel really in tune with that." The subject of folk music has emerged at various points during the day, with Robert and I both admitting our struggles and changing attitudes regarding English folk. In the 1960s, like me, he rejected most of it, James Brown's brand new bag being far more immediate. James Brown is still up there, but for the rest of it, now he's not so sure. I ask if he and Alfie had heard Rachel Unthank & The Winterset's new album, *The Bairns*, with its deeply moving version of Robert's "Sea Song"? The room explodes for a moment, yes and yes, Robert in wonderment that she has captured the core of his song so completely.

Backstage in Lincoln with
Robert Wyatt and Alfie Benge.

Rachel and Becky with Robert Wyatt.

FOLK

The Unthanks
The Songs of Robert Wyatt and
Antony & the Johnsons
(RABBLEROUSER)

The distance
between the
Unthanks' Geordie
folk canon and
the songbooks of
modern-day sophisticates Antony
Hegarty and Robert Wyatt proves
less than expected. The group's
chamber folk — stately piano, string
quartet, trumpet — is a perfect fit
for contemplative pieces such as
Wyatt's "Sea Song", while Hegarty's
"You Are My Sister" might have been
written for the Tyneside siblings.
The album is taken from a 2010
London show, but the Unthanks'
intertwining voices — cadent,
mournful, tender — never falter
and the between-songs banter
grounds an ethereal atmosphere. A
triumphant excursion. Neil Spencer

The Observer | 20.11.11

18

THE UNTHANKS GET TENDER
WITH BRASS

Adrian McNally

*First published on September 8th 2011 in The Guardian, Adrian discusses folk and brass traditions, and becoming a father
four weeks before the premiere of The Unthanks with Brighouse and Rastrick Band at Durham Cathedral.*

He's the best. A lovely midsummer's baby. Beautiful like his mum; Rachel Unthank by night. My son was born nine whole pounds exactly. Bigger and older looking than the other babies on the ward. Not a wrinkle on him; skin feather-soft and sweet. Calm, like his dad, apart from the occasional outburst, like his dad.

I can't think about the brass project without thinking about our George, who came into our world a couple of weeks late, just four weeks before the premiere of our collaboration with National Champions of Great Britain, Brighouse and Rastrick Brass Band. Two very steep learning curves to negotiate at once. Never had a baby before. Never written for brass before. In fact I don't even read or write music.

We're getting quite used to saying "yes please" to things we don't know how to do, and then worrying about "how" later. How usually involves me sat at the piano,

with Niopha Keegan, our fiddle player, patientl[y] scribing my whims, line by line, bar by bar. Learning is a good time to create I find. It's much easier to avoi[d] clichés when you don't know what you're doing.

George is named after Rachel's dad. Our baby bo[y] certainly has the lungs of his shanty singing, prou[d] granddaddy. I'm sat with George junior now, an[d] Rachel; a sleeping beauty on either side, mother an[d] baby resting on a quiet summer's afternoon after [a] successful feed. In the first week, I visited Rachel an[d] George at Hexham's Maternity Unit by day, then wen[t] home alone and wrote for brass by night. Four week[s] later, we had four short rehearsals with the world'[s] oldest public subscription band and found ourselve[s] on stage in front of 1200 people inside the Potter-esque Durham Cathedral. There is disbelief now abou[t] how we both managed — me to write ninety minute[s] of orchestral scores in three weeks, Rachel to take the stage so soon after giving birth. I will be foreve[r] n awe of her courage, and while her body may have ways of making her forget the pain so that she might have another, I will never stop respecting or stop being impressed by her resolve. Frightfully underprepared though we were, looking to the left of my piano to see a 30-piece orchestra, to the right 1200 people packed into the finest bit of Norman architecture standing, and in the middle, my wife, undertaking our biggest musical adventure to date just four weeks after giving birth, my fears were replaced by a realisation that this would probably be one of the best moments of my life.

It's a life that started in a small South Yorkshire pit village called South Hiendley, two doors from my childhood friend and bandmate Chris Price, and about two miles from Grimethorpe, home of the most famous colliery band in the world. Brass band music was part of the fabric, and something I absorbed as a child, which is probably why I find it so emotive as an adult. I couldn't think of an opportunity in music that I would be more excited and honoured by than this. The brass collective of instruments is surely the loudest of any instrument family, but for me it is in the restraint of this power, when brass is played tenderly, that beauty and honesty is found — a formidable giant is far more impressive when he is gentle! Add to my excitement a 20 year obsession with Miles Davies and especially Sketches Of Spain.

Folk song and brass-band music may be different musical disciplines but often both were designed to speak for — and be spoken by — the same people. Different types of music, but with similar heartbeats, similar content, plus folk music at its best is always about content and not style. The conventional musical and visual vernacular of folk music has been of use to everyone from Goldfrapp to Audi since we have been making music as The Unthanks, as culture looks for depth and identity in homogenised times. But for us, folk music is an oral history, not a genre of music; a human exercise in sharing and empathy, without recourse to vernacular stylings. The form of folk song has always followed its function, its circumstance, shaped less by notions of authenticity and more by the practical options available to audience and performer and the musical influences of the time. Limiting musical colours to those we think of as "folkie" is like a storyteller using the same voice to tell all his stories. Why not brass?

Of the many social issues that Rachel and Becky Unthank have grown-up singing about, the working man is certainly one, and none more so than the coalminer. With the brass-band tradition steeped in pit history, we decided to make mining a focus of the repertoire for this project. Perhaps the highlight of this focus was finally getting to look at 'Trimdon Grange Explosion', a song by Tyneside pitman poet Tommy Armstrong, written about a mining tragedy in 1882, in which 74 people died, among them boys as young as 11. The song speaks of Mrs Burnett, who lost all three of her sons. Another woman found herself attending the funeral of her betrothed on the day she was to have married him. One man, a father of two young children, was working his last shift before emigrating to America. A miner himself, Tommy Armstrong wrote many poems about Durham life. Strikes and fatal accidents were so commonplace that he became relied upon, almost like a preacher might be, to express his community's experiences.

Some people might say that the mining industry in our country is dead and gone, so what's the point of singing mining songs any more. For me, performing folk songs to an audience is an exercise in shared empathy, whereby a pile of people get to share an emotion together at one moment, happy or sad, rather like the function a church might once have had, or a community pub, or the family house. I don't believe that our capacity for empathy is limited to things that we can relate to from firsthand experience. If that were the case, we wouldn't have been captivated by the Chilean mining disaster. When journalists write things about "modernising folk music and bringing it into the 21st century", it drives me nuts. A story is capable of touching us, of teaching us, whether it is from another century, another continent or an industry we long since lost the fight over. All we need to do is tell the story well so that people will want to listen. And as an arranger, whether it's a brass band or The Unthanks at my disposal, I'm not trying to modernise, I'm simply looking to bring out the beauty and truth in a song that was there all along.

Our collaboration with the massed ranks of "Briggus" also included new compositions, commissioned by Durham Brass Festival and The Barbican in London. I wrote a four-movement work (not bad for a Barnsley lad!) called 'The Father's Suite' to celebrate the birth of our son. It was composed partly from a piece I wrote as a boy and another piece I remember from my childhood that my dad wrote. Sandwiched in the middle is a piece of spoken word set to music — an archive recording of Tyneside miner Jack Elliott, one of the Elliott's of Birtley, the north east's first family of folk, who set up Birtley Folk Club in 1962, which is still run by Jack's daughter Doreen. Jack speaks about raising children and their role in society, which couldn't be any more resonant right now. "If they hurt society, they hurt themselves, for the simple reason they're a member of society", he says. He also makes some barbed comments about religion, which I almost included, but got scared because the first performance was in Durham Cathedral!

Possibly the most remarkable discovery in this project was finding that brass bands are still amateur. There appears to be next to no funding for the art form. Consequently, the men and women of Brighouse and Rastrick — world class musicians — all have full time jobs, and so by the time they have practised in the band twice a week and performed three times at the weekend, they have little free time to speak of at all, and most have family lives to juggle. The likes of the world famous Grimethorpe Colliery Band had more freedom to perform when the pit was open and they were all miners! Back then, they'd be excused from

their shifts to play whenever the band was engaged to perform, whereas now they're fitting in shows at the weekends and during the summer holidays. More should be done to protect, promote and celebrate this tradition, surely?

Twelve weeks later, we have more brass shows to relish and a son who is all smiles and has slept right through for three weeks now. Profoundly intense surges of emotion are a daily occurrence: the instinct to protect, the power of love for one's own son or daughter. There is happiness, excitement, euphoric joy; but there is also deep, dawning realisation that no, it isn't possible without feeling it firsthand, to know and understand what it is to be a mother or father, which disproves my point about being able to empathise without having experienced! In most cases, we can imagine how we would feel in the same position. But not this. This is incredible. It is the point, for me at least.

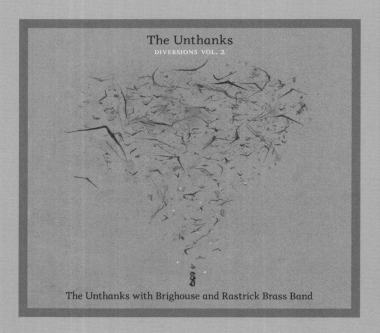

The Unthanks
DIVERSIONS VOL. 2

The Unthanks with Brighouse and Rastrick Brass Band

The Unthanks

Corbridge
Northumberland

Dear Unthank Girls
              I want to say "Thank you" for your brilliant, intensely moving track "King of Rome", including the sensitive backing by the Brighouse and Raistrick band. It touched me deeply- an 87 year old widower.

              80 years past, in my Lancashire textile home town, I was for a couple of years a willing helper at a nearby pigeon loft (Lancashire, for cree). Owned by a cotton-worker mate of my Dad's

              Each week I took our chosen birds to the local Pigeon Club for race-registration, before they were sent to strange and far-away places, like Rennes, in France, or San Sebastian, in Spain.

              And on Saturdays,sitting at our loft, waiting for their return. A 7-9 year old working class lad absolutely enthralled with the mystery of the birds' return. Exactly the feeling expressed by your "I can't fly, but me pigeons can".

              Thank you girls, for this moving track. Briefly, I was young again. I shall be sending, separately, my account for Kleenex.

              And in passing, my additional, if belated thanks, for the BBC documentary you made earlier, concerning clog-dancing.My old Grandad was a clog-dancer, into his 70's. (Latterly, after he'd had a "gill" of bitter!). I was then too young to understand his demonstration of folk-dance. I should have learned myself, whilst I still had a talented tutor. A challenger, for Jackie Toaduff?

              Many, many thanks,Unthanks, for your wonderful, sensitive singing. Just standing; no gyrating and twisting about. The music says it all. Wonderful. A joy.

Yours sincerely,

James W Foulds.

With "Briggus" at The Barbican, London.

Brighouse and Rastrick
at Leeds Town Hall.

The Unthanks with Brighouse & Rastrick Brass Band

Northumbrian sisters Rachel and Becky Unthank released their first album Cruel Sister in 2005, under the name of Rachel Unthank & The Winterset. An exquisite blend of traditional and modern folk, it was named MOJO Folk Album of the Year. Follow up The Bairns was nominated for the 2008 Mercury Music Prize and also saw them win the BBC Radio 2 Horizon Award for best newcomer, alongside three nominations for Folk Awards. Extraordinary singers, the sisters' voices intertwine beautifully. Live their humour does too, while never detracting from the quality and reverence they show for the English tradition. Now regrouped as The Unthanks, they have released three further albums and received eight more Radio 2 Folk Award nominations, including three Best Live Act nominations in a

row. Always looking to diversify, their paradoxical journey of staunch traditionalism and musical adventure continues with a collaboration with the Brighouse & Rastrick Brass Band. National Champions of Great Britain they are regarded by many as the best and most consistent public subscription band in the world. With a focus on the folk songbook of the coal mining industry, The Unthanks sing material from their past and current repertoire, with arrangements re-imagined for the massed ranks of brass, as well as especially written and arranged material. Premiered in 2011 at Durham Cathedral, this moving collaboration stole the show at this year's BBC Radio 2 Folk Awards.

Saturday Stage 1

Cambridge Folk Festival
26, 27, 28, 29 July 2012
Cherry Hinton Hall

Souvenir Programme

Promoted by
CAMBRIDGE
CITY COUNCIL

£3.50

Saturday Stage 2

AN ARTIST WRITES...

No 9. Glen Hansard, Singer, Songwriter and Actor, Ireland

About two years ago, just after arriving home from tour, I was home one evening enjoying a bath. The radio was on and a show called "The Blue of the Night" was playing some experimental classical music. I was half tuned in when a song came on that immediately caught my ear and heart off-guard. I turned it up and was transported, time stood still. Suddenly I found myself out of the bath, looking for a pen and paper to catch in the quiet presenter's voice a name for the song. It was "The Father's Song", a version by The Unthanks. I bundled up and went downstairs to follow up on the song online where I found The Unthanks' Diversions Vol. 2 with Brighouse and Rastrick Brass Band. I immediately listened to the song again, playing it for my girlfriend. We both sat there quietly listening, stumbling together upon the gold. I held her in my arms and we both started bawling; a deep and guttural cry, a release. A flood of emotion that we'd held inside ourselves since childhood days had just been unexpectedly freed through this song. We stood quiet for a long time, allowing the tears find their way out in this moment that could not be rushed in its absolute and devastating beauty.

After a cup of tea and some uncontrollable laughter we listened to the rest of the album. It was already clear that whoever this band were, they were our people. The hefty moment we had just experienced took wings with "The King of Rome", a song about a racing pigeon. With its Northern English directness, its hues of Ken Loach and Mike Leigh and the brass arrangements that give it such a majestic and emotional width and breadth, it was a favourite in our home from the very start and still is.

Another song I am moved to mention is "The Happiness or Otherwise of Society", a powerful piece of archive recording with a man named Jack Elliot speaking of raising his kids with a sense of social responsibility.

This acts as an intro to "The Father's Song", the beautiful lullaby written by Ewan McColl, which on this record has been reharmonised and opened up in a whole new way by The Unthanks. It is the absolute gem of this great record.

I'm grateful that the radio can still surprise us sometimes, and it is only when a DJ is given the freedom to play what truly inspires them. Truth of emotion carries through the airwaves and goes much further.

The Unthanks
Songs from the Shipyards

Commissioned by Tyneside Cinema, Songs from the Shipyards is a beautiful
and powerful audio visual work that traces the story of the shipyards through
a new 60 minute film by internationally acclaimed filmmaker Richard Fenwick,
accompanied with music and song from The Unthanks, performed live
- a moving illustration of Britain's industrial journey in microcosm.
The tour is focused on places with a history of shipbuilding.

OCTOBER 2012

Mitchell Theatre, Glasgow
Tyneside Cinema, Newcastle upon Tyne
Tyneside Cinema, Newcastle upon Tyne
The Ropework, Hull
The Forum, Barrow in Furness
The Arc, Stockton
The Mac, Belfast
The Pavillion, Dublin
The New Continental, Preston
Gorilla, Manchester
The South Bank, London
Couryard Theatre, RSC Stratford Upon Avon
Harbour Lights Picturehouse, Southampton
St George's, Bristol

NOVEMBER 2012

De La Warr Pavillion, Bexhill
The Epstien, Liverpool

The Unthanks DIVERSIONS VOL. 3
Songs from the Shipyards
(RabbleRouser Music, rel: Monday 5th November)

19
SONGS FROM THE SHIPYARDS

From the sleeve notes of Diversions Vol. 2:

Song from the Shipyards is a Tyneside Cinema commissioned film by Richard Fenwick. It's a beautiful and moving film, tracing the story of shipbuilding, illustrating Britain's industrial journey in microcosm.

The Unthanks were commissioned to create and perform a live soundtrack to the film. This record features 'the best' from that soundtrack, in nonsequential order. Some songs feature here as excerpts, exactly as they did in the soundtrack, while others are performed in full, when perhaps we only performed a couple of verses in the film soundtrack.

In the piece The Romantic Tees, we should point out that while the featured poetry from Graeme Miles sites the River Tees as the subject, the background sound from the film is from the River Tyne! Even more

confusingly if you have seen the film, for our li performances, we adapted Graeme's poetry from 'th romantic Tees' to 'the romantic Tyne', to fit the film using the voice of Rachel and Becky's father, Georg Unthank. As we were performing it to images of th Tyne, we felt the need to adapt it. When it came recording it for this album however, we took th decision to revert to Graeme's original prose ar voice. I used the tone and rhythm in Graeme's speec as the creative source of the piece, in much the sam way that composers like Steve Reich used sampled ar looped speech patterns back in the 60's and 70's as th starting point of creation. While 'Tyne' is truer to th footage, I feel that without the film, the piece has mo musical integrity with Graeme's original words an delivery. Graeme's voice is a sampled piece of soun taken out of the context it was originally intended fo

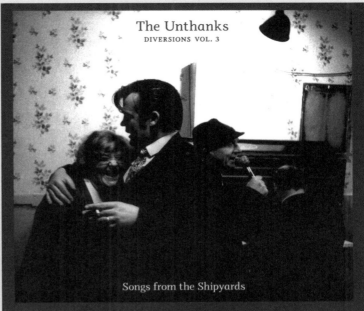

The Unthanks
DIVERSIONS VOL. 3

Songs from the Shipyards

nd looped to create something new. The recording of George Unthank was recorded subsequent to the creative process, spoken to fit the music, rather than he music fitting the words. It may seem like a trivial point, but it's very important to me that the music is heard to be inspired by the intonation of speech, and not the other way around.

All that said, the integrity of the piece is still undermined by that fact that the film audio behind the music is from he Tyne! I like to think that it is a coming together of rival northeasterly regions - the Unthanks sisters; brought up 200 yards from the banks of the Tyne by parents raised on Teeside, embodying harmony across he NorthEast!

So, Graeme Miles is clearly pointing to the absurdity of regarding a great industrial river as 'romantic'. My hope for the piece was to highlight the absurdity of romanticising not just the river, but industry as a whole; in this case shipbuilding of course. Impressions and accounts of our industrial past often tread the line between proud memories and rose tinted glasses; between the respect we have for the people who worked hard and the danger of glorifying their lives as honest, decent and proper; between describing them as great days and remembering that they were tough and dangerous days; between the pride for what the workers achieved and the reality of the wealth it created being siphoned away from their communities. And finally, the emotional complexity for those communities of having created something great, only to be completely deserted when the going got tough. How is it best for history to remember that? Graeme's absurd question has many different answers, and asks many more.

Adrian McNally, The Unthanks

TV make-up for Shipyards video shoot.

AN ARTIST WRITES...

No 10. Rosanne Cash, Singer songwriter and author.

No. Rosanne Cash, Singer songwriter and author, America. Elvis (Costello) said, "Have you heard The Unthanks? You have to get their record."Since I trust his musical recommendations implicitly, I got the first record and have been a fan since.

Dear Unthanks, do you know how many times *Songs From The Shipyards* has reset my internal compass and reconnected me to the Mystery? Thank you for that, and for all you are.

PS Thanks, Elvis.

Newcastle's independant Tyneside Cinema, commissioners of the project, Songs From the Shipyards.

Adrian on the Shipyards video shoot.

With George, Blast Studio, Newcastle.

For our sponsers, Port of Tyne.

George with his odd-mother Lucy
outside Vale studios, Worcestershire.

With the handsome Sam Lee, Howard Assembly Rooms, Leeds.

CO-PRODUCED AT sounduk

sounduk.net

A Time And Place

UK Tour 17 – 19 September 2014

Musical meditations on the First World War

RACHEL UNTHANK
BECKY UNTHANK
SAM LEE
ADRIAN MCNALLY
and more

Video design by
MATTHEW J WATKINS

"HAUNTING, ORIGINAL AND MAGNIFICENT"
— THE GUARDIAN

A Time and Place presents an evening of music inspired by the folk song, stories and poetry of the First World War created for audiences today.

"JUST BEAUTIFUL"
— LAUREN LAVERNE, BBC 6Music

Known for their ability to take traditional repertoire and reinvent it for contemporary ears, Mercury Prize nominated folk artists Sam Lee, Rachel and Becky Unthank collaborate for the first time in this poignant project to mark the centenary of the First World War.

As part of an 11 strong line-up they will perform original repertoire from the time alongside new material inspired by personal stories and arrangements to First World War poetry, all against the backdrop of Matthew J Watkins striking video design.

TOUR DATES

17 SEP | 7.30PM | BIR MINGHAM Town Hall
thsh.co.uk

18 SEP | 7.30PM | LONDON Barbican
barbican.org.uk

19 SEP | 7.45PM | LEEDS Howard Assembly Room
operanorth.co.uk

"LEE'S UNIQUE TAKE ON FOLK MUSIC NEEDS TO BE HEARD."
— THE GUARDIAN

MORE INFORMATION at sounduk.net
/soundukarts @soundukarts /timeandplace

Part of

LED BY BMW

Funded by

Supported using public funding by
ARTS COUNCIL ENGLAND
LOTTERY FUNDED

PRS

Co-Produced by

sounduk   opera north   barbican

IWANTDESIGN.COM

One million stories.
One great night.
**Great North
Run Million
Opening Ceremony**
Thursday 4th September

Not your average soundcheck - on the banks of the Tyne with Sting and Jimmy Nail.

20
SINGING WEEKENDS
Rachel Unthank

For seven years now, The Unthanks have hosted six winter weekends of singing, eating and walking on the Northumberland coast. Rachel and Becky lead workshops, there's food to write home about by Adrian (ably assisted by other band members and family), walks along beautiful heritage coastline to sing in cosy pubs, late night stories around crackling fires, sometimes a special guest and always an up–close mini concert from various Unthank members. In a growing culture of artists extorting cash out of their biggest fans by putting a hefty price tag on coming backstage for a quick chat and a photo, or offering to come round and do the washing up for every 50 copies of the new album you buy, the singing weekends are designed to disregard and undermine the conventional band/fan hierarchy. The waitress at breakfast might be one Unthank sister and the pot washer might be the other (or more frequently in truth, the sink will be occupied by fiddle–playing dynamo Niopha Keegan or Adrian's long–suffering mum). It's an inclusive experience, designed to bring people together for the joy of group singing and good company. For many, it has become an annual Northumberland pilgrimage, some having never missed a year, with each weekend developing its own personality and traditions. Rachel Unthank thinks back to how the idea came about and discusses the soul–nourishing, holistic benefits of singing your heart out, together.

Singing and performing in a band is amazing, such a privilege. I still pinch myself. I love trying to draw an audience into the story of a song and delight in the immediacy of performing live. The thrill of singing with my sister, weaving harmonies and tales, how we rely so implicitly on each other, Adrian, Chris, Niopha and the rest of the band. It always feels fragile and exciting, we all must play our part or it could all fall apart. And although sometimes exhausting, the wonder and fun of touring is in seeing new places, meeting new people, experiencing different scenarios that you just wouldn't encounter at home.

But we miss home. We miss our families, our friends, the landscape and familiar places, walking the beaches of Northumberland, eating and drinking and sharing significant time with significant others. We miss those occasions — the yearly rituals in the folk calendar and those that only happen when the right people are gathered together at a family party or festival singing session that we know will be special and yet can't make.

The singing weekends are partly borne out of the things that we miss from life while on the road. For example singing together in a packed pub with people with whom you have a common repertoire of songs, where you become a tiny part of something much bigger, almost invisible, but playing your part and adding towards the whole. This is a very different way of singing from standing on a big stage with nowhere to hide. Singing like this, together and not in performance, is a holistic experience. It is unquantifiably uplifting and nourishes you and feeds your soul in a different way. There is a true sense of community in shared song, a shared experience. Some of these occasions are on annual dates in the calendar, such as a Whitby Folk Week or the carols at Christmas, and so if we miss them because we're away, it's a whole year before they come back round.

So, seven years ago, when Adrian suggested that we may need to find some work for ourselves during one sparse winter, I had a think. Fuelled by philosophical meanderings with Becky, about our love of group singing, our wish to find a way to promote this, a longing to do some of those things that we missed from the road, my rusty cogs slowly turned. What if, for one weekend, we could entice enough people to come to our favourite part of a far flung corner of Northumberland, to sing with us, in the winter? Mmmmm. Would it work? I lured my mam, with a promise of a walk on the beach, to come and scope out a bunkhouse up near Seahouses.

It could not have been a more perfect setting. From the window you can see Bamburgh Castle, the Farne Islands and the North Sea. It's a stone's throw from our favourite sweeping beaches, and even more exciting, our favourite pubs, nestled near harbours and coves – family pubs with great beer and a positivity towards singing punters. Maybe this was also the opportunity to purge the not-so-secret hankering to run a restaurant that Adrian harboured. He could do the cooking with help of band members Chris and Niopha, providing an outlet for his mouthwatering kitchen spectaculars.

It grew from there. Mam and Becky would make cakes to welcome arriving singing weekenders. Dad and Jim (Mageean, Mam's partner) would come and help with the singing and help create that singing session pub atmosphere that they so love themselves, after a blustery walk on the beach. And, surely Adrian's parents wouldn't want to miss out on late night singing and socialising, in return for a little bit of washing up?!

Seven years on, we now run seven singing weekends during the winter months and their popularity continues to astound us. There is certainly more than a bit of washing up and onion chopping to do, and the

continued support of our families and a good few other roped-in helpers along the way has been invaluable.

The most striking and reaffirming thing for me continues to be something that we learnt in our very first weekend, and that is how singing together

a bonded whole that sounds like it has been singing together for years.

Some of my favourite moments - singing 'The Great Silkie of Sule Skerry' (a Silkie is seal in the sea, man or woman on land) to the wind and sea on a cold, wild beach; singing the song 'Magpie' under the shadow of Dunstanburgh Castle; drinking real ale after been blown along golden sands, by steely seas, packed together joyously singing in the pub; singing wassail songs huddled around blazing braziers of fire in the dark night air, mug of mulled cider in hand; eating, drinking, laughing, crying, making memories with lovely, like-minded people.

And singing. All that singing.

A FAN WRITES...

No 9. Fiona Monteith-Preston

The Unthanks and their music have had a huge impact on my life. I stumbled across them at my very first ever visit to Cambridge Folk Festival in 2007. These four (at the time) young women on the mainstage, singing beautifully constructed songs in their own accents – that of my adopted North East – they held the crowd in the palm of their collective hand as they launched their new album *The Bairns*. Instantly, I became a "fan" and sought out their live shows whenever they were playing nearby. I was fascinated by the way that Rachel and Becky's totally different vocal qualities worked so fantastically well with each other, with discovering local songs along the way that were completely new to me and watching the evolution of the band – even when they let the boys in – and how this changed the feel of the music, but yet didn't as at its core were still the same two contrasting, gorgeous voices.

I attended the first ever Singing Weekend in 2011 – agonising long and hard as to whether I should go, as I had only really sung in the shower and when forced to at typical Scottish family parties – heck, I didn't even know if I could sing properly in tune. That very first meeting with the band on arrival, when totally unnecessarily they each came up and introduced themselves (in my head I was saying back "Yes I know you are Rachel and you are Niopha!"). Becky asked the next morning whether I would like my bacon in a brown or white roll and my internal voice was saying "Oh My God, Becky Unthank is asking me what kind of roll I want". I came away from that weekend on a high, having realised I must be singing roughly in tune as I couldn't hear my voice singing anything different to those around me, having had an absolute blast learning new songs and having met a great bunch of friendly, encouraging, down to earth people – the band, the extended Unthank family and the other participants. I had so much fun, I went out and joined a choir a few days later and then another choir and a few more singing weekends and a couple of instruments and …well, I can't imagine not having music and song as such a huge part of my life.

I now wait on each new album and project with delightful anticipation, although how the sheer beauty of *Mount The Air* can be toppled, well, I'll wait and see.

All this beautiful, uplifting (even if the songs themselves are dark and sombre at times), gorgeous music has been truly life-affirming, and for that I must say a huge "Thank You" to The Unthanks, all because I happened to be in the right place at the right time on one sunny afternoon in Cambridge.

for a few hours so quickly breaks down any barriers or social inhibition, and can make a group of strangers into long lost friends. After the first evening singing together, and giving that little bit of yourself that singing requires, any nervous, awkward silences are replaced by laughter and the babbling of lively conversation. And, by the end of the weekend, the group feels like

Tar Barrel In Dale is the song written by dad, George Unthank, about the New Year's Eve fire tradition in Allendale, Northumberland. Our performance of it on BBC 6 Music for Mark Radcliffe and Stuart Maconie's Christmas Roadshow is becoming a tradition in itself, and its a favourite at the singing weekends. Here is the four-part vocal arrangement of the chorus, written out by Niopha Keegan.

A FAN WRITES...

No 10. Alice Bentley

The Unthanks, through their music, have spun a web of connections between people across time and space: between those whose lives are told in the songs and all of us who hear them.

Then there are we lucky, lucky people who have made the winter journey to Northumberland, and been fed with song, and laughter, and harmony, and food, and wild weather, and cold starlit nights, before being released back into the world Unthanked and connected. Coming first as strangers, each year we return and reconnect, and each year the net becomes richer and connections have flourished outside and beyond the yearly winter gatherings, and we bring the songs away with us and the net spreads ever wider through the seasons and around the world.

And we don't half laugh... Thank you!

George Unthank sings Tar Barrel In Dale.

THE PLACE THAT INSPIRES ME

Whether it's the roots of home or a wild escape from the rat race, most artists have a place that unlocks their imaginative flow or provides them with material to draw from. We asked writers, musicians, artists and directors to tell us about their creative hotspots

MAIN PORTRAIT BY GARY CALTON

'If you listen closely to our albums you can hear the cows'

⦿ THE NORTH EAST
RACHEL AND BECKY UNTHANK, MUSICIANS

We grew up on the banks of the Tyne in a little village called Ryton. Our parents are from Teesside but moved to Tyneside, and with Northumberland a stone's throw away and Newcastle just along the road, we feel very connected to the whole of the north-east. Our parents have always been really into folk music and we were brought up with lots of north-eastern traditions: we both still go clog-dancing every week and our dad did rapper dancing – a type of sword dancing that came out of the pit villages.

We draw on a lot on the traditional songs and stories of the north-east in our music – songs about border battles and the mining industry, about the river and the sea. This area feels inexhaustible as a source of inspiration. We're noted for singing in our accents, and why wouldn't

we? There's such a strong sense of identity here, and so much history and culture to draw from.

It's only recently that we've started to write songs of our own. Usually we look for songs in old songbooks or talk to knowledgeable people in the area. But sometimes going out for a walk is the best inspiration. One of our favourite walks begins in Ryton: you go down the hill into an area called the Willows, where we used to play as kids, then past the ponds, along by the river, through the forest, through the graveyard and back into the village. It's really beautiful down there.

Another walk we both love is up along the Northumberland coast – you get great big, beautiful beaches up there that are usually quite empty, even in the summer. So you start in the village of Craster, which is famous for its kippers, and walk up the coast past

Dunstanburgh castle and along Embleton Bay, where the sand is a lovely orange-golden colour. If you keep going around the corner, the sand becomes silvery and you get to Low-Newton-by-the-Sea, which is one of our favourite places in the world. There's a square of houses open to the sea and in the corner is a wonderful pub called the Ship Inn, which does fabulous crab sandwiches and has its own microbrewery. It's a good place to be.

On the subject of favourite pubs, there's a really good one in Newcastle called the Cumberland Arms. It's in the Ouseburn Valley, an industrial area of the city that's becoming a hangout for artists and musicians. The Cumberland Arms has always been a hub of music – our dad used to take us to Irish sessions there when we were kids. Lots of bands play there and we practise clog-dancing in the top room every Wednesday. It's changed hands over the years, but if anything it's got more

wonderful – maybe that's because we're allowed to drink the beer now.

Our studio is in a little hamlet called Aydon, where Rachel lives. We used to record at home, and we're pretty certain that if you listen closely to our albums you can hear the cows from the next-door farm. The studio is in a lovely old granary that belongs to the neighbours. It's definitely an inspiring place to rehearse. There were times when we ended up practising in sticky indie-rock studios and we were like, "Ugh, get me out of this boy environment." Here you can step out the door and be in the fresh countryside air. We've got our bunting up. It's brilliant.

The folk scene in the north-east has a very cohesive identity. It's not buried: it's very much alive. The tunes and traditions are in everyone's vocabulary. There are lots of sad tales but we sing silly songs too – our dad certainly does. It definitely feels like we've got our own thing going on up here.
Interview by Killian Fox

21
MOUNT THE AIR

Unseen alternative versions of Natalie Rae Reid's artwork for Mount the Air

AN ARTIST WRITES...

No 11. Martin Freeman, Actor

Music, for me, is like an anaesthetic.
Which is sometimes dangerous, because I can neglect all kinds of
everyday grown-up responsibilities, from paying bills to putting
the wash on (again) because I've been listening to some bloke
playing a piano for the last two hours. I do find it very hard to
focus on anything else once I've got a record on. Or headphones.
Life becomes just fine. I'll make that boring call later. The dog
doesn't actually need to be walked today, does he?

So, there are downsides of the anaesthetic. Things that need to be
done can slide. You are more or less in an 'other' state, where you
are the star of your own film. Or pop video.
But, like a real anaesthetic, music can be a necessary barrier to
pain, and on top of that, it can truly be a healer.
A couple of years ago, I was going through a very tough time in
my personal life, working on the other side of the world, and
missing home, family, and England.
The music of The Unthanks at that time really helped. It made me
cry and smile. And it somehow made me feel at home, and closer
to family. It was doing the most profound things for me that art
can do –it opened me up, it whisked me away and yes, it kind of
healed me. At least for moments.
And I will take that over EVERYTHING.

This group is capable of such beauty that sometimes I can hardly
bear to listen to them. And sometimes, when I know I need it, I'll
listen to them to open me up and clean me out.

I could bang on about them in a muso technical way, because
they are very good indeed at that business. But it's the effect they
have on me that makes me really love them.

If you haven't checked them properly, have a go. It may make
your life slightly better for a bit.

Lizzie, Moseley Festival 2015

Long standing viola play Becca Spencer on the Mount The Air tour, 2015.

Previously unseen photos from Sarah Mason's Making of Mount The Air shoot.

"I joke sometimes that I have a morbid dread of folk music, but when I first heard Rachel Unthank's singing,
I realised that the beauty was in the root and the branch too. Each new Unthanks record is deeper and richer.
Adrian McNally's delicate orchestrations frame Becky Unthank's voice so beautifully.
It is hard to choose just one song from *Mount The Air*. I hope you hear it all."

Elvis Costello (choosing 'Flutter' for his Mojo covermount CD)

Unthanks air their new album to invited guests

> The Unthanks' new album. launched in Northumberland   Simon Greener

Sam Wonfor
Culture Writer
sam.wonfor@ncjmedia.co.uk

FOLK siblings The Unthanks launched their latest album at a special event in Northumberland yesterday.

An audience of invited guests enjoyed a special and intimate playing of the new release from the award-winning Northumberland folk group – their first studio long player for four years.

Maximo Park's Paul Smith and award-winning children's author David Almond, as well as a few lucky competition winners, were among those who had gathered for the occasion in the remote studio where the album was recorded near Corbridge.

"We wanted to celebrate the album as an art form – giving it time to be listened to from beginning to end, and mark and celebrate all the work we have put into it," said Rachel Unthank, who leads the band with sister Becky.

"We thought it might be nice to invite people up to the studio where it was recorded to hear it with us."

As well as being treated to the first full public unveiling of Mount The Air, which is released today, guests also got to enjoy a banquet of a buffet prepared by the band.

"Of course we're nervous about it," laughed Rachel, (talking about the album, not the buffet). "I don't think you can not be nervous about something which you've invested so much time and work in."

In addition, Becky said this album offered another layer of anxiety for the band, because it's the first one on which they have all had a writing credit.

She said: "In the past, somebody might say they didn't like our singing, but they couldn't get at us for the songs because we were mostly singing someone else's words – we were just the messenger! This record is a lot more exposing in that way I suppose, but that makes it exciting too."

Although Mount The Air is the first studio album in a while for the Mercury Music Prize-nominated and BBC Folk Award-winners, Rachel was quick to point out they have kept themselves busy with other things during that time – like the acclaimed Songs from the Shipyards project, their live and recorded collaboration with Brighouse and Rastrick Brass Band and working with Sting on the music for The Last Ship. Rachel has also become a mother of two sons with husband and the band's pianist and producer, Adrian McNally.

She said: "When you're working on a project-based album, you're kind of working to an agenda or a framework. But when it's a studio album for the band, it's just about what you want to express and explore. It feels really good to be releasing an Unthanks album."

And the assembled audience seemed to agree.

Jade Kirton-Darling, North East MEP for Labour, said: "The album is extremely beautiful. It is like the geography of the North East in musical form. The instruments represent the landscape and their voices are like the wind running through it."

Fan and competition winner Fiona Monteith-Preston added: "It is beautiful. The arrangements are stunning and complement Becky and Rachel's voices."

AN ARTIST WRITES...

No 12. Geoff Travis, Founder Of Rough Trade Records

...the Carter Family, the Everly Brothers, the Von Trapp Family, the Jackson Five, the Osmonds, the Beach Boys, the Staple Singers, Rachel and Becky Unthank.

...sometimes blood is thicker than water and when two voices are mingled together it produces something as powerful as magic. That's what I hear when these two sisters sing.

...add to this an understanding of where they came from, their sense of the history of this island and a deep intuitive understanding of what WB Yeats once described as trying to "hold in a single thought reality and justice".

...add to this a work ethic second to none and you have a set of musicians under the name The Unthanks who comprise a travelling troupe of the highest order, bringing grace and joy and truth to a land that is sorely in need of these things.

The London launch. Clockwise from top right: Isn't that Martin Freeman over there on the decks?; Rachel failing to conceal excitement, with Martin and Niopha; Robert with Adrian; Robert Wyatt and Alfie Benge; Robert Wyatt chatting with Geoff Travis (Rough Trade)

The Unthanks, Newcastle City Hall

"I HAVE some notices for tonight... a bit like a parish council meeting," says Rachel Unthank. She proceeds to do audience members' birthdays as part of this good-natured and affectionate homecoming gig.

Unlike any parish meeting I ever attended as a young reporter, the band's debut at the City Hall features the exquisite voices and nifty clog-dancing footwork of sisters Rachel and Becky (along with some very pretty dresses).

Stockton's strident harmonisers The Young 'Uns open proceedings with Billy Bragg's Between the Wars, "as relevant now as it was 30 years ago".

Nominated for a Radio 2 Folk Award, the trio bring a robust levity (along with some toilet humour) to both halves of the show, matched by the lively banter of The Unthanks.

The sisters are touring their new album Mount the Air with an eight-piece band, including manager and pianist Adrian McNally (Rachel's husband) and violinist Niopha Keegan, a long-time collaborator.

A string quartet, alongside bassist, drummer and superb trumpeter Victoria Rule, provide the brilliant musicianship required to carry off the lengthy instrumental passages featured on The Unthanks' new tracks.

They open their set with an elegant interpretation of the bleak Hawthorn, by Charles Causley, and continue in melancholic spirit with Becky's beautiful original tune, Flutter.

The soaring and swelling highpoints of this gig include the joyous title track of the album, based on a traditional song and developed by Becky and Adrian.

Also utterly beguiling is Last Lullaby, developed from the folk song Golden Slumbers by Rachel, now a mum of two boys.

Niopha's tune For Dad, featuring her voice as a little girl, is haunting in its poignancy, but as ever it's the Unthank dreamy harmonies which are spellbinding.

With quite a back catalogue to choose from, The Unthanks also present some of their Antony and the Johnsons and Robert Wyatt interpretations, completing the encore agreeably with 2011's Last.

■ **The Unthanks also play Middlesbrough Town Hall on March 19.**

Tamzin Mackie

The Journal
17.3.15

Top to bottom: Becky with the goods; with Paul Hartnoll (Orbital); Martin Freeman with Adrian; an engaged Hannah Moulette

A FAN WRITES...

No 11. Brian Smith

If back in 1980, after going to my first gig (The Jam) at the age of 14, somebody said, that in over 35 years' time, I'd be watching a clogdancing, five piece folk band, singing in a 100 capacity theatre in Peebles, and that said, could reduce the most unemotional guy in that theatre to tears with a song called "Hymn for Syria", I would have told them to take a running jump.

35 years later it DID happen, that is what the music this group makes has the power to do, at an Unthanks gig you go through the wringer of emotion, laughter, tears, happy, sad, up, down, In my book the greatest folk band this country has EVER produced.

The Peebles gig wasn't the first time I had seen the band but it was without doubt, my favourite show, a week later I went to Manchester to see the Stone Roses in front of 60,000, the Roses never came close to that night in Peebles . Thank you!

MAJOR TOUR AND NEW ALBUM ANNOUNCED FOR 2015
"I'm glad to be around at the same time as them. They make my heart beat faster." Martin Freeman

The UNTHANKS

February 2015
21 **Southampton** Turner Sims
22 **Exeter** Corn Exchange
24 **Yeovil** Octagon Theatre
25 **Bristol** Colston Hall
26 **Cardiff** St. Davids Hall
27 **Nottingham** Albert Hall
28 **Sheffield** City Hall

March 2015
01 **Liverpool** Philharmonic Hall
03 **Bury St. Edmonds** The Apex
04 **Brighton** Dome
05 **Ashford** Revelation St. Marys
06 **Norwich** Open
07 **London** The Roundhouse
08 **Warwick** Arts Centre

10 **Leeds** Irish Centre
11 **Manchester** The Ritz
12 **Dublin** TBA
13 **Belfast** Empire
14 **Newcastle** City Hall
19 **Middlesborough** Town Hall
20 **Edinburgh** Queens Hall

Tickets on sale now.

Tour features 10 piece ensemble • www.the-unthanks.com

The Unthanks

Mount The Air

UK and Ireland tour in support of their first studio album in four years, out 09.02.15

"They make my heart beat faster. I'm glad to be around at the same time as them." Martin Freeman
"There really is no better folk band in the land" Q Magazine

February 2015
21 **Southampton** Turner Sims
22 **Exeter** Corn Exchange
24 **Yeovil** Octagon Theatre
25 **Bristol** Colston Hall
26 **Cardiff** St. Davids Hall
27 **Nottingham** Albert Hall
28 **Sheffield** City Hall

March 2015
01 **Liverpool** Philharmonic Hall
03 **Bury St. Edmonds** The Apex
04 **Brighton** Dome

05 **Ashford** Revelation St. Marys
06 **Norwich** Open
07 **London** The Roundhouse
08 **Warwick** Arts Centre
10 **Leeds** Irish Centre
11 **Manchester** The Ritz
12 **Dublin** National Concert Hall
13 **Belfast** Empire
14 **Newcastle** City Hall
19 **Middlesbrough** Town Hall
20 **Edinburgh** Queens Hall

Tour features 10 piece ensemble
www.the-unthanks.com

RABBLE ROUSER

A FAN WRITES...

No 12. Sandra Stafford

Well, I must have been living under a stone! Until the BBC2 Folk Awards this year (2016), I had never heard of the Unthanks. But those sounds took me straight back to my childhood (I'm 60 now) and my Nanna's voice, her accent, the fact that she sang so beautifully, that she told me her story, like it was a novel – the landscape of her birthplace, the farm she lived on and how hard she worked, the complexity of her family unit (her mother was 'a right one'), and why she left (ran away) to come south to London in the 1920s, where she went into service. And I feel emotional just writing this, because I wish I'd paid more attention to her and her story. I guess this is the first time I've experienced such a powerful link between lyrics/songs/performance and my own personal family history. So thank you for that. And thank you for an unbelievable performance of 'Mount The Air' at St George's Bristol in June 2016. It will stay with me forever.

JOHN GRANT   BILLY BRAGG   THE UNTHANKS
THE WEDDING PRESENT   DAN CROLL   THE FELICE BROTHERS
IBIBIO SOUND MACHINE   HONEYBLOOD   BLACK RIVERS
EMMY THE GREAT   DAMIEN DEMPSEY   JAMES YORKSTON
DIAGRAMS   MENACE BEACH   KIRAN LEONARD   THE PICTISH TRAIL
THE LOST BROTHERS   LISA O'NEILL   FATHERSON   ELIZA SHADDAD
CURTIS ELLER   ROZI PLAIN   CATTLE AND CANE   SERIOUS SAM BARRETT
FURS   MAIA   DEBORAH ROSE

WITH MUCH MORE MUSIC STILL TO COME

DEER SHED FESTIVAL 6
UP IN THE AIR

THE FAMILY FRIENDLY MUSIC, ARTS AND SCIENCE FESTIVAL 24 - 26TH JULY 2015

Gratuitous modern social media shot.

Advian and Niopha check the scores, Middlesborough Town Hall.

Camp drumming with Martin, London 2015.

Mount The Air shoot outtake.

Lizzie with Joel Borkin (Unthanks live sound)

Joel wearing Becky's fox jumper

With Eliza Carthy, Damien Dempsey and lots of MacColls, Ewan MacColl tribute, Barbican, London, 2015.

A FAN WRITES...

No 13. Robert Kingsbury-Barker, London

Early in 2015 my mum was diagnosed with terminal cancer. Near the end of her life she was looked after in a hospice located, by a weird coincidence, in Unthank Road in Norwich. Living in London I spent many hours driving to and from Norfolk, and my one constant musical companion during those bleak drives was 'Mount The Air'. By any standards this is an astonishing album, but to me it's also a constant reminder that no matter how dark things are, love and beauty are still there for anyone who looks for it. Thanks for everything you've already done, and here's to many more years to come!

Backstage session for Cerys Matthews at Glastonbury 2015.

The Roundhouse London, Mount The Air tour, March 2015.

A FAN WRITES...

No 14. Juha Koivisto, Finland

The planning for the trip started right after the "Kulturfestivalen" was added to the tour dates. That's 6 month prior. Tried to get a friend to join me, but had no luck. Stockholm is about 10 hour cruise ship journey from where I reside. Booked the cheapest cabin I could find, which probably wasn't the best idea. It had no windows and the engines were creating a lot of unpleasant noise. Thankfully the deck outside was open for everybody. The weather was amazing.

Upon arrival I checked into hostel and went outside to visit the record stores. Finally the night came and performance began. There seemed to be a supernatural element to all of this, since I did not know anybody in the city. The freedom hidden within anonymity and the music lifted my ordinary essence to greater heights. The possibilities opened up in an instant and reminded me of original source of happiness.

The song 'Mount The Air" spoke to me like never before and then the band announced that they would be meeting fans nearby the stage. Besides getting picture with Becky I had the opportunity to chat with Adrian and Rachel. I told them how the feeling of spiritual kinship is expressed through their music, how it hits deep within and how hopefully someday they will perform in Finland.

The Stockholm summer night was breathtakingly beautiful and everything seemed to be full of love while I walked back to the hostel. The thought "did this all really happen?" echoed multiple times inside my head before falling asleep. I felt the need to check my camera a few times and the pictures were still there to remind me of a great evening with a great band.

A FAN WRITES...

No 15. Geoff Read

I have to confess an occasionally embarrassing problem. Certain musical things such as Richard Thompson's guitar, Ben Folds' melodies and, most of all, the perfect vocal harmonies of Rachel and Becky Unthank have a direct line to my tear ducts. Couple this with the fact that all three have associations of wonderful evenings spent with my nearest and dearest watching them perform live and I can get real messy, real quick. For this one, there was no way I wasn't going to be up close so I staked my place near the front with my sons Jake and Tom flanking me. Damn, they were incredible from the start. Adrian McNally and an astonishingly gifted group of string, brass and percussion players create a perfect soundscape for those two beautiful, oh so different but flawlessly complementary voices to work their usual magic on me. Tracks I knew and adored from their most recent album *Mount The Air* took on a new perspective, an added layer of beauty and meaning. As the sunlight breaking the clouds refracted through my teary eyes to create a kaleidoscopic halo around Rachel and Becky, they introduced their next song – my favourite from the album, 'Magpie'. "This is for a very special man called Geoff Read" they said. WTF? That's my name. Am I just fantasising? An excited whoop and nudge in the ribs from Jake gives me a clue. He'd emailed the band, explaining how much I love them, how much he appreciates what I do for him and Tom, and asking politely if they'd mind doing a 'shout out' for me. It says so much about The Unthanks that they remembered and took the time to do this in the middle of a major set. It says even more about Jake that he made the request in the first place – and I know that Tom would have done the same. If the intention was to make me feel very loved and create a memory that will last forever, it certainly succeeded. A distillation of the End Of The Road spirit in one stage announcement.

Innocency in Safety – a token from The Foundling Museum,
which inspired the lyric "Innocent and safe from his future in war"
in Adrian's song Foundling from Mount The Air.

One July night in 2014, I came home from tour to find a note in my letterbox:

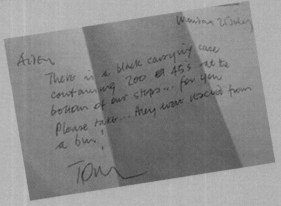

I nipped downstairs and found this:

A case of more than 200 vintage 45 records. Rock'n'roll and R&B from the 1950s and 60s, all in mint condition. My neighbour, Tom, had noticed them at the recycling bins one morning and assumed that an unwitting de-clutterer had abandoned them. I suspected otherwise: they were too good, too rare, too organised, too loved. I spent the next few weeks contacting collectors and DJs around Edinburgh asking whether anyone knew of a case of stolen records. Nothing.

Over the next few months I became fairly attached to those records. The music they contained began featuring at gatherings at my flat. On one particular night – the night Lau finished recording our album *The Bell That Never Rang* with producer Joan (As Policewoman) Wasser – the band went out for a celebratory meal, headed back to my flat for a few drams, subjected Joan to some hardcore trad tunes (solo bagpipes, unaccompanied Sheila Stewart) then let her take over the DJing. Expertly, ecstatically, she played records from the mysterious collection until it was time to catch her flight back to New York the next morning.

By now it was December and the records had been in my living room for five months or so. I kept checking in with various collectors and DJs but still no word of who might have lost the vinyl. Some collectors started offering me very decent money to buy the lot. Friends advised me to put the collection on eBay, but somehow I couldn't quite let the story end there.

The year swung around, spring arrived, the records were still with me. Toward the end of March I went to an Unthanks concert at the Queen's Hall. This is home territory for me: it's the stage Lau has played every winter for the past ten years. I've also known Becky and Rachel since we used to meet at the Whitby Folk Week l as teenagers –I would troupe down from Argyll, initially with The Caledonia Ramblers, then with Tabache.

Whitby was a formative kind of place for me, mainly because it was the first gathering where I played folk music with people roughly my own age. Before then, in Oban, I'd been pretty active at fiddle competitions and the local Strathspey and Reel Society but I had always felt the age gap. Arriving in Whitby and meeting other teenagers up for tunes and craic was a game changer. Today when I listen to Rachel and Becky singing, I still have happy memories of those Whitby days, and hearing them in my home venue was doubly heartwarming. (Lau and The Unthanks would go on to play a double-header at Celtic Connections some months later, but let's stay with the night in question for the moment.)

After the Queen's Hall concert there was the customary trip to The Royal Oak (a tune-inclined public house) for the enlivened. I seem to remember Becky almost missing the tour bus for wherever next. Around 3.30am, I wandered home through a messy Friday-night Cowgate carrying a vinyl copy of The Unthanks' *Mount The Air* under my arm.

A chap began walking alongside me and he spotted the record under my arm. We got talking –about music and vinyl and all sorts. He told me he was a DJ who plays mainly 50s and 60s rock'n'roll and R&B. He went on to tell me that about a year earlier, walking home one night after a club gig, he had put down his case of favourite records and, for whatever reason, had walked off without them. He had never recovered them. He seemed genuinely upset just recounting the experience.

It was late and my mind was racing. "I've got your records," I said. "I've been trying to give them back to you for eight months." He thought I was winding him up. "Come with me," I told him, and he did, and five minutes later we were in my living room and I was showing him the case of vinyl and he was holding his hands up to his face. "I'll turn around!" he shouted. "Name any track and I'll tell you the artist and the year it was released!" I told him there was no need; "I believe they're yours,"I said. But he insisted, and sure enough he could name them all.

A few months later, Andy played a DJ set at my 40th birthday with those same records.

Memories from making two television programmes for BBC4
on summer and winter customs in England.

Stockholm, summer 2015.

By kind permission of The Chancellor of the Exchequer

Rt Hon George Osborne MP

Dr Thérèse Coffey MP and Aldeburgh Music

invite you to a reception for

FRIDAY AFTERNOONS

to celebrate this national singing project
encouraging young people to sing

and to announce future plans

at 11 Downing Street, London SW1A 2AB

on 8 October 2013, 5–6.30pm

|||||||||||||||||||||||||||||
|||||||||||||||||||||||||||||
Aldeburgh Music

ARTS COUNCIL ENGLAND   BOOSEY & HAWKES   charanga   bpi   britten

RSVP Wendy Andrews at wandrews@aldeburgh.co.uk by Friday 27 September

For security reasons please bring this invitation and photo ID e.g. driving licence or passport
The use of mobile phones is prohibited in 11 Downing Street

Inspired by the composer Benjamin Britten, Friday Afternoons will involve well over 100,000 children
all around the UK and the world, singing Britten's *Friday Afternoons* songs on the 100th anniversary
of his birth, Friday 22 November 2013.

Above: An invite to Downing St.
We weren't free, so we didn't have
to decide whether to go!

Right: Singing with Voice Squad
and Martin Carthy, Drogheda, Ireland.

AN ARTIST WRITES...

No 14. Maxine Peake, Actress and Writer

I was first alerted to The Unthanks when I was in a play many years ago (name dropping now) with Jan Ravens. We we're doing Lillian Hellman's *The Children's Hour* at The Royal Exchange in Manchester. Jan and myself were having a good chinwag about music –our likes and dislikes –and she asked "Have you heard of Rachel Unthank & the Winterset?" I hadn't, so off I went to investigate.

There are few times when you hear an album or discover a band and they stalk immediately to the heart of everything you love and hold dear.

Their exceptional skill and musicianship is one thing but there is something extremely spiritual that is manifest in their music. It's very hard to articulate but to listen to an album or spend an evening at one of their gigs is like witnessing a seance. The history and emotion of their songs fills you to the brim. It's always a very emotional experience, with many tears shed, but as many through joy as from being touched by the sadness.

Politically I have always been led to believe rightly or wrongly that we are on the same page, as the compassion and empathy always speaks volumes to me.

They stride the traditional and contemporary worlds of music with a lightness of touch that is nothing short of magical.

A new friendship. Maxine Peake and our junior Arther at our annual appearance on Stuart MacConie and Mark Radcliffe's BBC 6 Music Christmas Roadshow, singing Tar Barrel In Dale.

AN ARTIST WRITES...

No 15. Philip Selway (Radiohead), Drummer, Singer and Songwriter

The Unthanks have covered a lot of ground in the past decade and watching them evolve over this period has been truly inspiring. I first came across them at the BBC Folk Awards in 2008 in their first incarnation as Rachel Unthank&The Winterset. I was hooked by their singular and infectious take on English folk music. Although I feel that they've stayed true to this tradition, they've never been defined or confined by the genre. Instead, they've used it as a springboard to explore all kinds of music and to continue to grow as artists. Throughout all of these developments, they have, however, remained recognisably themselves; they seem to be a band comfortable in their own skin but never complacent.

Fast forward to the BBC Folk Awards in 2016. In my opinion, The Unthanks produced the stand out performance of the evening in amongst a stellar bill. For me, it summed up the scope and ambition of their music and also the distance they've covered as a band. Adrian McNally's nuanced arrangements moved in a supple and sensuous groove, with a subtly complex interplay between strings, brass, piano and rhythm section. And at the centre of it all, Rachel and Becky's gorgeous voices still spoke straight to the heart, a direct line back to their origins.

I like music that's laced with misery; I'm in Radiohead after all. However, it needs to be delivered with heart, honesty, intelligence and good tunes to really hit home. The Unthanks have all of these in abundance.

Crows' Bones

SOME LIVING,
SOME DEAD,
SOME NEITHER.

opera north

An unmissable journey into the dark heart of folk song

Performers

Accordion — Martin Green (Lau)

Voice — Becky Unthank (The Unthanks)

Voice & noises — Inge Thomson (Karine Polwart Band)

Nyckelharpa — Niklas Roswall (All Sweden nyckelharpa champion)

Dates

Spitalfields Music Winter Festival
at Shoreditch Church, London
Thu 12 Dec 7.00pm

The Brewery, Kendal
Fri 13 Dec 8.00pm

National Centre for Early Music, York
Sat 14 Dec 7.30pm

The Stables, Milton Keynes
Mon 16 Dec 8.00pm

St. George's, Bristol
Tue 17 Dec 7.30pm

The Gate, Cardiff
Wed 18 Dec 7.15pm

Crows' Bones is a mesmerising exploration of ghost songs (old and new), pinpointing the very essence of what is most beautiful and unsettling within the traditional folk genre. Led by Lau accordionist Martin Green, this world-class band of musical luminaries includes Becky Unthank, virtuoso nyckelharpist Niklas Roswall and singer/multi instrumentalist Inge Thomson.

Drawing on songs of murder, visitations and unnatural happenings, *Crows' Bones* takes you on an unmissable journey into the dark heart of folk song.

'Thomson and Unthanks' voices are both distinctively otherworldly in themselves ... while Green and Roswall's instrumental contributions ranged from delicately disquieting atmospherics to nigh-on orchestral-scale ominous grandeur'
★★★★★ The Scotsman

Tickets and more info:
operanorth.co.uk

Martin Green is currently producing an album of the music from *Crows' Bones* with Portishead's Adrian Utley.

Commissioned and produced by Opera North Projects.

'A must see'
★★★★
The Herald

Crows' Bones

By Martin Green (Lau)

With Becky Unthank, Inge Thomson
and Niklas Roswall

AN ARTIST WRITES...

No 16. Conor O'Brien (Villagers), Singer Songwriter, Ireland

Listening to The Unthanks is like living in a deep, dark dream. The Song is forever in service to a communication of the sheer weight of meaning and emotion, which they attach in a manner that I find extremely pleasing to the soul. In other words, a lot of musicians and singers choose to perform songs about the trials of life and love and everything in between, but very few manage to convey the sense of fundamental urgency which is so often inextricably linked to the emotional filters we develop in order to survive within the confines of our inner worlds. I can hear my heart screaming when I listen to The Unthanks. There is something so natural about their approach to performance and arrangement that it seems trite to try to analyse it or to separate it into core elements. It is here to be experienced as a whole and can only be understood as such. When they sing of liberty, I can feel the incarceration from which the word gains its power and when they lull me to sleep with the most gentle of tones, I am violently woken to the memory of when I first heard the ever-present magic of human harmony.

Becky singing in Martin Green's
Crows' Bones project.

Packing off the Memory Box, Dec 2015.

Some time members Dan Rogers (bass) and Nick Byrne (cello).

Artist Natalie Rae Reid signing prints.

Stamping, sticking and signing. The making of the Memory Box, with Cally.

SSD CONCERTS AND THE UNTHANKS PRESENT

Home Gathering

The Unthanks
PLUS SPECIAL GUESTS

the Baghdaddies
Alasdair Roberts
Rob Heron & the Teapad Orchestra
Twelfth Day

PLUS: DJING FROM PAUL SMITH (MAXIMO PARK)
RAPPER SWORD DANCE · CLOG
the unthanks singing weekenders!

SATURDAY 22ND AUGUST
THE STEPHENSON BOILER SHOP
NEWCASTLE NE1 3PD

TICKET PRICE £22.50 OVER AT SEE TICKETS

Home Gathering –
The Newcastle festival
curated by us, two years in.

Change of Venue! Now at Hoults Yard

Hoults Yard
Walker Rd NE6 2HL
16–17th September 2016

Home Gathering

FRIDAY: RICHARD HAWLEY / THE YOUNG'UNS
SATURDAY: THE UNTHANKS / KITTY, DAISY & LEWIS

THE MOULETTES / RICHARD DAWSON / GET THE BLESSING / HYDE & BEAST /
MARRY WATERSON / THE HEADHUNTERS / THE FURROW COLLECTIVE /
LIVERPOOL STRING QUARTET PLAY STEVE REICH'S DIFFERENT TRAINS /
TIM & RHONA DALLING / PHIL & CATH TYLER / RAEVENNAN HUSBANDES /
THE HORSE LOOM / ROB HERON DJ / NEWCASTLE KINGSMEN & CLOG

Curated by The Unthanks, an adventurous bill of headline acts, intimate performances, dance,
flash mob style surprises and artisan food and drink. See website for details of venue change.

WEEKEND TICKET: SOLD OUT / FRIDAY ONLY: SOLD OUT / **SATURDAY ONLY – Just a handful of tickets left! £30**

PRESENTED BY **SSD CONCERTS** AND **THE UNTHANKS**   WWW.HOMEGATHERING.CO.UK

Hexham Abbey, Christmas 2015.

"There really is no better folk band in the land" Q Magazine
"They make my heart beat faster. I'm glad to be around at the same time as them" Martin Freeman

THE-UNTHANKS.COM

A FAN WRITES...

No 18. Josh and Clare Langton

Happy Birthday (Un)Thanks to Storm Desmond!

Yes the time we travelled up to Hexham to see The Unthanks for Clare's birthday celebrations was a weekend never to forget, the weekend Storm Desmond decided he would join us. The day of the gig was Friday 4th December 2015, coincidentally the same day the storm was named 'Desmond', and oh how he did play havoc with the weekend!

We finished work around 4pm and left what had been a sunny day in Manchester (yes it doesn't always rain here) and it boded well for the weekend... Oh how wrong we were. High winds and rain set in the further North we drove but this did not deter these two intrepid Unthanks travellers. On our arrival we were greeted by the Christmas tree lights waving frantically in the park across from our hotel setting the scene for the late 10.30pm concert. Sat amidst the stone walls of the 1300 year old historic Abbey the whistling winds created a haunting atmosphere and the evening culminated in a fabulous repertoire from The Unthanks team of troubadours. As the clock struck midnight we battled the wind and rain on the short walk back to our hotel and fell into the bar soaking wet.

The excitement and atmosphere of the previous night's events turned to fear the following day when making our way home via Corbridge and then Consett the severity of the weather that Desmond had conjured up, as if from nowhere, forced us into a small village called Eastgate(A689) where the roads in all directions were blocked due to floods and fallen trees. Thankfully there was a pub, there's always a pub and The Cross Keys Inn was to be our refuge for the night. The kind hospitality of the owners was well received by two shaken travellers. The winds tore through whilst the river alongside the Inn rose increasingly higher and with continued reports of misery and flooding brought to the Inn door by local villagers, we remained huddled by a cosy fire safe from the elements with the ale tasting all that more extra special.

The bright sunshine and birdsong the following morning belied the truth of the devastation Desmond had wrought. Homeward bound we managed to avoid the worst of the damage not realising the true extent until we arrived home later that Sunday evening where the news reports revealed the full destruction some unfortunate folk had been dealt.

Would we do it all again? For such an emotionally charged, beautiful evening in the breathtaking surroundings of Hexham Abbey, in the company of the wonderful Unthanks? Hell yeah!

Special moments removed from daily life such as the weekend of the 4thDecember 2015 are thrown up unexpectedly but can enhance your life in ways that our daily routines do not allow. Six months later, with much better weather, we travelled to New Galloway in Scotland to soak up another fabulous Unthanks weekend but that's another story.

Music transcends transports and testifies that we are here, the spiritual experience of the abbey and the harsh realities of nature have enriched our lives and when songs from The Unthanks are heard again and again these special moments are revisited and that is the true and lasting gift of music.

Thank you for the memory.

Fareweel regality.

AN ARTIST WRITES...

No 17. Charles Hazlewood, Conductor

When I think of the Unthanks I think of fairy dust, of warmth, of truth, of generosity; organic and whole, yet playful. There is something about the way they tell stories (I mean musical ones) that is honest, full of wonder, poetically beautiful, poetically to the point. In an age of click-tracked and air-brushed music which doesn't (can't) breathe, The Unthanks are earthy, wayward (in a good way), and irreverently persuasive. Who else can get a large crowd to sing three=part harmony while clog dancing and riding the sonic wave of a symphony orchestra? And with a big grin? I first met them in a barn on my farm where we were filming a series about the birth of British music. We were wrestling John Gay's (coruscating proto-socialist but largely impotent with age) *The Beggar's Opera* to the ground and attempting to breathe new vigour into it, to reclaim it for now. With their folky, earthed gutsiness, fabulous instincts and wide-open zest for adventure, we were flying in minutes. Like fairies with big boots. Or clogs.

And since, there have been collaborations with full orchestra (terra firma for me, and very quickly for them) and much else besides.

Note to self: don't ask Rachel and Becky to sing ska.

A FAN WRITES...

No 17. Andrew Aston

Well where to start... my first show was at Warwick Arts at the outset of the *Mount The Air* launch... my close long-time but somewhat older friend Graham had been a fan for a while – singing weekend, the works. He kept telling me that as I had persuaded him to see the likes of Julian Cope, Otis Gibbs and the Polyphonic Spree then I had to see his favourite band... In truth I resisted as the bar was too high, but my love of the Warwick Arts venue and my enjoyment of the few bits I had heard over the years persuaded me.

Before the show I picked up the CD from the library and it started to grow but it hit home hardest when my 7-year-old kept asking me to replay it. I know no other 7-year-old who balances classical music with Kid Carpet, Bill Drummond and Taylor Swift with a little Johnny Cash thrown in!

Things started well. The Young'uns got things off to a rousing start, but the first note to the end of the first set from the Unthanks literally left me speechless... the 10 piece set up, Victoria Rule's trumpet playing, the harmonies, simply like nothing I had ever heard. The second half somehow matched it without the brilliant coda of 'Mount The Air' bringing things full circle.

What struck me after, though, was the interaction between the band and the fans. I had not experienced such a warm collective after a show. I have now seen them several times since, twice with my young daughter Teagan, and in truth each time gets better and better.

To the next ten years. The world needs you, and the joy you bring in these uncertain times...

Stalwart singing weekender and 6Music DJ and John Peel Archivist Wee Davey spinning 78s on a grammophone around the fire.

A FAN WRITES...

No 20. Janet Ulma

Sometimes grief, like the sea, rolls over you in waves and leaves you feeling untethered. I first listened to The Unthanks a few months after my mum died. The sisters' beautiful voices soothed me and anchored me, gave me a renewed sense of connection to the Northeast where I grew up. *Mount The Air* was my first album, and I can't stop listening to it. In particular I am mesmerised by the lyrics of the title track –changing into animal form! and into another! - and the melody is just beautiful. The knowledge that this music will always be there for me is deeply comforting.

With all good wishes

AN ARTIST WRITES...

No 18. Stephen Mangan, actor.

The Unthanks have delighted, surprised and moved me for years. They need to be cryogenically frozen at some point and kept in a safe location for the nation's benefit. Then thawed out at times of national crisis. Balm for the soul.

DISCOGRAPHY 2005 - 2015

ALBUMS

CRUEL SISTER

THE BAIRNS

RR005 RabbleRouser Music 2005
UK Release 11.05.05

01 On A Monday Morning
02 January Man
03 Fair Rosamund
04 Cruel Sister
05 Rap Her To Bank
06 Raven Girl
07 Twenty Long Weeks
08 The Fair Flower Of Northumberland
09 The Greatham Calling On Song
10 River Man
11 Bonny At Morn
12 John Dead
13 Troubled Waters

Rachel Unthank (voice, cello)
Becky Unthank (voice)
Belinda O'Hooley (piano, voice)
Jackie Oates (five-stringed viola, voice)

Additional musicians:
Ben Green (voice), Bryony Griffith (fiddle), Kevin Hall
(voice), Will Hampson (melodeon), Beth Hardy (voice), Mike
Hockenhull (banjo), David Kosky (guitar), Adrian McNally
(guitar, voice), Colin Mather (voice), Rosie Morton (clàrsach),
Brian Pearce (voice), Chris Sherburn (concertina), Julian
Sutton (melodeon), George Unthank (voice), Mat Unthank
(voice), Pat Unthank (voice), John Winton (voice), The Keelers
(George Unthank, Jim Mageean, Alan Fitzsimmons and Peter
Wood) sing vocals on the introduction to John Dead.

Recorded, produced and mixed by Adrian McNally
Recorded in many locations
Mixed & mastered at Panda Studios, Robin Hood's Bay with
Ollie Knight
Cover illustration by Becky Unthank. Sleeve design by Steven
Wainwright, incorporating photographs by Stephen Redfern and
Adrian McNally

RabbleRouser Music 2007
UK Release 20.08.07
Licenses – UK: EMI Records Ltd 2007. Europe: Rough Trade
2008. North America: Ryko Disc 2008. Australia: 2008 Shock
Records

01 Felton Lonnin
02 Lull I
03 Blue Bleezing Blind Drunk
04 I Wish
05 Blue's Gaen Oot o'the Fashion—The Wedding O' Blythe—
When the Tide Comes In—Blue's Gaen Oot o'the Fashion—The
Lad With the Trousers On—The Sailors Are All at the Bar
06 Lull II: My Lad's A Canny Lad
07 Blackbird
08 Lull III: A Minor Place
09 Sea Song
10 Whitethorn
11 Lull IV: Can't Stop It Raining
12 My Donald
13 Ma Bonny Lad
14 Fareweel Regality
15 Newcastle Lullaby

Rachel Unthank (voice, cello, ukulele, feet)
Becky Unthank (vocals, feet)
Belinda O'Hooley (piano, voice)
Niopha Keegan (fiddle, voice)

Additional musicians:
Neil Harland (double bass), Julian Sutton (melodeon),
String section on Felton Lonnin: Iona Brown (violin), Andre
Swanepoel (violin), Michael Gerrard (viola), Rosie Biss (cello)

Recorded, produced and mixed on location by Adrian McNally
between January and March 2007.
Mixed at Blast Studios, Newcastle
Mastered by Adrian McNally and Denis Blackham, Skye
Mastering
Sleeve design by Steven Wainwright with photographs taken at
Beamish Museum, Co. Durham by Karen Melvin

HERE'S THE TENDER COMING

RabbleRouser Music 2009
UK Release 14.09.09
Licenses – UK: EMI Records Ltd. Europe/North America:
2009 Rough Trade. Australia: 2010 Shock Records

01 Because He Was A Bonny Lad
02 Sad February
03 Annachie Gordon
04 Lucky Gilchrist
05 The Testimony Of Patience Kershaw
06 Living By The Water
07 Where've Yer Bin Dick?
08 Nobody Knew She Was There
09 Flowers Of The Town
10 Not Much Luck In Our House
11 At First She Starts
12 Here's the Tender Coming
13 Betsy Bell (hidden track)

Rachel Unthank (voice, cello, ukulele, clogs)
Becky Unthank (voice, feet, autoharp)
Niopha Keegan (violin, voice, accordion, mandolin)
Adrian McNally (piano, dampened piano, plucked piano,
drums, marimba, chime bars, autoharp, Wu-Han tam tam,
Chinese temple gongs, tubular bells, backing voice)
Chris Price (guitar, bass, ukulele, dulcitone, marimba, backing
voice)

Additional musicians:
Jo Silverston (solo cello), Rosie Biss (quartet cello), Mike
Gerrard (viola), Andre Swanepoel (violin), Iona Brown (violin),
Jenny Chang (violin), Dan Rogers (bowed double bass), Graham
Hardy (trumpet, flugelhorn), Simon Tarrant (trumpet), Chris
Hibberd (trombone), Adam Sinclair (drums, cymbals, shaky
egg), Julian Sutton (melodeon), Neil Harland (double bass),
Shelley Thomson (backing voice), Jane Pollinger (backing
voice).

Recorded by Adam Sinclair at Blast Studios, Newcastle, between
April and June 2009
Produced and Mixed by Adrian McNally
Mastered by Adrian McNally and Denis Blackham, Skye
Mastering
Sleeve design by Helen Thomas and Steven Wainwright using
photographs by Alex Teller

LAST

RRM010 RabbleRouser Music 2011
UK Release 14.03.11
Licenses – UK: EMI Records Ltd. Rest of the World: Rough
Trade

01 Gan To The Kye
02 The Gallowgate Lad
03 Queen Of Hearts
04 Last
05 Give Away Your Heart
06 No One Knows I'm Gone
07 My Laddie Sits Ower Late Up
08 Canny Hobbie Elliot
09 Starless
10 Close The Coalhouse Door
11 Last (Reprise)

Rachel Unthank (voice, kalimba)
Becky Unthank (voice)
Niopha Keegan (violin, voice)
Adrian McNally (piano, dulcitone, voice, drums)
Chris Price (bass, acoustic and electric guitar, ukulele)

Additional musicians:
Ros Stephen (violin), Becca Spencer (viola), Jo Silverston
(cello), Lizzie Jones (trumpet), Dean Ravera (double bass), Alex
Neilson (drums), Julian Sutton (melodeon)

Produced and Mixed by Adrian McNally
Sound engineered by Adrian McNally and Thom Lewis
Mastered by Denis Blackham
Sleeve Design by Steven Wainwright with photos by Alex Telfer.
The front cover incorporates an illustration from an 1863
edition of *Harper's Weekly* by American artist Winslow Homer
whose career included painting for two years in the North East
of England.

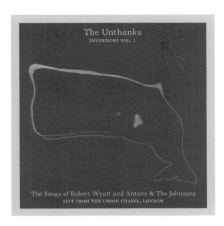

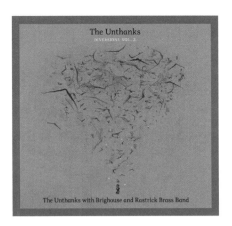

DIVERSIONS VOL 1:
THE SONGS OF ROBERT WYATT AND ANTONY & THE JOHNSONS

LIVE FROM THE UNION CHAPEL, LONDON.

RRM009 RabbleRouser Music 2011
Released 28.11.11
Licenses: Rest of the World – Rough Trade.

Songs By Antony & The Johnsons
01 Bird Gerhl
02 Man Is The Baby
03 You Are My Sister
04 For Today I Am a Boy
05 Paddy's Gone
06 Spiralling

Songs By Robert Wyatt
07 Stay Tuned
08 Dondestan
09 Lullaby For Hamza
10 Lisp Service
11 Free Will And Testament
12 Out Of The Blue
13 Cuckoo Madame
14 Sea Song
15 Forest (excerpt)

Rachel Unthank (voice, feet, dulcitone)
Becky Unthank (voice, feet)
Adrian McNally (piano on Robert Wyatt set, drums on Antony set, harmonium, voice)
Chris Price (drums on Robert Wyatt set, electric bass on Antony set, voice)
Niopha Keegan (violin, accordion, voice)

Additional musicians:
Ros Stephen (violin, voice), Becca Spencer (viola, voice), Jo Silverston (cello, voice), Lizzie Jones (trumpet, voice), Dean Ravera (double bass), Jonny Kearney (piano on Antony set).
Recorded at the Union Chapel, Islington, London, on 8th and 9th December 2010
Mixed and Produced by Adrian McNally
Mastered by Denis Blackham
Designed by Steven Wainwright incorporating illustrations by Becky Unthank and photographs by Mark Winpenny

DIVERSIONS VOL 2:
THE UNTHANKS WITH BRIGHOUSE AND RASTRICK BRASS BAND

RRM010 RabbleRouser Music 2012
Released 30.07.12

01 The King Of Rome
02 Trimdon Grange Explosion
03 The Father's Suite:
    George
    The Happiness Or Otherwise Of Society
    The Father's Song
    George II
04 My Lagan Love
05 Queen Of Hearts
06 Gan To The Kye
07 Felton Lonnin
08 Blue Bleezing Blind Drunk
09 Newcastle Lullaby
10 Gresford (The Miner's Hymn)
11 Fareweel Regality

Rachel Unthank (voice)
Becky Unthank (voice)
Adrian McNally (piano, voice, drum on 'King Of Rome')
Chris Price (voice, including lead vocal on 'Queen Of Hearts', drums on 'Felton Lonnin', cymbals on 'King Of Rome')
Niopha Keegan (voice, including lead vocal on 'My Lagan Love')

Voice of Jack Elliott on 'The Father's Suite' taken from the BBC film *Death of a Miner*
Performed with Brighouse and Rastrick Brass Band, conducted by Sandy Smith
Recorded at Salford's The Lowry, at Leeds Town Hall, at Derby Assembly Rooms and St George's Bristol.
Produced by Adrian McNally
Mastered by Nigel Palmer, Lowland Masters
Illustration by Becky Unthank, depicting the character Charlie from 'The King of Rome'
Designed by Steven Wainwright and featuring photography by Graham Whitmore, Ken Drew and Jeff Goldberg

DIVERSIONS VOL 3:
SONGS FROM THE SHIPYARDS

RabbleRouser Music 2012
Released on 05.11.12

01 The Romantic Tees (Prelude)
02 A Great Northern River
03 Black Trade
04 Fairfield Crane
05 Big Steamers
06 All In A Day
07 The Romantic Tees
      i. The Romantic Tees
      ii. Tyne Slides By
      iii. The Looking Back Song
08 Shipbuilding
09 Monkey Dung Man
10 Taking On Men
11 Only Remembered

Rachel Unthank (voice)
Becky Unthank (voice)
Niopha Keegan (violin, voice)
Adrian McNally (piano, harmonium, drum, voice)
Chris Price (guitar, bass, voice)

Additional musicians on 'The Romantic Tees':
Keith Hill (vibraphone), Julian Sutton (melodeon)

Produced and mixed by Adrian McNally
Engineered by Adrian McNally and Chris D'Adda
Mastered by Denis Blackham, Skye Mastering
Sleeve Design by Steven Wainwright, with photographs by Keith
Pattison

MOUNT THE AIR

RRM015 RabbleRouser Music
Released on 09.02.15

01 Mount The Air
02 Madam
03 Died For Love
04 Flutter
05 Magpie
06 Foundling
07 Last Lullaby
08 Hawthorn
09 For Dad
10 The Poor Stranger
11 Waiting

Rachel Unthank (voice)
Becky Unthank (voice)
Adrian McNally (piano, voice, celeste, kalimba, Fender
Rhodes piano, chord organ, glockenspiel, Indian harmonium,
percussion)
Niopha Keegan (quartet violin, solo fiddle, voice)
Chris Price (electric bass, guitar, piano tinkles on Last Lullaby)

Additional musicians:
Lizzie Jones (trumpet, flugelhorn), Martin Douglas (drums,
percussion), Dan Rogers (double bass), Tom Arthurs (trumpet
on 'Mount The Air'), Kathleen Ord (violin), James Boyle
(violin), Gabriel Wait (cello), Nick Byrne (cello), Eilidh
Gillespie (flute), Esther Swift (harp)

Recorded, produced and mixed by Adrian McNally between
August 2012 and October 2014 at the Unthanks' studio in
Northumberland
Mastered by Denis Blackham, Skye Mastering
Designed by Steven Wainwright, incorporated photographs by
Sarah Mason and illustrations by Natalie Rae Reid

ARCHIVE TREASURES 2000-2015

RabbleRouser Music 2015
Released 11.12.15

1 2000 Miles (The Unthanks' 2015 Christmas single)
2 On A Monday Morning (live from TFF
Rudolstadt, Germany, 2009)
3 I Wish, I Wish (live from Melbourne, Australia, 2008)
4 Blue Bleezing Blind Drunk (live from Holywell Music
Room, Oxford, 2008)
5 Close The Coalhouse Door (live from Tyne Theatre and
Opera House, Newcastle upon Tyne, 2011)
6 Alifib/Alifie (live from Brighton Dome, 2012)
7 The Gallowgate Lad (live from Tyne Theatre and Opera
House, Newcastle upon Tyne, 2011)
8 Felton Lonnin (from BBC Radio 1 Rob Da Bank session)
9 Tar Barrel In Dale (performed live on Radcliffe and
Maconie, BBC Radio 2, 23 December 2008)
10 Queen Of Hearts (alternative demo, 2009)
11 Sexy Sadie (from *MOJO Presents the White Album Recovered*, *MOJO*
79, 2008)
12 A Dream Of A Tree In A Spanish Graveyard (feat. Ian
MacMillan, from *Harbour Of Songs*, 2012)
13 Oak, Ash And Thorn (from the *Oak Ash Thorn* tribute album,
2011)
14 The Unthank Family Band (recorded at Hartlepool Folk
Club, 2000)

Rachel Unthank (voice, feet)
Becky Unthank (voice, feet)
Adrian McNally (piano, drums, rhodes, celeste and sleigh bells,
voice)
Niopha Keegan (violin, voice, accordion, mandolin)
Chris Price (bass, drums, guitar, voice)

Additional Musicians:
Becca Spencer (viola), Lizzie Jones (trumpet), Stef Conner
(piano), Dean Ravera (double bass), Jo Silverston (cello, saw),
Anna Jenkins (violin), Gabriel Waite (cello), Ed Cross (violin),
Chrissie Slater (viola), Neil Harland (double bass), Julian
Sutton (melodeon), Adam Sinclair (drums), Ian McMillan
(spoken voice), George Unthank (voice), Matthew Unthank
(violin), Annie Whitehead (trombone), Alex Neilson (drums)
Produced by Adrian McNally
Mastered by Denis Blackham, Skye Mastering
Designed by Cally with illustrations by Natalie Rae Reid

SINGLES

The songs 'Felton Lonnin' (radio edit), 'Last' (radio edit),
'Flutter' and 'Died For Love' were singles but never released in a
physical single format.

Lucky Gilchrist
Rabble Rouser Music under exclusive license to EMI Records
Ltd. Released 30.11.09
The single (released on CD but billed as a double A side
plus bonus track) was the first as The Unthanks, but featured
two tracks originally credited to Rachel Unthank & The
Winterset; 'Tar Barrel in Dale' (the other A side), taken from
a live performance on Radcliffe and Maconie, BBC Radio
2, 23.12.08; and 'Sexy Sadie' (the bonus track), recorded
in studios at York University, first appearing on the MOJO
covermount CD album of Beatles covers, *MOJO Presents the
White Album Recovered*. These two tracks were the only recordings
released at the time to feature temporary Winterset member Stef
Conner (she later appears on live recordings released on Archive
Treasures), providing vocals on Tar Barrel in Dale and piano on
Sexy Sadie, the later being a crossover moment, featuring Chris
Price's debut recording with the band (on bass) and Adrian
McNally's drum debut, before laying a finger on the piano.

Mount The Air (Single Version)
RRM012 RabbleRouser Music 2014. Released 08.12.14
Limited edition 10" vinyl single. Exclusive B side: Died For Love
(Live Demo Version)

2000 Miles
RabbleRouser Music (2015). Released 11.12.15
Limited edition 7" vinyl single only released as an item in *The
Memory Box*.
B side: Tar Barrel In Dale

RECORDINGS BY THE UNTHANKS ON OTHER RECORDS

OAK, ASH AND THORN (Folk Police Recordings 2011)
'Oak, Ash and Thorn' The Unthanks
Rachel and Becky Unthank (voice) Niopha Keegan (voice, violin) Adrian McNally (piano, drums), Chris Price (guitar, bass)

HARBOUR OF SONGS (Stables Trading 2012)

01   House of Wood – Raevennan Husbandes
02   White Fish Authority – Nick Hemming (The Leisure Society)
03   The Ruler – Nick Hornby and Adrian McNally
04   Dressing Up – Jonny Kearney
05   My Rola-Bola Board – Alasdair Roberts
06   A Dream of a Tree in a Spanish Graveyard – Ian McMillan and The Unthanks
07   Carved in Two – Lucy Farrell
08   Steve Tilston – Sail On By
09   Pampelmüsse & The Conjurer's Stool – Hannah Moulette
10   Delayed Reaction – Villagers
11   Simple Wooden Box – Sarah Blasko
12   The Tiny Mouse – Janis Ian
13   Shed Song – Ralph McTell

Recorded, produced, curated and arranged by Adrian McNally

Adrian McNally (piano on tracks 03, 06, 07, 08, 09; Wurlitzer electric piano on 3, 10; voice on 03, 06, 09; string arrangements on 02, 03, 04, 07, 08, 11)
Rachel and Becky Unthank (voice on 02, 03, 05, 06, 08, 10)
Niopha Keegan (voice on 03, 05, 06; violin on 02, 03, 05, 07, 08, 11, 12)
Chris Price (bass on 02; guitars on 06; voice on 03, 06)

THE JOY OF LIVING - A TRIBUTE TO EWAN MACCOLL
(Cooking Vinyl 2015)
Cannily, Cannily – The Unthanks

Rachel and Becky Unthank (voice), Adrian McNally (piano)

RECORDINGS FEATURING CURRENT MEMBERS OF THE UNTHANKS

COAST TO COAST
Simon Haworth (Fellside Recordings 1998)
Rachel Unthank (vocals, 'cello)

TAKING ROUTES
Simon Haworth (Fellside Recordings 2003)
Rachel Unthank (vocals, 'cello)

MELODEON CRIMES
Julian Sutton (Resilient Records 2005)
Rachel Unthank ('cello)

THE NORTH FARM SESSIONS (EP)
Jonny Kearney & Lucy Farrell (RabbleRouser Music 2010)
Rachel Unthank and Adrian McNally (backing vocals)
Also recorded and produced by Adrian McNally

KITE – JONNY KEARNEY & LUCY FARRELL
(RabbleRouser Music 2011)
Adrian McNally (piano on 'Winter Got Lost', 'Peggy Gordon'; drums, keyboards and tuned perscussion on 'A Dream'; string arrangements on 'Winter Got Lost' and 'Down In Adairsville'), Chris Price (ukelele on 'Stand Up Show')
Recorded and produced by Adrian McNally

CONSTELLATIONS
The Moulettes (Navigator Records 2014)
Rachel and Becky Unthank (voice on 'Elegy')

THE LAST SHIP
Sting (A&M 2013)
Becky Unthank (voice on 'So To Speak')
Rachel Unthank (voice on 'Peggy's Song'*, clogs on 'What Have We Got')
*Song appears on Super Deluxe version of *The Last Ship* only

8.58
Paul Hartnoll (ACP Recordings 2015)
Rachel and Becky Unthank (voice on 'A Forest')

CROWS BONES
Martin Green, Becky Unthank, Inge Thomson and Niklas Roswall (Reveal Records 2014)
Features Becky Unthank (voice) throughout.

The real battle is between artistic integrity and the forces that impede creative expression. Traditional music has always experienced change and been enriched by innovation, while at the same time maintaining continuity. The issue that is of utmost importance is that innovation, change, tradition and continuity all be tempered by integrity, humility and understanding. These issues are the issues of all artistic pursuit and therefore universal, as is the very core of the music itself.

Martin Hayes,
from the sleeve notes of The Lonesome Touch 1997